CW00923857

LUCY DELAP

Feminisms
A Global History

A PELICAN BOOK

PELICAN BOOKS

UK | USA | Canada | Ireland | Australia
India | New Zealand | South Africa

Penguin Books is part of the Penguin Random House group of companies whose addresses can be found at global.penguinrandomhouse.com.

First published in hardback in 2020
Published in paperback 2021

006

Book design by Matthew Young
Set in 11/16.13 pt FreightText Pro
Typeset by Jouve (UK), Milton Keynes
Printed and bound in Great Britain by
Clays Ltd, Elcograf S.p.A.

The authorized representative in the EEA is Penguin Random House Ireland, Morrison Chambers, 32 Nassau Street, Dublin D02 YH68

A CIP catalogue record for this book is available from the British Library

ISBN: 978-0-141-98598-5

Contents

List of Illustrations

List of Abbreviations

BUGA-UP: Billboard Utilising Graffitists Against Unhealthy Promotions
CEDAW: Convention on the Elimination of All Forms of Discrimination Against Women
CLIT: Collective Lesbian International Terrors
DCWLM: District of Columbia Women's Liberation Movement
ERA: Equal Rights Amendment
FEN: Feminist Economic Network
FFCU: Feminist Federal Credit Union
ICW: International Council of Women
IWSA: International Woman Suffrage Alliance
NAACP: National Association for the Advancement of Colored People
NGO: Non-Governmental Organization
NOW: National Organization for Women
NUSEC: National Union of Societies for Equal Citizenship
NUWSS: National Union of Women's Suffrage Societies
NWRO: National Welfare Rights Organization
oob: off our backs
RAWA: Revolutionary Association for the Women of Afghanistan

SPEW: Society for the Promotion of the Employment of Women

WCTU: Women's Christian Temperance Union

WIDF: Women's International Democratic Federation

WIN: Women in Nigeria

WSPU: Women's Social and Political Union

WTUL: Women's Trade Union League

UN: United Nations

YWCA: Young Women's Christian Association

Introduction

In January 1886, a woman in the British-ruled Gold Coast (now Ghana) took up a pen to write an incendiary letter to the *Western Echo*, a local newspaper founded the previous year.

> We Ladies of Africa in general are not only sadly misrepresented but are made the foot-ball of every white seal that comes to our Coast . . . We have been sadly abused by people of such description, and because we have said nothing they continue to abuse us with impunity . . . Although we have not white or angelic faces we are capable of as high a degree of culture as any white lady.[1]

The letter speaks eloquently of her feelings of being kicked around by European colonists, of lack of respect for her culture, and the abuse and impunity of colonial governance as it impacted upon women. The writer was not just angry – she also offered some satirical wordplay, terming white male power 'Just Ass' rather than 'Justice'. Her name does not survive, yet her willingness to speak for 'we Ladies of Africa' draws our attention to her imagined community of African womanhood. Her forthrightness and breadth of vision were helped by local factors – the long-standing African-owned press in the Gold Coast – as well as the global reach of the women's movements of her day.

1886 was a moment of intense colonial expansion. Some of the major European powers were annexing African and Asian territory at speed, giving rise to a violent world order in which racial hierarchies and norms of sexuality became more strongly policed, and which radicals, nationalists and anti-colonialists would contest over the coming century. It was also a moment when women's education was flourishing throughout the globe, their access to (or coercion into) paid employment was growing, and the spread of the bicycle was inaugurating new mobilities and anxieties that would be epitomized in the bloomer-wearing 'new woman' cyclist. It offers a way into a larger story of the profound transformations of how women thought about and inhabited their bodies and lives. Our story ranges both back and forward from 1886, to encompass 250 years of attempts to politicize the injustices of gender.

All who challenge the wrongs faced by women have approached it in ways deeply shaped by their own historical moment. Their ability to name themselves – as feminists, women, ladies or sisters – is always provisional. Their politics have been organized around divides of class, caste, ethnicity, religion, sexuality, nationality and age. No naming of an individual as feminist can be taken for granted. Nor can we impose 'feminism' as a label onto the activism of women and men who would not have recognized it, or who actively rejected it.

We can use 'feminism' as an entry point to understand better how campaigns over 'women's rights', 'new womanhood', 'the awakening of women' or 'women's liberation' might have shared concerns and tactics. But I will also be telling the story of the limits of feminism, its blind spots and silencings, its specificities and complicities. Even the idea of 'women' (or, as nineteenth-century commentators often preferred, 'woman') has proved controversial. And 'gender', understood as the cultural and social organization of biological sex, has only become a commonly used term in the late twentieth century. This book traces out how feminists and activist women related to nationalism, religious doctrines, imperialism, utopianism and racial thinking. My aim is to offer feminist inspiration, showing how unexpected linkages and resonances emerge across different feminist generations and epochs. Inspiration must be set alongside a different story of conflicts and tensions. Feminist coalitions have long had their limits, and feminist concerns of the past don't always mesh easily with urgent contemporary efforts to make visible and stamp out the injuries of gender.

Feminism seeks an alliance that spans more than half of humanity. There may have never been such an ambitious movement in human history. But what do feminists want? All share the insight that being a woman means disadvantage vis-à-vis men, and that this can be addressed through struggle. But the resulting political claims have varied dramatically over time and proceeded under many different names. Feminism is best understood as an overlapping, internally complex set of actions, questions and demands that has been in formulation since the eighteenth century or even earlier. Its concerns change over time. A century ago, British socialist-feminist Ethel Snowden described feminism as a project seeking the purity of men and women through harnessing 'those instinctive feminine forces which make for the protection of the race'. Twenty-first-century feminists are unlikely to identify with this rhetoric, and Snowden's race politics would have been contested by the anonymous Gold Coast letter-writer. There is nonetheless remarkable freshness and relevance to the feminist debates of the past when viewed through the lens of contemporary feminist concerns. Snowden's insistence, for example, that women have an equal right to fight in the military resonates with today's hard-fought campaigns to gain equality in battlefield operations.

Feminists have been motivated by the terrible realities of women's lack of control over their bodies – the rapes, sexual abuses, unwilling pregnancies and the relentless pressures of the male gaze. They have drawn attention to women's poverty, their exclusion from safer and better-paid jobs, their vulnerabilities through marriage or motherhood, their illiteracy. They have shown the cost of women's lack of legal rights, that have taken the form of loss of custody of their children, forced labour, lack of medical resources and land rights, and women's vulnerability in conditions of occupation, war and famine. The costs and human misery of gender inequalities have been and remain incalculable. Yet feminist activism has also been creative and empowering, creating coalitions and inspiring commitment to change. Ideas and dreams have taken shape as campaigns and protests; individuals have found hope, resilience and justice.

Feminism has been repeatedly written off as a political movement that has achieved its aims – only to come back with renewed force as another generation of women angrily name their malaise. Today's campaigners have deep interest in what some ambivalently term 'the F word'. But many are uncertain as to how their activism relates to feminist history: some embrace 'foremothers' such as Concepción Arenal, Mary Wollstonecraft or Funmilayo Ransome-Kuti. Others repudiate the past and stress the uniqueness of 'their' feminism.

The ambivalence about the term, and the content of the feminist past, is unsurprising. The historical organizing frame of 'feminist waves' has not proved up to the job of making sense of the complexities of feminist history. Talk of first, second, third and fourth waves of feminism, or variants such as 'new feminism' or riot grrrl, have not always mapped easily onto women's experiences. And for many women, their activism has been so bound up in other movements – socialist, nationalist, anti-colonialist – that the term 'feminism' has been rejected as too divisive, too Euro-American, too white, too middle-class.

There will be some familiar stories in what follows, of suffrage militancy and stone-throwing protests; of radical feminist celebration of women's power and solidarity. But there is no assumption that feminism looks the same in each place or time. A theme running through the book will be a central paradox of feminism: as a movement, feminism insists on women's inclusion in all areas of social and political life and demands the radical transformation of those exclusionary structures; but feminism has its own forms of marginalization and has struggled to extend its boundaries to all women on equal terms. Black, working-class, lesbian, trans and bisexual, disabled, non-Western and non-Christian women have often been shut out of what theorist Chela Sandoval has termed 'hegemonic feminism'.[2] Despite its cosmopolitan origins, charted in the chapters that follow, 'feminism' has often been associated with a Western model of emancipated womanhood. The voices of those with different backgrounds or goals have not always been listened to, and feminist campaigning has not always met their needs. Archival materials, where they document feminism at all, tend to lean towards the story that more powerful and privileged feminists have wanted to tell. As Adele Murdolo comments, 'very few documents exist in the feminist archive that readily reveal a conflictual and racially or ethnically divided movement.'[3]

Feminist battles have sometimes been regarded as already won, victories realized at the moment of enfranchisement, or where pioneering women finally achieved rights to practise medicine, to have custody of their children or to drive. In the 1990s, there was much talk of a 'post-feminist world' in which political power, economic success and cultural riches were all for women's taking. But this confidence that feminism had done its work has diminished considerably in the last decade of economic austerity, brutal wars and authoritarian politics. In 2013, prominent Nigerian novelist Chimamanda Ngozi Adichie gave a TED Talk which declared, 'We should all be feminists.' She published this clarion call in 2014, and her words were also sampled by pop icon Beyoncé, who had toured under a giant projection of the word 'feminist' in 2013. The published version of 'We Should All Be Feminists' was given to every sixteen-year-old in Sweden shortly after it came out. Yet anti-feminist and misogynist rhetoric has dominated recent political debates. In 2016, Hillary Clinton failed to win the American presidential election, having faced intense negative coverage over her appearance. She and other female politicians faced vitriol from their opponent Donald Trump, who declared of Carly Fiorina in his own Republican Party: 'Look at that face!' and 'Would anyone vote for that?' His words prompted millions of women across the world to march in early 2017. They were incensed by Trump's boasts of having 'grabbed women by the pussy', and coined the slogan 'pussy grabs back'. Across the globe, the pink 'pussy hat' became ubiquitous at protests and marches, echoing the red 'liberty cap' or '*bonnet rouge*' of republican *citoyennes* during the French Revolution. 2017 was also the year that a major American dictionary, Merriam-Webster, declared 'feminism' to be its most looked-up word. A global poll showed that only in Japan did a majority of respondents disagree with the statement: 'I advocate and support equal opportunities for women – I do more than just think about these things, I actually speak up and out to change things for women in my country.'[4] Talk of post-feminism seems unconvincing in the face of these social and political trends.

Coined in the late nineteenth century, 'feminism' has always been a controversial term. An American comic newspaper called it the 'New Name for Masher' and pictured a man making unwelcome advances to a woman while declaring, 'Pay no attention to me, mademoiselle, I'm only a feminist.'[5] It took some time to gain a more stable meaning as a person campaigning against injustice to women. Rebecca West, who began writing for a feminist journal, *The Freewoman*, at the age of twenty in 1911, defined being a feminist as what people called her 'whenever I express sentiments that differentiate me from a *doormat*'. But she nonetheless wrote under a pseudonym, for fear of embarrassing her family.

It has not only been women who have been inspired by

ideas of equality, 'gender justice' and living different lives. Throughout this book, we will meet men who have worked to advance women's rights, often through deep personal investment in feminist goals as also benefiting men. Indeed, the very term 'feminist' became used in the late nineteenth century to replace the idea of 'the women's movement' with a more open-ended identity that was open to both sexes. In 1906, at a meeting of the International Council of Women in Paris, a Monsieur Legendre interrupted the meeting, declaring himself to be the feminist candidate in a recent local election; participants were not impressed, and newspapers reported him as being 'ruthlessly expelled' from this women-only gathering.[6] He was not the only man to stand on a feminist ticket in twentieth-century elections. George Lansbury, who went on to lead the British Labour Party, stood as a women's suffrage candidate in Middlesbrough in 1906, and in Bow and Bromley in 1913. Accused of seeking 'petticoat government', Lansbury lost both elections, but his commitment was undiminished. He was imprisoned for inciting violence in the women's suffrage cause later in 1913, where he joined the hunger strike which was widely used by women prisoners to protest their incarceration. In more recent years, campaigners have produced t-shirts for all, including in men's sizes, emblazoned with 'This is what a feminist looks like'. This slogan was taken up by United States former president Barack Obama in 2016, though for many men, being a feminist is still something they approach with ambivalence and anxiety.

For some women and men, feminism has proved a transformative, explosive, life changing way of seeing the world. For others, it has elicited responses of visceral repudiation, laughter, ambivalence and irony. Impoverished women claiming welfare rights, Black women protesting police violence and housing conditions, working-class women in labour unions calling for equal pay and safe workplaces, or men meeting in men's groups have often opted for other labels, such as 'anti-sexist', 'womanist' and 'social justice campaigner'. Those who preferred other names for their activism should not be claimed as 'feminists'. But their motivations, and why they avoided this label, are important to historians of feminisms, who must cast their net widely in documenting activism against gender injustice.[7]

The 'When' of Feminism

Being a feminist has been projected back into past centuries with mixed success. There have been efforts to claim figures such as the late-medieval writer Christine de Pizan, or even the ancient Alexandrian philosopher Hypatia, as 'feminists'. Of course, these historical actors did not think in these terms, and it is misleading to approach them through our much later ideological concerns. Instead, we should ask what terms and concepts they used to think about men and women. A division of the world into two sexes cannot be taken for granted. In some parts of the world, it is not clear that there was a clearly recognizable concept of 'woman'. As historians of China have argued, the category of 'female persons' (*funü*) was a relatively late invention and related directly to family status. In many contexts, female persons were profoundly subdivided – into 'wives' and 'courtesans' in Qing China. The same might be said about the class divide of 'women' and 'ladies' in nineteenth-century Britain.

Local diversity has meant that the emergence of organized demands for change happened in very different ways all over the world. Where they existed, 'feminists' spoke for different groups and in diverse registers. 'The women's movement' or 'woman question' was the terminology of nineteenth-century Europe and the Americas, while 'women's awakening' was widely debated in Middle Eastern and North African countries in the early twentieth century. Others in this period preferred to talk of the 'new woman' as a symbol of new forms of economic and cultural opportunity for women. Chinese radicals variously made demands in the name of women's rights (*funüjie*) and gender equality (*nannü pingdeng*). Feminism does not map in any straightforward way onto these terrains, and historians of feminism must take care not to erase the local specificity of struggles and activism. However, it would be a mistake to simply look at all these debates and movements in isolation; they often shared key ideas or drew inspiration from each other's struggles. We can chart the rich interweaving of global debates on the relationship between gender and power, at the same time as recognizing feminism as a deeply historical and context-specific phenomenon.

Though it was often defined in highly various ways, 'feminism' as a term was adopted globally in the early twentieth century. It might refer to women's 'rights' as well as to campaigns of women's advancement, protection and equality. A single issue of a magazine titled *La Aurora Feminista* (*The Feminist Dawn*) was published in Chile in 1904, the same year that Rosika Schwimmer (1877–1948) founded the Feministák Egyesülete (Feminist Association) in Hungary; a Centro Feminista was founded the following year in Buenos Aires,

Argentina. An Asociación Feminista Filipina was founded in the Philippines in 1905; Filipina women saw feminism as carving out a civic role for women, attempting to improve the regulation of women's work and preventing early marriage.[8] In the same year, Argentina hosted the first International Feminine Congress, and saw the publication in La Plata of the journal *La Nueva Mujer* (*The New Woman*). The motto of the Congress had been 'Let Us Work', and the emphasis of Latin American feminism in these early years was on social service and the protection of women by the state. Its critics accused feminists of being *marimacho* – half man, half woman. But the term 'feminism' was flexible enough to be adopted by religious conservatives such as Laura Correa de Bustos, who published an account of '*feminismo Christiano*' (Christian feminism) in the Uruguayan capital Montevideo in 1907.[9]

In Britain, the suffrage movement is often assumed to speak for feminist concerns of the period. However, contributors to the first British magazine that called itself 'feminist', *The Freewoman*, used 'feminism' in 1911 to distinguish their beliefs from the suffrage campaign for votes for women. By 'feminist', its avant-garde editors indicated a term open to both sexes, and one which rejected conventional political institutions. They sought revolutionary change; one editor, Dora Marsden, declared controversially that 'rebels armed with rifles' would be most likely to gain respect. Other terms were also available – French radicals experimented with '*éclaireuse*' ('trailblazer') to capture a sense of pioneering women, 'liberated from all that still burdens the bulk of their companions'.[10] German-speaking activists wavered between '*Feminismus*' (feminism) and '*Frauenbewegung*' (women's movement), fearing that the former term had implications of 'free love' or British suffrage militancy.[11] Feminism has often been a 'loanword', deployed in a wide variety of places to label different kinds of gender politics; there was talk of feminism as '*feminizumu*' in Japan in 1910. Russian activists however preferred the term '*ravnopravki*' or 'equal righters' when, in the heady revolutionary days of 1905, they founded the Union of Equal Rights for Women.[12] Across the world, there was fascination with this new concept, as well as suspicion of European or American influences.

Sometimes external labels stuck. The British media mocked early-twentieth-century militants by terming them 'suffragettes', but this name was embraced with enthusiasm by those throwing stones for the right to vote. 'Bra burners' was an insult of the 1970s, but activists came up with their own puns and subversive reappropriations: Harpies Bizarre, Hags, Lavender Menace, the Monstrous Regiment, the Society for Cutting Up Men.

The meaning of 'feminist' has continued to evolve, and to be controversial. Activists in the 1970s and 80s often preferred to talk of 'women's liberation', since they associated 'feminist' with reformist 'liberal' politics of parliamentary rights and suffrage. Feminists in France associated with the 'Psych et Po' (Psychoanalysis and Politics) grouping disliked 'feminist' as an American import connoting confrontation. They preferred to talk of '*femmes en lutte*' ('women in the struggle') as a means of capturing their distinctive stress on feminine difference and maternal qualities. Late-twentieth-century Japanese activists have preferred to talk about a 'gender-free' society. By the twenty-first century, many activists across the world have felt the need to routinely preface their feminism with other flags, resulting in labels such as 'intersectional feminism' or 'trans-friendly feminism'.

Despite the many varieties of feminisms, one of the overarching feminist dreams has been of a movement that could span all women: 'Helping each other, all of one mind', as the Chinese banner declared at the 1913 conference of the International Woman Suffrage Alliance. This fantasy has carried with it the paradox of an abstract political agenda that, in its very inclusivity, ignores concrete exclusions. Talk of 'black feminism' or 'Chicana feminism' has sometimes attempted to solve this problem, but critics have argued that this simply foregrounds the exclusion of black or Chicana women from the ethnically unmarked feminist 'mainstream'. African American writer Alice Walker coined the term 'womanism' in 1984, and this has been taken up by some black women. 'Womanist' (or 'womynist' for those who preferred to entirely excise the 'man' lurking in 'woman') runs the same risks as 'feminist' of universalizing its claims. But it does provide a useful reminder of the limits and exclusions of feminism as an affiliation. As the African American activist Frances Watkins Harper (1825–1911) put it succinctly as far back as 1866: 'You white women speak here of rights. I speak of wrongs.' Harper wanted the women's movement to challenge the racial segregation of streetcars, but her white peers were reluctant to take on issues of racial exclusion. As an African American woman and a former domestic servant, she continued: 'I, as a colored woman, have had in this country an education which has made me feel as if I were in the situation of Ishmael, my hand against every man, and every man's hand against me.'[13]

She and her fellow African American activists formed the National Association of Colored Women in 1897, preferring, in an environment of growing racial exclusion, to organize separately from white women and without embracing 'feminism' as a platform.

These debates over naming and belonging suggest the need to look closely at the historically variable labelling of gender activism, and to think hard about the work different names do. We need not engage in a competitive struggle to identify the first, or the truest, feminists. Instead, we can trace out experiences of exclusion and difference amongst gender and social justice activists, and chart their passionate, painful or strategic coalitions.

Despite the renewed interest in what feminism 'means' in the present day, it is important to recognize that its meaning has been mobile. Feminist symbols and slogans have been malleable, reshaped in formats that were useable for different audiences. *Feminisms: A Global History* will explore traditions that include Islamic, black, indigenous and lesbian feminisms. More controversially, it will also explore men's identification with feminism, in order to probe long-standing tensions over who is being addressed by feminism, and who can be part of the movement.

Why Global?

Why should we approach feminism from a global perspective? Histories of feminisms have often been organized around a 'civilizational' and Eurocentric model. In these stories, feminism can be dated back to the European writers of the seventeenth century, such as Aphra Behn, François

Poullain de la Barre and Sarah Fyge, who began to think about women as an 'enslaved class'. Such writers were inspired by ideas of women's spiritual equality within mostly Protestant religious traditions. When they talked of 'enslavement', they rarely considered women who were literally enslaved on the plantations and estates of the Americas and Caribbean. They began to find ways to name and renounce experiences of rape and forced marriage – though again, without reference to the prevalence of such experiences for the enslaved. These intellectuals have often been viewed as significant 'foremothers' for the history of feminisms.

In older histories, the baton was usually then passed to women who experienced the American and French revolutions in the late eighteenth century, such as Abigail Adams and Olympe de Gouges. De Gouges, who proclaimed the rights of women in her *Declaration of the Rights of Woman and the Female Citizen* (1791), is often named with the British writer Mary Wollstonecraft as the initiators of ideas and polemics that are recognizably feminist. Their influence is then traced onwards, through the more activist nineteenth century, during which campaigns flourished on women's education, property rights and suffrage, and into the twentieth century. Only recently have figures such as former slave and poet Phyllis Wheatley (*c.* 1753–84) been added to this story. Feminist history has often been structured around a limited cast of mostly white and educated foremothers. This has led to lineages of inheritance that not only risk misreading earlier versions of feminist thought and action, but have also been organized around the desire to show 'who was first'. Simply put, the earliest texts that can be read as 'feminist' have been used to establish a national priority, where white citizens of imperial powers such as France, Britain or the United States came to be taken as originating points.

The writing of global or world history has for decades now challenged this kind of account. Historians have proposed ways of understanding the global that take alternative starting points and new thinkers. We might take as an originating feminist moment the 1799 Rasheed (Rosetta) Women's Conference, where a group of Egyptian women, radicalized by protesting the 1798 French invasion at Alexandria, met to discuss the conditions of women's employment and family status. Alternatively, a starting point might be the rights given to indigenous female householders to vote in Sierra Leone in 1792 – a right lost when their country became a British Crown Colony in 1808. Indigenous and settler women gained voting rights in New Zealand from 1893, well ahead of their European and American counterparts. These perspectives help challenge the assumed priority of European feminisms.

Global histories of feminism have focused on the large-scale structures that underpinned ideas about the 'woman question', women's rights and women's emancipation. There has been deep attention to the role of empires, for example, in shaping the nineteenth- and twentieth-century women's movements and producing a world in which liberty and citizenship were denied to colonized populations. Colonized peoples underwent mass migrations within systems of indentured and forced labour. Women in many settings found their access to land and trading rights curtailed. Women of imperial powers used the rhetoric of racial and civilizational advancement to become authorities on colonized women. They used the roles of missionary, settler and wife to travel, describe the lives of non-Western women, and intervene in how they were treated, sometimes in the name of equality or feminism. For later decades, when empires began to be dismantled, it was the geopolitical contests of the Cold War that helped to authorize and shape women's and feminist activism.

The nineteenth and twentieth centuries were also dominated by the development of nationalism, and this meant that women's status and freedoms were often tied to debates about national progress. Within such debates, the problematic idea of 'backwardness' as a means to capture local discontent with women's circumstances features prominently. In Brazil, for example, the imagined European or North American emancipated, educated woman was used to make claims for the advancement of the nation or region. The editor of the Brazilian women's rights newspaper, *O Jornal das Senhoras* (*The Ladies' Journal*), noted in the journal's first editorial in 1852:

> in France, England, Italy, Spain, the United States, and in Portugal itself, cases abound of women dedicated to literature who contribute to various newspapers. Perchance shall South America alone stay stationary in its ideas when the entire world marches toward progress and moves toward the moral and material improvement of society?

O Jornal das Senhoras had been founded in Rio de Janeiro and was edited by the Argentinian-born Juana Paula Manso de Noronha (1819–75). Manso saw *O Jornal das Senhoras* as a platform to work for the 'social betterment and the moral emancipation of women'. While it was rhetorically useful for Manso to draw a contrast between 'advanced' and 'backward' regions, in reality the kinds of reforms actually (or imagined to be) taking place in nations such as Britain, France and the United States were also evident in Brazil. The first university college for women in Britain, Girton College in Cambridge, opened in 1869. Women were given the right to enter higher education only a decade later in 1879 in Brazil – in the same year that the French state resolved to provide *lycées* (secondary education) for French girls. Women's suffrage was seriously debated in the Brazilian Constitutional Congress of 1891, paralleling similar debates in Britain and the United States. And despite her rhetoric of backwardness, Manso was convinced that Europe need not take the lead, since 'the banner of enlightenment waves gracefully in the perfumed breeze of the tropics'.[14]

Manso's mobility across national borders reminds us that histories of feminism cannot be located only within single nation states, regions or empires. Global influences have been based on the migration of individuals, as refugees, students, exiles and workers. An early women's suffrage petition in Britain, for example, was organized by Anne Knight of the Sheffield Female Political Association in 1851 after she had spent time with French activist Jeanne Deroin in Paris during the revolutionary days of 1848; in turn, Deroin published Harriet Taylor Mill's 1851 essay 'The Enfranchisement of Women' in her journal *L'Almanach des Femmes* in 1852. With the rise of technologies of travel and communications in the nineteenth century, some women were peripatetic across multiple nations – historian Bonnie Anderson, for example, tracks the Jewish abolitionist and suffragist Ernestine Rose (1810–92) across Poland, Berlin, Paris, London and New

York as she fled an arranged marriage and immersed herself in socialist and feminist activism.[15]

Historians have become newly attentive to the deliberate cultivation of transnational spaces, in the pages of globally circulating periodicals, in conventions, conferences, alliances and federations. Sometimes transnationalism was a deliberate tactic, witnessed in the global mobilization undertaken by bodies such as the Women's Christian Temperance Union in the nineteenth century. International organizations such as the International Council of Women helped foster important elements of global governance, such as the League of Nations Commission on the Legal Status of Women (1937). The 'left-feminist' Women's International Democratic Federation built up similar networks of campaigning and mobility in the second half of the twentieth century, which later helped inform the influential United Nations (UN) World Conferences on Women in Mexico City (1975), Copenhagen (1980), Nairobi (1985) and Beijing (1995).[16]

A global history approach also allows us to see the interactions between globally famous texts and local intellectual or activist traditions.[17] John Stuart Mill's important book, *The Subjection of Women*, for example, was published in Britain in 1869, in the context of Mill's recent attempts to get a women's suffrage bill through the Houses of Parliament, where he sat as the Member for the City and Westminster. It was quickly translated into many languages, including into Spanish by a Chilean woman, Martina Barros Borgaño, in 1872, and published in the Chilean journal *Revista de Santiago* as *La Esclavitud de la Mujer*. The Chilean women's movement drew on European texts but retained its own distinctive emphases.

In Chile, where few men voted, the most pressing question was not suffrage but the economic exploitation of women drawn into industry, and this perspective reshaped the meaning of Mill's ideas about the 'slavery' of women.

Feminism is better understood as a conversation rather than an import; but a conversation with many registers. It has taken place under unequal conditions, where some voices are amplified and some are routinely ignored.[18] The idea of 'entangled histories' has been used by global historians to capture the ways in which ideas, people and texts crossed and re-crossed borders to create multiple 'intersections'; historian Kathryn Gleadle invites us to think of feminist history as a non-linear rhizome root structure, full of unexpected growth points, dead ends and patterns of influence.[19] Some of this patterning stretched over time; feminists and others sustained critical dialogue with earlier texts and reworked their ideas. The assumed priority of white, educated Euro-American women has turned out to be a myth.[20] In the following chapters, I highlight specific local constellations of ideas that allowed for feminist dreams, ideas and actions to be developed and contested. There may sometimes be faint lines of influence, but there is just as likely to be repudiation and innovation. Rather than trying to find origins in Europe, I work with a more diffuse idea of 'mosaic feminism', built up from inherited fragments but offering distinctive patterns and pictures. Like mosaics, the view from afar and the close reading of feminisms may give a very different picture. And like mosaics, feminist coalitions were built up from the bits and pieces available – other movements, committed individuals, actions and ideas. Some mosaics have been long-lived;

others have crumbled, and their tiles have been reused, or have disappeared from view.

The familiar centring of Europe is displaced and 'provincialized' by telling the histories of other networks and sites, such as the importance of Japan in hosting Chinese exiles in the early twentieth century, creating a site of powerful exchange. International campaigners and writers on suffrage, temperance, anti-colonialism and peace questions are also brought into view, displacing those located firmly within the nation state. Throughout the book, I alternate between wide-angle summaries of different feminist beliefs or campaigns, and close scrutiny of the lives of individual women who fought against gender inequities. In doing so, I hope to draw out some important new ways of reading feminist practices and ideas across historical time. Influenced by Kimberly Springer's concept of 'politics in the cracks', I suggest that we look not only at the shards and fragments that make up a mosaic, but also at the gaps between the pieces. Springer's work on black feminist organizations such as the Third World Women's Alliance describes a politics created in 'the cracks' – snatched moments between the demands of everyday work and care. Black women's organizing also fell between the civil rights and the women's movements, awkwardly or creatively showing up the intersections of class, gender and race.[21] Springer's 'interstitial' politics draws our attention to concerns that did not fit easily into existing feminist politics, and the opportunities and dislocations that resulted. In a similar spirit, we might ask what makes the mosaic stable, or what erodes its patterns. Or investigate how dreams, campaigns, spaces and places, emotions and songs could provide a kind of feminist 'cement', embedding a politics into its historical shape, and giving way over time so that mosaic pieces might drop out and new patterns can emerge.

Metaphors of mosaics and conversations give a sense of the richness of feminist debates. But it is important also to maintain in view the discord, violence and trouble that have also characterized feminism. As the feminist philosopher bell hooks has observed, 'women can and do participate in politics of domination, as perpetrators as well as victims.'[22] Some of the global systems that emerged around the same historical moment as the 'woman question' and feminism – systems such as imperialism, missionary and settler colonialism, indentured labour, nationalism – were projects that relied on violence and subordination. The world is not, historically, a freely traversed space for all. While we as twenty-first-century observers might take a global perspective on the feminist past, this privilege was not available to the historical actors themselves. A global history of feminism, as historian Mrinalini Sinha has insisted, will not simply pluralize our picture so that we think in terms of 'feminisms'.[23] Instead, our account of feminisms must acknowledge what Sinha terms the 'discrepant histories of different women's movements', marked by contests, conflicts and power-play.

Theory, Activism and Useability

What have feminisms been used for? What uses might they have today? The idea of 'useable history' offers a means of thinking about history in dialogue with the present – a history which can help clarify questions of feminist strategy, priority and focus in the contemporary moment by showing how dilemmas and campaigns were shaped in the past. Feminist ideas and campaigns have been used to redistribute domestic labour, to transform how children are raised and educated, how art and music are created, how 'work' is categorized and rewarded, how legal systems operate. Without wanting to claim that history offers direct repeats or recapitulations, we can look back to feminisms past and find precursors to problems today. We might ask, historically who could reside in the category 'feminist'? Who gets left out? What kinds of differences did feminism make to individuals, to societies or to nations?

Thinking about useability does not mean that we should explore the feminist past only for contemporary inspiration. Instead, we can also grasp the specificity and distinctiveness of how, say, religion informed feminism in the late eighteenth century, or how nation-building provided a specific context to the development of women's movements in early-twentieth-century China or the Middle East. A useable history is not one that judges the past by today's standards. Instead, useability reminds us of the variable ways in which feminisms have been put to use, rhetorically, intellectually and materially, in the lives of historical actors.[24] And inevitably, each reader will bring their own questions and determine what is useable for them. Useable feminisms must be non-doctrinaire and open-ended, shaped but not determined by the encounter between past and present.

There may be aspects of the feminist past that make us uncomfortable today. But the idea of useability acknowledges the need for a historical underpinning to today's activism.[25] Feminists have long been caught in an awkward position in relation to their history; moments of rejection of what mothers or grandmothers believed in are motivated by a need to rebel, to declare a new era and to shake off inheritances. Novelties such as social media platforms can make contemporary feminists feel that the #CuéntaLo (Tell It) or #MeToo moments are very different from preceding feminist upsurges. But at the same time, there has always been a strongly historical aspect to feminist movements, sometimes imbued with nostalgia for the past. And only a brief look back reveals strong shared themes, around sexual harassment at work and in the street, and challenges to male violence, impunity and disrespect for women.

For many, a book about feminist history will be at least partly an intellectual journey. Feminism has always been, amongst other things, an invitation to think hard about how and why society is organized, and why (some) men have louder voices, more resources and more authority than women. Feminist thinkers have been engaged with the big ideas of modern times – they have challenged the liberal self, the social contract, accounts of democratic citizenship, state and nation, as well as socialist ideas of revolution. Feminism has intersected with and contributed to anarchist critiques, as well as ecological, theological and critical race scholarship. Indeed, as higher education has expanded in the late twentieth century, feminism has become an established part of the academic landscape across much of the world. Yet theory was also produced at the cutting edge of protest, consciousness-raising and campaigning. It has often been intended to be useable in activism, as well as in personal life transformation.

The ways in which history is written have changed and

pluralized over the past twenty years. There has been a flourishing of work in cultural history, as well as the development of new approaches to the study of material culture, space, capitalism and the emotions, to name but a few recent growth areas. This book is informed by these new approaches and expands feminist history beyond its typical location within intellectual and social movement analyses. I won't attempt to tell a continuous story that spans the feminist movements of the last two centuries – such an undertaking would be impossibly large. Instead, I offer some new jumping-off points, rooted in recent innovative histories. Chapter 1, on feminist dreams, is informed by the turn towards literary and psychoanalytic thinking, which takes seriously our dreams and the creative and unconscious work they might do. Chapter 2 recognizes the theoretical resources that feminists have created, by discussing how patriarchy and other terms have captured the persistent gender patterns within human social organization. It also examines the influence of long-standing intellectual traditions such as republicanism, and the more recent development of ideas of intersectionality and sexism. Inspired by the increasing scholarly interest in how location and space shape social movements, Chapter 3 explores the idea of a feminist place. It locates feminism in spaces of work and worship, and charts attempts to craft spaces of refuge and safety. Chapter 4 looks at some feminist objects. Where previous histories have understood feminism as an ideology, or best captured through biographies of people, this chapter foregrounds the material and visual culture of feminism, in the political statements of badges and posters, as well as everyday objects such as the mundane yet powerful book and hat pin. Chapter 5 extends material culture into the 'look' of feminist clothing and fashion, while Chapter 6 draws on new work on emotions to think about the feelings occasioned by feminisms. Chapter 7 reminds us of the strong activist dimension that has always threaded through the history of feminisms and looks at the ways protests have been executed across both bodies and space. And Chapter 8 explores aural dimensions of feminism, thinking about the chants, songs and musical innovations linked to activism.

These new perspectives root feminist history to some of the most innovative areas of historical research and shake up our sense of the uses of feminism. They take us across continents, and show why universal definitions of feminism, spanning time and place, aren't going to work. Instead, I invite us to examine 'feminisms' across a global canvas, spanning 250 years. The resulting stories are less about gender equality than about gender justice – demands for an environment in which all can thrive. This could mean paying a fair wage, kicking out colonial occupiers or embracing Goddess spirituality. It sometimes meant conflicts between different feminist goals and dreams. I argue that we can find inspiration in the feminist past, as well as a fuller understanding of why Chimamanda Ngozi Adichie's invitation for 'us' to all 'be feminists' is never going to be a straightforward task.

CHAPTER 1

Dreams

When I was a graduate student in the 1990s, first embarking on study of the history of feminisms, a chance encounter in a seminar one evening challenged me to think hard about what kinds of dreams might motivate feminists. A senior colleague sat next to me, and we both listened to a debate about feminist philosophy. Or perhaps I listened, but I also have a powerful visual memory of her rainbow socks that, like gloves, had a space for all her toes. She was joyously unconventional in her self-presentation. We got talking about feminism, and I was genuinely shocked when she told me that her vision of feminism was that it would erase gender entirely. Her dream was of a world where male and female were simply irrelevant categories. Today, with gender-queer, trans and gender-neutral forms of identity being experimentally or vigorously taken up, this dream might be less transgressive, and my own views have become less conventional. But it was an important moment for me, because it made clear the diversity of utopian hopes attached to feminism, and my own investment in existing categories of male and female. Dreams are powerful ways of inviting ideas of change and otherness. The late-eighteenth-century writer Mary Wollstonecraft called them 'wild wishes', and these moments of imagination are revealing of what brought women and men to feminist consciousness.

Dreams offer a very personal, intimate sense of what has motivated feminist activism. They are shaped by the circumstances of the dreamer – their family, experiences of labour and employment, their reading, their emotional states. But dreams are also linked to the historical moment – by what can be imagined in the context, say, of occupation, revolution, urbanization or famine. It might be imagined that feminist dreams started small, centred on equality with men or the attainment of specific rights such as child custody. But a glance at the diversity of dreams and dreamers in the decades of the late eighteenth and nineteenth centuries would suggest otherwise. The dreams of Charles Fourier (1772–1837) and his followers are suggestive of the ambition and startling heterodoxy of earlier visions of a new gender order. Fourier argued that human happiness required meaningful labour and the free expression of desire. He reflected on the corrupted sexual mores of his time:

> Is not a young woman a piece of merchandise put up for sale to the highest bidder? Is she not tyrannized by prejudice from childhood and obliged to consent to any marriage that may be arranged for her? People try to persuade her that she is only bound by chains of flowers. But can she really doubt her degradation?[1]

Fourier proposed instead another feminist dream – an ideal society termed 'Harmony', characterized by creative, attractive work, organized cooperatively so that all workers – men, women and children – had a diversity of tasks, suited to their inclinations. In sexual matters, all would be free to express their 'host of amorous innovations which we cannot yet imagine'. Women were to share in the governing of Harmony, which, Fourier forecast, would span the globe. But the means of achieving this goal were vague, which was why later thinkers termed this a utopia rather than a serious socialist prospect. His followers insisted on the abolition of marriage, property and conventional motherhood in favour of 'passional equilibrium' in their communities of the 1830s and 40s in France, Spain, Algeria, the United States and other nations. Their unruly experiments remind us that there has been no increase over time in the radicalism of feminist thinking.

In this chapter, I look at some diverse sources and sites of feminist dreaming, including those advocating separation from men, those prioritizing love and sexuality at the heart of their vision, and those 'advancing the race'. Well-developed literary or science-fiction fantasies are set alongside unconscious and chaotic fragments of dream life. Dreams are both a site of restless utopianism and, at times, an indicator of the uneasiness and conflict that frequently accompanied visions of a new life.

Ladyland and Herland

In 1905, a 25-year-old Bengali woman, Rokeya Sakhawat Hossain, published *Sultana's Dream*, a fictional account of a feminist utopia, a technologically advanced country she named 'Ladyland'. In her vision, men had been placed in the seclusion of the *zenana* or harem and women now ruled, without veils or purdah. Ladyland was a garden-like setting, where women's expertise and technologies had been harnessed for plenty. She imagined universities in Ladyland run by women, whose research enabled ecologically sustainable agriculture. Crucially, she stressed women's access to plentiful water, perhaps influenced by Mughal cultural and garden traditions, as well as her experiences of the environmental depredations of the British colonial occupation of India. In the 'real world', Rokeya declared, men's use of science had been reserved for military purposes. Nonetheless, her female monarchs were strong and willing to enforce their rule; she imagined them using heat-ray weaponry to beat back armies of men from neighbouring lands.

This was not a secular vision, but the religion the Muslim-born Rokeya supported was unorthodox. She described it as based on love and truth, with a redefinition of 'sacred' relations. In Bengali society, 'sacred relationships' were those with immediate family, where intermarriage was forbidden. Rokeya playfully insisted that, in Ladyland, the 'sacred' was enlarged as if *all* were 'family', so that men and women could freely interact without any sexual connotations. Rokeya's critique of purdah and veiling did not cast Islam as a site of constraint. Like many others, she based her politics on ideas of the restoration of women's rights that Islamic religion had offered: 'What we want is neither alms, nor a gift of favour. Our claim is nothing more than what Islam gave us 1300 years ago.'[2]

In her lifetime, Rokeya (1880–1932) was frustrated by Bengali Muslim women's seeming compliance with purdah: 'Why do you allow yourselves to be shut up? You have neglected the duty you owe to yourselves and you have lost your natural rights . . .' She passionately supported women's education as the route to freedom for her female contemporaries, and went on herself to have a career in social work and women's education.[3] For her, women's seclusion through purdah and veiling was 'a silent killer like carbon monoxide gas'. In this rejection of purdah, Rokeya's views were compatible with the majority of colonial commentators, who saw the seclusion of Muslim women, as well as Hindu child marriage and 'widow burning' as primitive or savage practices. Rokeya chose to write *Sultana's Dream* in English, and her utopia was first published in the *Indian Ladies Magazine*. This Christian, English-language journal may indicate her imagined audience of educated colonial elites. She positioned herself as part of elite indigenous circles, whose interventions aimed to 'modernize' the domestic practices of British-ruled India. Nonetheless, Rokeya also published extensively in Bengali journals, and founded a branch of a welfare association for Muslim women, the Anjuman-e-Khawateen-e-Islam (Muslim Women's Association). She also translated and cited progressive feminist tales and texts from Afghanistan and Britain, and campaigned for women's education in the interwar years.[4]

Rokeya's vision of a community of women governed by autonomous self-rule shared much with the dreams of another major feminist figure, but one who came from a very different cultural background. Charlotte Perkins Gilman (1860–1935) was one of the most important and visible feminists of the early twentieth century, who campaigned on a bewildering variety of issues, spanning dress reform, suffrage, sex reform, birth control and prostitution. Like Rokeya, Gilman presented feminism as a dream of a different future. She had been born into a family linked through her father to well-known activists for social causes and women's suffrage, such as her abolitionist great-aunt Harriet Beecher Stowe. But her father abandoned his wife and children, and Gilman's early years were spent in poverty and marginalization. Her brother was sent to college, but Gilman was not. She was forced to become resourceful and independent even after marriage in 1884. Her material challenges were intensified after she took the relatively unusual step of separating from her husband in 1888. These qualities served her well, in a career of extraordinarily prolific writing. She published single-handed a monthly periodical, *The Forerunner*, from 1909 to 1916, in which she wrote every editorial, article, book review, poem and story. She even wrote her own advertisements, such as a glowing endorsement for the Wisconsin 'Holeproof Hosiery Company' in 1909, which informed her readers: 'I wore them and wore them and wore them, till I was so tired of those deathless, impervious, unnaturally whole stockings that I gave them away!'

Gilman promoted feminism with a light touch, aiming to reach out to 'ordinary' women readers. She termed feminism a form of humanism, promoting 'the development of human qualities and functions among women'. Fiction helped her imagine alternatives to women's economic dependency, and her most elaborate utopia, *Herland*, was published in 1915, a decade after Rokeya's Ladyland. *Herland* was written during the heightened tension of the suffrage campaign, and the growing devastation of global warfare in the First World War. It envisaged a women-only community where the racial advancement of humanity (or 'race work') was undertaken without the constraints of male domination. Gilman was highly influenced by theories of matriarchal or 'gynaecocentric' culture as the early form in which human society had evolved. Sociologists and ethnographers had argued that kinship and property-owning motives had led to an overthrow by men of women's social dominance in the earliest human societies. This overthrow gave rise to what Gilman termed an 'androcentric' society in which 'parasitic', non-working women were subjugated by men.

This phase of human evolution, Gilman believed, was now over – both women and 'the race' would benefit from a more egalitarian society in which sex selection based on love would lead to a 'higher race'. *Herland* was a means of imagining how this might come about and its consequences. Gilman depicted a science-fiction utopia of a South American society of women who had slaughtered their menfolk in the distant past. After two thousand years of reproduction by parthenogenesis (single-sex reproduction), in which only daughters were born, Herland society had evolved humanist values. Its women were enabled to be intelligent, physically active and completely autonomous of men. Motherhood was valued above all else, and was placed at the heart of society – whether expressed through personal motherhood or the 'social motherhood' of care towards society:

> the longed-for motherhood was not only a personal joy, but a nation's hope . . . Each girl holds it close and dear, an exquisite joy, a crowning honor, the most intimate, most personal, most precious thing.

In Gilman's Herland, sex relations were banished. Dress was unencumbering and aesthetically pleasing: 'short hair, hatless, loose, and shining; a suit of some light firm stuff, the closest of tunics and kneebreeches, met by trim gaiters'. Ever practical, Gilman also stressed the inclusion of roomy pockets in this idealized dress. Herland residents lived semi-communally, each with their own bedroom, reception room and bathroom. For Gilman, who had been forced to give up custody of her daughter when her marriage had broken down and who lived a semi-peripatetic life of lecturing and campaigning in bedsits and lodgings, this vision must have helped sustain her own hopes for change.

Gilman's novel was not just a paean to a female-centred lifestyle. It was given shape by the plot device of the discovery of Herland by three American men, and their efforts to capture its women into couple relationships. Their early efforts to entice women using cheap jewellery failed, and their assumptions were quickly unseated, as the central (male) narrator reported:

> Jeff, with his gentle romantic old-fashioned notions of women as clinging vines. Terry, with his clear decided practical theories that there were two kinds of women – those he wanted and those he didn't.

The residents of Herland surrounded each interloper

> in great numbers, evidently indifferent to what he might think, evidently determined on some purpose of their own regarding him, and apparently well able to enforce their purpose.

The narrator marvelled at their physique:

> Fishwives and market women might show similar strength, but it was coarse and heavy. These were merely athletic – light and powerful.

Despite their attempts to use guns to enforce their demands for marital partners, the male visitors were captured and forced to a reluctant respect for Herland society and its forms of 'higher comradeship'. They eventually were married into the Herland society, and Gilman depicted their slow realization that the 'hyper femininity' of the old world might be a damaging condition for both women and men.

Consistently through her publications and lectures, Gilman stressed the shared interests both sexes had in feminist reform based on mutual love and respect. But she remained aware of how fragile this could be and used *Herland* to raise the issue of marital rape, at a time when husbands could disregard the sexual consent of their wives with the full support of the courts (a situation only reformed across all jurisdictions of the United States in 1993). Gilman depicted one of the American male visitors, Terry, attempting to enforce his 'conjugal rights' against the wishes of Herland inhabitants, with his rationale: 'There never was a woman yet that did not enjoy being MASTERED.' But Terry's attempt to enforce sex with his wife led to the expulsion of all three from Herland at the conclusion of Gilman's utopian text.

Gilman's conclusions were seemingly pessimistic; yet historians have noted her strong desire to involve men as agents of feminist change, and her optimism that male violence and coercion would ultimately fail when set against the demands of the human race.[5] Her advocacy of male sexual restraint came to seem naïve and 'Victorian' when set against the new sexual precepts of psychoanalysis, as well as the sexual informality and experiment that pervaded the mid-twentieth-century United States. Nonetheless, her utopia of short-haired, physically liberated and mentally alert women, living lives of emotional and sexual liberty from men, remains a compelling dream of a feminist future.

A Great Love

Both Rokeya and Gilman envisaged women's liberation through the abandonment of sexual links to men. Gilman's life as a divorced travelling lecturer reflected the new possibilities for some women to live without men and become emotionally centred on other women. Increasing numbers of women across Europe and the United States experienced lives of singleness, and while some mourned this, others found women-centred lives to be loving and fulfilling. But the exclusion of men was probably not a majority goal, and most who dreamt of a feminist future still included men in various forms and roles. Alexandra Kollontai (1872–1952) was one such dreamer. She was passionately committed to the transformative power of love and sex between men and women, but nonetheless imagined a very different world in which love might flourish.

Kollontai was born to a wealthy Russian father and a peasant-born Finnish mother. The social distance between her parents created huge obstacles to their marriage. Kollontai was always aware of the tensions for those trying to realize a 'love match' in late-nineteenth-century Russia, and became fascinated by the power of love. She rejected her parents' attempts to impose a conventional bourgeois feminine role on their daughter, and embarked on a rebellious marriage herself – but one that was to prove deeply unhappy. Despite the birth of a son, Kollontai became increasingly politically

Figure 1.1
On the left, Alexandra Kollontai, Marxist revolutionary, writer and, after the Bolshevik Revolution, People's Commissar for Social Welfare (1917–18)

active in Marxist circles in St Petersburg. She was hugely impressed by the strikes amongst women textile workers in 1896, and became convinced of the need to engage women in socialist struggle. She left her husband in 1898, after five years of marriage, and embarked on a life of political organizing.

Feminist attempts to gain access to suffrage and the professions in Russia seemed marginal to Kollontai.[6] Instead, she founded a women factory workers' club and became heavily involved in revolutionary agitation. This work threatened her safety in Tsarist Russia, and leaving her son with her parents, she went into exile in Germany, Switzerland and Scandinavia. It was perhaps during her extensive travels in Europe and the United States that she gained further exposure to ideas of individual self-fulfilment in love relationships. She viewed women's status as key to Communism, and confidently expected a transformed world after an anticipated Communist revolution.

In *Working Woman and Mother* (1914), Kollontai compared the life chances of four women who shared the same name – Mashenka. They comprised a factory owner's wife, a laundress, a maid and a dye worker. She was enraged by the material inequalities of their lives, and imagined an end to the class hierarchies that created 'parasites' and workers. Instead, Kollontai asked her readers to 'Imagine a society, a people, a community, where there are no longer Mashenka ladies and Mashenka laundresses', where human needs 'will be taken care of by society, which is like one large, friendly family'.[7]

Kollontai saw enormous possibility for women in the changes promised by the Bolshevik Revolution. Indeed, her earlier writing saw these changes as inevitable, rooted in Marxist interpretations of economic systems:

> But such a society, surely, is only to be found in fairy tales? Could such a society ever exist? The science of economics and the history of society and the state show that such a society must and will come into being. However hard the rich capitalists, factory-owners, landowners and men of property fight, the fairy-tale will come true.[8]

After the Bolshevik Revolution of 1917, in which she was on the Petrograd Soviet executive committee, she became a high-profile agitator. Kollontai's forecasts of collective housekeeping, the new morality and new womanhood were widely publicized within the Soviet Union, and her writing was also translated by revolutionaries of the May Fourth movement in China in the 1920s. Yet her dream of inevitable change downplayed the obstacles of male power and seemed to leave little space for women's agency. A dream might be inspirational, but if it offered no opportunities for women to do anything to bring about its realization, then it remained a chimera.

Kollontai recognized some of the limitations of her earlier dreams of women's transformed lives when she was writing a few years after the Bolshevik Revolution. She had been able to experiment with some of her dreams when, in 1917, she became the first People's Commissar for Social Welfare in Vladimir Lenin's government. She founded the Zhenotdel (Women's Department) in 1919, and insisted on women's literacy and reproductive rights in the early Soviet Union. Abortion was legalized in 1920, though Stalin was to criminalize it again in 1936. In the chaotic years after the revolution, Kollontai had not found it easy to realize her dreams, and she eventually fell out with the Bolshevik leadership. Her novels and short stories, written in the 1920s after she had gone into semi-exile, revealed her growing awareness of how complex change in the gender order would be. Unlike many of her revolutionary peers, Kollontai's dream evolved beyond a vision of higher living standards for her Mashenkas. Her later utopian writing centred on a society where all could experience 'great love' – the transformative potential of which she believed would change the entire social order. She sought sexual liberation, and saw (heterosexual) desire as a transcendent force:

> only when words were no longer adequate would they discover the ultimate expression of their feelings in sexual passion, that bright burning force which was so very beautiful, which encompassed the colour of her dreams.[9]

Nonetheless, Kollontai recognized that love and desire were difficult emotions to control, which could carry significant costs for women. Her personal life also reflected her emphasis on love; she lived out a transgressive and unconventional love affair with Aleksandr Shliapnikov, a metalworker, and then Pavel Dybenko, a much younger working-class revolutionary whom she married in 1917. She was forced to face the limits of both her dreams and their realization in the difficult climate of the 1920s, when the sexual and emotional transformation Kollontai sought was eclipsed by the realities of economic and political crisis. Kollontai was sidelined by Lenin over her support for worker control and was required to leave the Soviet Union and take up diplomatic posts in Scandinavia and Mexico. It was during the 1920s that she wrote her fictional explorations of women's lives under Communism and gained global notoriety as an identifiable face of 'free love'. Just as the reputation of the British writer Mary Wollstonecraft was dominated by accusations of sexual immorality when her love affairs and pregnancy outside of marriage become widely known, so Kollontai became known as a subversive promoter of sexual excess. She was notorious for her analogy between sex and drinking water; Lenin's reported response was scathing and stigmatizing: 'thirst must be satisfied. But will the normal person in normal circumstances lie down in the gutter and drink out of a puddle, or out of a glass with a rim greasy from many lips?' Whatever Kollontai's intentions, both dreaming of and living an alternative life risked being subject to exclusion and silencing.

Unlike many utopian writers, Kollontai projected her fiction into the past, before the Bolshevik Revolution, or into the contemporary moment of the revolution itself. Her stories centred on female characters who loved men, and were committed to new kinds of living. Kollontai's utopia was not futuristic, but remained utopian in imagining a transformed human psyche, able to love, to enjoy sexual passion, and to balance passionate self-realization with a commitment to the collective good. In 'A Great Love', a short story written in 1923, Vasilisa Malygina was presented as a working-class Communist activist attempting to set up communal houses. Vasilisa was the lover and then wife of an anarchist-turned-Bolshevik, Vladimir, and their relationship was a complex one of desire, friendship and frustration. Vasilisa, like many of the other heroines Kollontai created, struggled to combine stormy individual love relationships with working for revolution. She rejected the patriarchal premium on virginity, and had sexual relationships with several men; yet she was tortured by the survival of older ideas of sexual respectability, which her lovers sometimes hypocritically maintained. Eventually, the worker-heroine left her unfaithful husband and returned to her Party work; Kollontai's heroines were unfailingly happier when relieved of their demanding lovers. Vasilisa had related to men in an almost maternal fashion, and Kollontai's men seemed childlike in their emotional dependence on women.

In 'A Great Love', Vasilisa's passionate love for Vladimir eventually turned into friendship, and she was even able to feel sisterhood with his new lover, if shot through with pity at the mistress's bourgeois reliance on loving a single man. But Kollontai acknowledged women's reproductive vulnerabilities by concluding 'A Great Love' with Vasilisa discovering that she was pregnant. She was perhaps naïvely optimistic about the prospects of raising a child by relying on collective Soviet provision. Kollontai's *Working Woman and Mother* had made confident forecasts:

> When Mashenka, who is now neither a lady nor a servant but simply a citizen, becomes pregnant, she does not have to worry about what will happen to her or her child. Society, that big happy family, will look after everything. A special home with a garden and flowers will be ready to welcome her . . . Children will grow up in the kindergarten, the children's colony, the crèche and the school under the care of experienced nurses. When the mother wants to be with her children, she only has to say the word; and when she has no time, she knows they are in good hands.[10]

The reality of life in the post-revolution Soviet Union was less rosy, but Kollontai maintained her sense of optimism in the imagined pregnancy and motherhood of Vasilisa. Perhaps her own relative privilege, and the limited impact of her own motherhood on her political activism, had left her with little imagination for the actual experiences of women raising children outside of conventional familial structures.

Though all written within a space of twenty years, Rokeya's, Gilman's and Kollontai's feminist utopias differed dramatically in how they imagined the relationships between women and men, reflective of their different cultural, religious and political contexts. In the intellectual work of Charlotte Perkins Gilman, her spirituality and vision was woven together with Darwinian and eugenic concerns into a formation Gilman termed 'the larger feminism'. The dreams of Rokeya Hossain had developed a transcendently visionary and unorthodoxly Islamic version of a feminist dream. Alexandra Kollontai was also interested in spiritual transcendence through the power of love, though she preferred a secular, Marxist framework for this. Though these figures were also rooted in specific local campaigning around causes such as women's suffrage, reproductive rights and education, all were keen to explore imagined and sometimes fantastical worlds of changed gender relations. They shared an emphasis on women's meaningful, universal labour as key to a feminist future. This feature was common in the utopian socialist tradition, and in Kollontai's work it was most closely linked to a Marxist vision of the rule of workers. Employment brought economic independence, and most feminists acknowledged this as an important goal. But women's labour – projects of creative, socially useful activity – was a key underlying goal shared across these different feminist dreams.

Actualizing Utopia

These dreams of feminist utopias reflect a rich period in the late nineteenth and early twentieth centuries when both sexes were able to imagine different kinds of social organization. There have also been attempts to live out such dreams in more concrete terms. Nineteenth-century radicals experimented widely with 'model' and utopian communities and insisted on their ability to turn dreams into reality. Pandita Ramabai (1858–1922) was one such dreamer, who was convinced of the need for her Indian female peers to live autonomously, in supportive communities of women. She was a high-profile social reformer, whose life had been shaped by the unusual decision of her father, a high-caste Brahmin Sanskrit teacher, to extend his scriptural knowledge to his wife and daughter. Ramabai undertook a precarious, unorthodox life of pilgrimage with her parents and siblings. Her father resisted offers of an arranged marriage; Ramabai eventually chose her own husband at the relatively late age of twenty-two, after her parents had died of starvation during the Madras famine of 1877, and her brother had also died unexpectedly. She had been a celebrated example of traditions of Hindu scholarship in Calcutta before her marriage, though her choice to marry outside of her caste and in a civil ceremony caused controversy. She went on to take a profound interest in issues affecting Indian women. As historian Padma Anagol has argued, Ramabai's establishment of Arya Mahila Samaj (Arya Women's Society) in 1882 in the Indian state of Maharashtra gave her a platform to testify to colonial authorities on issues of women's subordination and the need for reform.[11]

Early marriage and widowhood had become prominent issues of gender justice and equity for Ramabai, who was herself widowed after only two years of marriage and left to support a daughter. It was this experience that led her to promote widows' homes, particularly aimed at those widowed in their childhood or youth. First opened in 1889, Ramabai's home was termed Sharada Sadan (Home of the Goddess of Learning), and aimed at economic self-sufficiency for women, through craft and agricultural activities.

Like many other women's movement activists, Ramabai was intensely committed to the power of literacy and print culture for realizing feminist dreams. Sharada Sadan, she declared, was to have libraries of the best books on science and literature. In addition, 'Lectureships should also be established in the libraries . . . to open the eyes and ears of those who long have dwelt in the prison-house of ignorance.'[12] Ramabai helped set up a women-run printing press, and encouraged the publication of women's journals. She promoted opportunities for the employment of Indian women in teaching and nursing, and remarriage for widows. And while she had initially presented her work as securing the futures of high-caste women, she remained alert to the needs of the less educated and privileged. Given her own tragic experiences of famine, she was particularly proactive in offering rescue to women made vulnerable by the repeated famines of colonial India. Her feminist commitment was organized around the idea of women's self-reliance, underpinned by a strong sense of the transformative power of women's education.

Ramabai had travelled extensively in Britain and North

America in an attempt to study medicine, and to fundraise for her widows' homes. Her lectures were supported by publications, including *The High-Caste Hindu Woman*, which she published in English in 1887. Ramabai was successful in raising money, partly through the establishment of the Ramabai Association of America.[13] Engaging with suffragists, temperance activists and abolitionists, Ramabai was able to construct a coalition of supporters that gave her opportunities to support socially marginalized Indian women.

However, such support came at a cost; Ramabai's work was introduced in terms that exoticized Indian women and presented them as victims. One of her sponsors, Rachel L. Bodley, was Dean of the Woman's Medical College of Pennsylvania. Bodley had helped train Anandibai Joshee (1865–87), the first Hindu woman to gain a medical degree, despite having been married at the age of nine. Joshee's pregnancy at thirteen and loss of her son at birth had inspired her to seek medical training. Bodley supported Joshee, but found it impossible not to see Indian women as powerless victims. Commissioned to write the introduction to Ramabai's *The High-Caste Hindu Woman*, Bodley offered a melodramatic presentation:

> The silence of a thousand years has been broken, and the reader of this unpretending little volume catches the first utterances of the unfamiliar voice. Throbbing with woe, they are revealed in the following pages to intelligent, educated, happy English and American women.

Ramabai herself seemed to follow Bodley's lead, and described Hindu women in highly pejorative terms:

> They have been so cruelly cropped in their early days that self-reliance and energy are dead within them; helpless victims of indolence and false timidity, they are easily frightened out of their wits, and have little or no strength to withstand the trials and difficulties which must be encountered by a person on her way towards progress . . . Is it not the duty of our Western sisters to teach them how they may become self-reliant?[14]

Despite her talk of Indian women's timidity, Ramabai herself developed a reputation as a disputatious, unorthodox character who would not play the part of victimized Indian womanhood. Controversially, she had converted to Christianity during a visit to Britain, and offered Sharada Sadan residents instruction in both Hinduism and Christianity. However, she rejected key elements of Anglican ritual and theology, refusing to wear a crucifix or endorse the divinity and resurrection of Christ; instead, she preferred to indigenize Christianity by composing Marathi and Hindi psalms, and translating the Bible into Marathi. She was also convinced of the very low impact that Western interventions through missionaries and charity might have on Indian women's situation. In her view, the 'zenana missionaries' from abroad could never overcome the scale of India. In order to effect change, Ramabai insisted, 'women teachers of our own nationality' must be prioritized.

When it came to the administration of the Sharada Sadan, it proved difficult for Ramabai to exercise authority in the complex environment of colonial India. Her activities were in competition with British and American missionaries, as well as Anglican Church authorities and colonial government. Ramabai sought authority within the homes she founded, only to find herself sidelined by committees of wealthy American funders. She also challenged the ritual authority of Brahmins, and as a Christian woman was an unwelcome presence. Her widows' home became boycotted by influential Maharashtra Hindus, for fear of the threat of Christian conversion by inmates. Her tolerance of a multifaith environment and championing of women's spiritual freedoms were always suspected of being a form of subversive Christian mission, particularly when Ramabai extended the home's membership from upper-class widows to the less educated rural women who had faced starvation during famine years. The managing committee eventually restricted Ramabai from spaces in the home such as kitchens, dining rooms and the living accommodation of Hindu residents.

The dream of a space of personal and religious freedom for women was extremely hard to implement in the tense environment of interfaith interactions. Ramabai's attempts to create women-run spaces of sanctuary and opportunity were undercut by patriarchal opposition, but also by religious sectarianism and the interests of colonial powers. Nonetheless, her agency and determination were inspirational to later activists. In Indonesia, a schoolgirl called Kartini read about Ramabai, and recorded that she

> trembled with excitement; not alone for white woman is it possible to attain an independent position, the brown Indian too can make herself free. For days I thought of her, and I have never been able to forget her.'[15]

Kartini (1879–1904) went on to become the first woman to openly contest polygamy and campaign for women's education in the Dutch East Indies (present-day Indonesia) via her correspondence with Dutch women. Abandoning plans to train as a teacher in Tokyo, she became the third wife of an Indonesian chief in 1903 and died the following year, aged twenty-five, after the birth of her son. Despite a life cut short, her outspoken support for expanded opportunities for Indonesian women has made her an important figure for later Indonesian activists.

The Limits of Dreams

So far, the feminist dreams examined here have been utopias, expressed in fiction and fantasy, and occasionally in everyday lives. But dreams are not always straightforwardly utopian or aspirational. The dreams of nighttime hours can be ambivalent, and full of unconscious tensions that remind us of the difficulty of living with feminist principles. Recalibrating the relationships between men and women meant rethinking the most intimate realms. Unsurprisingly, this provoked some ambivalence and distress that emerged in the dream lives of women and men imagining a different world.

Very few dreams are recorded in historical archives, and we have to treat those that are written down as only a very approximate record of what might actually pass through our dreaming minds. And, of course, those written down are those the dreamer chooses to share. We gain an extraordinary glimpse of the unconscious wishes of a key feminist thinker in a letter written by the nineteenth-century British philosopher, politician and champion of women's rights, John Stuart Mill (1806–73), describing one of his dreams.

Mill had published a philosophical and ethical case for women's equality in 1869, *The Subjection of Woman*. He attempted to push for women's suffrage by sponsoring a women's suffrage amendment to the 1867 Reform Bill that was about to enfranchise a new swathe of working-class British men. His contributions to women's suffrage remind us of an important thread running through this book – that men have been active and influential as feminists. The idea that only women can be feminists is a claim that must be historicized – at certain points in time, and in certain places, this was a deeply held belief. But it is far from being true of all periods, and Mill joins other figures, such as American former slave and suffragist Frederick Douglass and China's Jin Tianhe, as high-profile supporters of wider opportunities for women. Mill, like many male feminists, drew inspiration from a female collaborator – in this case, his wife Harriet Taylor Mill. He idealized her as having 'all but unrivalled wisdom', and the two wrote collaboratively on domestic violence and other campaigning issues.[16]

John Stuart Mill had a very specific vision of the ideal woman citizen. He celebrated the lives of married, domesticated women as the highest form of womanhood, despite the rising numbers of women in many European countries in the later nineteenth century who were unable to marry. The emigration of European men to countries such as the United States, Argentina, Australia and Canada had created gender imbalances in their countries of origin. This caused enormous public concern that unmarried women were socially and sexually 'surplus'. Mill's support for women's suffrage was based on his perception of the particular qualities of married women as citizens, and he was less supportive of single women, whom he considered to have failed to reach their highest fulfilment. Yet while the married woman was Mill's ideal, his account of feminine virtue depended on an 'asexual femininity as a moralizing force', Sandra Zerilli has argued.[17] Prudence, restraint and the suppression of lower appetites were core to this vision of citizenship, and Mill himself sustained a twenty-year passionate but celibate relationship with the already married Harriet. It was only after the death of her first husband that John Stuart Mill and Harriet Taylor were able to marry, and Mill maintained his critical position towards 'base passions' as social evils throughout his life.

His own dream life suggests something of the dissonance that sexual desire held for Mill. In 1857, he wrote to his wife Harriet about his dream of an imagined conversation at a dinner party, 'with a woman at my left hand and a young man opposite'. In Mill's dream, the young man declared:

> 'There are two excellent and rare things to find in a woman, a sincere friend and a sincere Magdalen.' I answered 'the best thing would be to find both in one' – on which the woman said 'no that would be *too* vain' – whereupon I broke out 'do you suppose when one speaks of what is good in itself, one must be thinking of one's own paltry self interest? No, I spoke of what is abstractly good and admirable.'[18]

A 'magdalen' was a euphemism for a promiscuous woman or one who sold sex. Mill's dream suggested that he was seeking a figure who could combine sensuality and desire with the intellectual equality and companionship he prized as citizen virtues – though he feared judgement of this as 'vain'.

Ambiguously, the reference to this combination as 'vain' could mean impossible ('in vain'), or an accusation of personal vanity. Dreams rarely offer clarity, though they can suggest tensions and unresolved feelings. In Mill's account of his dream, he went on to correct his dream character: 'he had quoted it wrong and [that] the *right* words were "*an innocent magdalen*" . . .'

The paradox of this concept – female sexual knowingness combined with innocence – again points to Mill's unconscious frustration and ambivalence over his gender politics. The impossible 'innocent magdalen' was a menacing, destabilizing figure. His letter to his wife continued, 'How queer to dream stupid mock mots, and of a kind totally unlike one's own ways or character.' He distanced himself from the dream by terming it 'droll' and 'ridiculous'. Nonetheless, it offers a tantalizing glimpse into the difficulties of sustaining a feminist position that for Mill, like Gilman and Rokeya, centred on sexual restraint and the promotion of reason over passion.

The dream of American feminist Doris Stevens gives us another vivid example of the tensions involved in living the feminist life. Stevens had joined the suffrage struggle in the United States through the National Women's Party, and she later featured prominently in the interwar efforts to raise women's influence on international policy, as head of the Inter-American Commission of Women (1928–39). She had married the well-known lawyer Dudley Field Malone in 1921 and declared her support for new kinds of marital relationships. Women should keep their names on marriage, she proposed, and should remain in paid employment. She hoped her marriage would be an example of how love and companionship might be possible – a lived example of the hopes Kollontai had expressed only a decade or so earlier, and which had seemed both utopian and realizable in the ferment of the Bolshevik Revolution.

But the relationship between Doris Stevens and her new husband did not take the form she had hoped for. He was emotionally abusive, belittling and isolating her. Malone had little understanding of women's needs for autonomy and fulfilling labour. He was also sexually unfaithful, and the couple eventually divorced in 1927. Doris had recorded in her diary a dream that she had had while living in Paris with Dudley; she had dreamt that on approaching a group of friends, Dudley had commented on her as a 'little wife – nice bitch she is'. Mortified by his behaviour, she had dreamt of impersonating a train, making 'chuff chuff' noises to mask his treatment and defuse the situation.[19] The dream reveals the psychic cost of trying to live outside the confines of conventionality. Doris was pilloried in the press after her divorce, as a woman whose aspirations to work and 'modern' love had destroyed her marriage.

Dreaming of Difference

The feminist dreams we've looked at spanned a relatively short time period – the 1880s to the 1920s – and show how the environments of British-ruled India, Soviet Russia and the United States could produce very different visions. Each feminist 'mosaic' has its unique pattern, though sometimes the same tile or colour is visible across time and space.

The impulse to find commonalities between feminisms became particularly pressing and troubling when framed by the concepts of sisterhood that pervaded ideas of women's liberation in the years after 1968. American feminist Adrienne Rich (1929–2012) published her poetry collection *Dream of a Common Language* in 1978. She was already a well-recognized poet, and a leading figure in the strand of the American women's liberation movement termed 'radical' for its celebration of women's autonomy, and their shared knowledge and interests rooted in motherhood and autonomous sexual desire. Rich's poems offered no simple call to unity, and her emphasis was on the disempowerment of women in the structures of language imposed on them by men. She was also well aware of the challenges that divides of race, ethnicity, sexuality and class posed to concepts of 'sisterhood'. But in one poem dedicated to black lesbian feminist Audre Lorde, Rich seems to be reaching out in female or maternal solidarity across the contentious racial divides between women:

> I stand convicted by all my convictions –
> You, too. We shrink from touching
> Our power, we shrink away, we starve ourselves
> And each other, we're scared shitless
> Of what it could be to take and use our love,
> Hose it on a city, on a world,
> To wield and guide its spray, destroying
> Poisons, parasites, rats, viruses –
> Like the terrible mothers we long and dread to be.[20]

Audre Lorde (1934–92) published a long conversation with Rich, taped in 1979 and published in 1981, about the power of writing to convey women's experiences and traumas. Their exchanges suggest the very deep racial tensions between American feminists, but also the possibility of creative energy through acknowledgement of difference. Rich had ended her poem dedicated to Lorde, 'Until we find each other, we are alone.'

But commonality proved hard to achieve. Lorde lost patience with having to constantly address, but seemingly never resolve, the racism of white American women. In 1979, she refused to engage further, in protest at the sapping of her activist energy by racism. In an open letter to another white radical feminist, Mary Daly, Lorde declared:

> I had decided never again to speak to white women about racism. I felt it was wasted energy because of destructive guilt and defensiveness, and because whatever I had to say might better be said by white women to one another at far less emotional cost to the speaker, and probably with a better hearing.[21]

It was a similar sense of futility that led Pratibha Parmar, a British Asian film maker and activist, to contribute a reflective piece titled 'Other Kinds of Dreams' to the magazine *Feminist Review* in 1989. Parmar had stressed on other occasions the strength that she drew from black feminist commitments to diversity, though she noted the defensiveness that this provoked amongst white feminists. To celebrate difference, based on specific experiences of oppression, could be productive; but could also easily end in the unproductive accumulation of 'oppressed identities' and a retreat into 'lifestyle "politics"'. Parmar proposed that, instead of organizing around shared oppressions, or 'partnership in misery', the concept of diaspora was the most productive way of capturing diversity, avoiding the essentialism of identities such as 'blackness' and 'whiteness'. Parmar cited the American poet June Jordan on the power of 'other kinds of dreams that have nothing to do with whether we are white or not white'.[22]

In 1871, the American suffragist Susan B. Anthony was lecturing to an audience in Salt Lake City, Utah. A bothersome male audience member tried to convey his views, and Anthony famously declared: 'Away with your man-visions. Women propose to reject them all and begin to dream dreams themselves.' The idea that women's dreams might differ from men's was deeply subversive. Yet the extent to which all women might share the *same* dreams has proved a defining concern of feminists, and an area of deep divisions. Dreams do not only envision innovations but can also suggest the limits and tensions embedded in hopes for change, as Ramabai discovered in her awkward attempts to create a women's shelter. Feminist visions of an imagined future have been radically plural. My colleague's vision of the erasure of gender, for example, was taken up in Ursula Le Guin's extraordinary 1969 novel of androgyny, *The Left Hand of Darkness*. But the erasure of gender can be another person's nightmare. There is no evidence that feminist dreamers of the early twentieth century such as Rokeya, Gilman and Kollontai read each other. They would likely not have recognized themselves as participating in any common 'feminist' movement or sharing any kind of identity. Placing their dreams alongside each other does not try to reconcile them. It shows instead the different registers of feminist utopian imagination in different places, as well as some resemblances and echoes that were shared across their dreams.

Sidestepping the impossible conundrum of feminist unity

and substituting looser, more provisional coalitions and mosaic patterns has been a productive move within recent feminist thinking. As feminist philosopher Iris Marion Young argued in 1997: 'we need to wake up to the challenge of understanding across difference rather than keep on dreaming about common dreams.'[23] Where Adrienne Rich had named her dream one of a 'common language', Lorde talked of 'the very house of difference'. Her own dream in *Zami: A New Spelling of My Name*, was of a sensual world in which women 'work together as friends and lovers', bridging the divisions between labour and love that so troubled the writings of Mill, Gilman and Kollontai. I shall give Lorde the last word here:

> Being women together was not enough. We were different.
> Being gay-girls together was not enough. We were different.
> Being Black together was not enough. We were different.
> Being Black women together was not enough. We were different.
> Being Black dykes together was not enough. We were different.[24]

CHAPTER 2

Ideas

Feminist dreams may have been utopian, but by imagination, speculation and fantasy about different futures, they showed up the violence, absurdities and contingencies of how gender was organized. They found purchase in feminist lives and campaigns, and inspired ideas, theory and analysis. This chapter looks at critical feminist intellectual innovations, and traces feminist borrowings from traditions as varied as Christianity, socialism, liberalism, constitutionalism, nationalism and republicanism. I focus on a key insight – that sexual difference is not a natural division but is imposed in different forms across time and space.

Ideas of gender are maintained through social and political structures. Some societies might work with a binary of male:female. Others might have multiple formulations of sex and gender, structured around age, social status, labour performed, spiritual role and so on. Early modern Japan, for example, provided opportunities for 'third sex' roles that young men or monks might take on; some Native American societies have been similarly organized around multiple genders. Some societies might see sexual difference as a foundational form of organization; others might see age, ethnicity or race as much more important. Scholars such as Ifi Amadiume, for example, have argued that hierarchies and groupings of age were more important than gender in the organization of some African societies, and this allowed for women to adopt transgressive or powerful roles such as 'female husband'.[1]

This idea of variability is really important because it leaves open the possibility of change – sexual difference is not a given but can take different forms. It is therefore open to challenge and change. History is so powerful for feminists because it demonstrates this variability over time and refuses the taken-for-granted nature of women's subordination. However, this idea of fluidity and variety in the organization of sexual difference has developed hand-in-hand with another feminist idea – that forms of socio-economic organization that disadvantage women are long-standing and hard to shift. Malign forms of socio-economic organization have been named variously by feminists as 'separate spheres', 'androcentrism', '*nannü*' or 'patriarchy'.

Recognizing enduring inequities and oppression has not prevented a more optimistic strand of thinking. Some feminists have taken heart and inspiration from the idea that women possess their own distinctive and long-standing characteristics, rooted for some in their maternity, or in ideas of 'women's culture' associated with more humane, peaceful or equitable forms of society. Here I will look at ideas of sexual difference, as well as the persistent nature of male domination, over the past two and a half centuries.

Women, Reason and Virtue

Eighteenth-century European debates over gender tended to dwell on the nature of women as a threat to the public good, due to their perceived love of luxury and gossip. In a century that stressed 'Enlightenment values' – the power of reason and education to transform humanity and support good government – femininity seemed to threaten ideas of progress. Some of the early contributors to debates on women in public life rejected this view and insisted upon women's intellectual and moral potential. The 'woman question', as it was often termed, was less about men's power over women, and rather, focused on the contested qualities of femininity.

Raised in elite circles in Aragon, Spain, Josefa Amar y Borbón (1749–1833) was a well-known translator and writer of the Spanish Enlightenment. She was celebrated for her contributions to Spain's literary culture at a time of national sensitivity to accusations of Spanish backwardness and ignorance. She wrote books on the 'woman question', which centred on women's education and appropriate role in public life. Her essay *Discourse in Defence of the Talents of Women, and Their Aptitude for Government and Other Positions in which Men Are Employed* was published in 1786, and called for all debate about the relative merits of women and men to cease until the two sexes were offered equal opportunities for education and self-cultivation. Subjected to flattery and tyranny, she argued, women were 'born and raised in absolute ignorance', their talents suffocated. Drawing on an Enlightenment faith in reason and education, Amar insisted that 'if ignorance were destroyed, slavery would be destroyed as well.' But she was not above poking fun at male conceit. When Eve ate the apple in the Garden of Eden, Amar observed, Eve sinned – but at least she showed curiosity. Adam ate only at Eve's command, 'through acquiescence'. The Christian narrative of the Fall, far from showing woman as sinful and transgressive, instead indicated for Amar that 'woman was ahead of man in her desire for knowledge.'[2]

Addressing progressives who were seeking to modernize and reform Spanish society, Amar demanded women's entry into the salons that flourished amongst her male peers. Termed 'economic societies', these were the spaces that hosted reformist debates. Like many writers of her age, Amar looked back to the achievements of past women of Ancient Greece, France, Russia and Spain. But she was also determined to counter the assumptions of the *philosophes* of her age. Jean-Jacques Rousseau's *Émile, or, On Education* (1762) had powerfully argued that women and men were profoundly different in their needs and social duties. Rousseau's sentimental view of women – that they were, at best, delightful helpmeets to men – was hugely influential in shaping eighteenth- and nineteenth-century assumptions about domesticity and submission as key feminine virtues. Amar was comfortable with the idea of women's orientation to household duties, but she insisted that rational education was necessary to the provision of care for their families. This was to include quite advanced skills – double-entry book-keeping, Latin and Greek, history and arithmetic. Her demands did not include political and civic rights – but by publishing under her own name and boldly demanding recognition of women as men's moral and intellectual equals, she became a central contributor to the 'woman question' in Spain. Her own actions during the Napoleonic Wars, when she braved heavy fighting to remove the wounded to safety, also suggested women's ability to serve their nation in unexpected ways.

Amar's writings on the 'woman question' still read today as incisive, funny and furious about how women were judged and treated. Her contributions, however, were eclipsed by the chaotic years in Spain during and after the loss of Spain's colonies and conflict with other European powers in the early nineteenth century. It did not help writers such as Amar that there was a political reaction against France after the Napoleonic invasions of other European countries in the early nineteenth century. 'Women's rights' became tainted by their association with French revolutionary discourse. Nonetheless, even in this period of backlash, the links between Spain and wider European debates on the 'woman question' were strong. In particular, and in spite of his French nationality, the utopian socialist Charles Fourier was important in continuing to promote women's equality to men. His ideas were influential upon women such as the Irish writer Anna Wheeler and, in the German state of Thuringia, Louise Otto. His edicts were taken up in experimental communities across Europe and the Americas, though for the women involved, the sexual subversiveness of Fourier's ideas made these communities risky and unsettled enterprises. Still, the desire to live according to new values kept 'Harmony' alive amongst groups all over the globe.

The global dissemination of 'sex radical' ideas was strengthened by the patterns of exile and migration that characterized the careers of nineteenth-century revolutionaries. In the revolutionary Andalusian city of Cadiz, for example, Fourier's ideas were propounded by Joaquín Abreu, a revolutionary figure who had spent some years in exile in France. Cadiz in 1812 had seen one of the first efforts in the world to write a constitution. Its authors asserted the liberal rights of a free press and demanded mass male suffrage under a constitutional monarchy. Though never enacted, it left a legacy of radical constitutionalism which was taken up and extended in feminist and early socialist directions. Female followers of Fourier based in Cadiz, such as Margarita López Morla, published a series of journals in the 1850s and 60s which offered translations both of Fourier's work and that of other European socialists who wrote on the 'woman question', such as the Polish radical Jan Czyński (1801–76). The Cadiz women echoed Fourier's call for social harmony to be achieved by co-operation and sexual freedom.[3] Fourier provided an important resource for these early feminist interventions in Spain because his ideas were easily adapted to local concerns. In Cadiz, this meant interest in agricultural reform and in the political traditions of republicanism, which emphasized participatory self-government and liberty.

The feminist contributions to journals in Cadiz were collected into book form by 'Rosa Marina' (possibly a pen-name), who published *La Mujer y la Sociedad* (*Woman and Society*) in 1857. This text provided an early manifesto in Spain that demanded the transformation of women's social status. Looking back to earlier writers such as Josefa Amar, 'Rosa Marina' based her calls for women's equality on Christian commitments to spiritual equality across the sexes. This produced a feminist language that resonated with the Roman Catholic religious setting of Spain. This conciliation of feminism and Christianity was to prove a persistent theme in nineteenth- and early-twentieth-century Spanish feminist texts.[4] Within its framework, 'Rosa Marina' claimed access to all forms of employment for women, even after marriage, as well as their legal autonomy. The distinctive utopian socialist stress on labour remained, though the sexual freedoms of Fourier's feminism became muted. Nor was there any particular recognition of how men benefited from a society organized around women's marginalization. Like many texts of the late eighteenth to mid-nineteenth century, the emphasis was on the benefits both sexes would receive when women attained equality with men.

This combination of Christian, Enlightenment and socialist thinking influenced Spanish nineteenth-century contributions on the 'woman question'. Despite internal tensions, it established a discourse that informed the debates that also flourished in Latin American countries. As in Spain, Latin Americans had witnessed war, sharp social change and constitutional upheavals in the late eighteenth and early nineteenth centuries. The region had seen the development of newspapers alongside growing industrial employment for working-class women. The changes, alongside controversies over constitutional reform, had fuelled a widespread debate on the 'woman question'.

In Brazil, for example, women's lives in the early nineteenth century were deeply constrained by a legal code which originated in the colonial power, Portugal, and declared women to be perpetual minors. Brazilian free women were likely to marry early and to lack education, though working-class women adopted many different family forms including, on occasion, female-headed households. Of course, some Brazilian women were not just legally minors, but were also personal *property*. Brazil was a slave-owning society until

1888. Slave women lived lives of deep privation, though some found leadership roles in the Afro-Brazilian churches.

Nineteenth-century Brazil was politically dominated by the coffee-growing planter class and Portuguese rule. It was only possible for exceptionally determined and mostly elite women to gain a voice in the public sphere. They include figures such as Nísia Floresta Brasileira Augusta (1810–85), who translated into Portuguese a text she believed to be Mary Wollstonecraft's *Vindication of the Rights of Woman* in 1832. The book, published as *Direitos das Mulheres e Injustiça dos Homens* (*Women's Rights and Men's Injustice*) turned out to be based not on Wollstonecraft but instead upon an eighteenth-century text of unclear authorship, *Woman Not Inferior to Man.*[5] This was an environment in which authorship could be fluid or indeterminate, and translators could play a substantial role in shaping a text.

Floresta, who took the name 'Brasileira' to emphasize her patriotism, was an unusually vocal supporter of women's rights across her publishing career of four decades. She had been briefly married at thirteen, then had two children with another man, only to be widowed, leaving her with a baby and toddler. She was forced to support herself by teaching and publishing in the Brazilian cities of Porto Alegre and Rio de Janeiro, as well as travelling in Europe. Floresta was deeply committed to women's education, but also to the wider responsibility that was so prominent in the republican tradition of women as producers and shapers of good citizens. These ideas were shaped by her friendship with French Positivist philosopher August Comte (1798–1857), who believed women to be a superior moral and regenerationist force. Floresta, like many of her peers, was incensed by eighteenth-century ideas of women as luxury-loving playthings. She insisted on women's powers of reason, with direct criticism of Rousseau and other philosophers. Her work celebrated feminine qualities of self-denial and maternal influence that, she argued, were essential to nation-building and human advancement.

Brazilian supporters of women's rights, like their contemporaries in Cadiz, drew on the powerful language of constitutionalism. Latin American countries were emerging as independent entities in the nineteenth century, after decades or centuries of absolutist colonial rule from Spain and Portugal. Constitutional conventions and congresses debated the kinds of written texts that might govern the political order, and this provided opportunities for supporters of women's citizenship to argue for their inclusion. Nonetheless, such claims continued to be framed in terms of preservation of family life and Christian morality – a '*progresso feminino*' ('feminine progress') rather than a more distinct and radical feminism.[6]

Floresta did not envisage women's roles as extending beyond the family. Unlike her socialist peers in Cadiz, she was uninterested in the lives of poor, indigenous and working-class women. Yet across the nineteenth century, the rise of women's employment (spanning manual labour in industry and, for middle-class women, professions such as school teaching) was an important factor that gave women more access to literacy, more resources and a stronger sense of their social and civic value in Brazilian society. The innovation of women's newspapers in the second half of the nineteenth century in Brazil and across Latin America was particularly important in articulating their rights and allowing women to participate in political debates. The kind of citizenship imagined was not one of domestic confinement, even if family life was at its centre. Brazil had been declared a republic in 1889, with a central commitment to the active role that citizens should take in serving their nation. In the years that followed, women's suffrage demands were framed in terms not simply of the duty of voting but also the right of women to stand for election and take a more active role in political life.

Patriarchy

Christian and liberal versions of republicanism offered important traditions that empowered radicals to argue for women's inclusion in existing structures. They were less useable, however, for those trying to identify the pervasive and structural nature of women's subordinate status. While male tyranny and exploitation of women was visible to many observers, it was rare for this to be understood as systemic. The metaphor of women's 'enslavement' by men was widely used by radicals of both sexes, inspired by the increasingly vocal and organized opposition to the Atlantic slave-trade, in which women had been very active. But men were largely portrayed as individual oppressors, and early texts that addressed the 'woman question' preferred to dwell on women's powers of reason, and how they could be better citizens and mothers.

As a more prominent and organized women's movement emerged at certain locations in the middle decades of the nineteenth century, thinkers and theorists of the women's movement began to experiment with a means to convey the depth and significance of men's oppression of women. Patriarchy has been the most successful such concept, conceived initially by ethnographers, popularized within the socialist movement and later taken up, reinterpreted and contested by feminists of many different kinds.

The idea of patriarchy as an overarching form of social organization that consistently put women under male domination was initially formulated in the nineteenth century by Lewis Henry Morgan (1818–81) in his account of human progress through 'savagery' to 'civilization', published under the title *Ancient Society* in 1877. Morgan's massive account of the complexities of human sexual and social organization was foundational to modern anthropology. It traced the evolution of humans from promiscuity to monogamy, and from matriarchy to patriarchy, based on his study of Native Americans and other indigenous peoples. Intellectually influenced by Charles Darwin, Morgan developed a linear account of 'civilization' as a progressive sequence of stages. 'Degraded' or promiscuous forms of group marriage were 'primitive', Morgan argued, but 'need not revolt the mind' because they were systems that would gradually, necessarily, give way to more 'civilized' forms of 'exclusive cohabitation' based on knowledge of paternity and private property.[7] Morgan was also deeply committed to the expansion of women's higher education and endowed a women's college in his will.

European socialists Karl Marx (1818–83) and Frederick Engels (1820–95) were influenced by Morgan, using his idea of patriarchy to explain the malign influence of property. Rights to ownership had caused men's exploitation of women's reproductive powers (their 'mother right'), and subverted early forms of matriarchal societies. In a reversal of typical nineteenth-century progress narratives, Engels named women as the first proletariat, created at the specific historical moment when, he argued, their labour became exploited by men. His 1884 book, *The Origin of the Family, Private Property, and the State: In the Light of the Researches of Lewis H. Morgan*, argued that women in early human societies had enjoyed 'a higher social position than women have ever enjoyed since . . .' Primitive communism was replaced by a condition of slavery or prostitution for women in more 'advanced' patriarchal societies:

> The lady of civilization, surrounded by false homage and estranged from all real work, has an infinitely lower social position than the hard-working woman of barbarism, who was regarded among her people as a real lady.[8]

There are echoes in Engels's criticism of 'the lady of civilization' of the eighteenth-century association between women and luxury. This strand of thinking was continued in later accounts of women's 'parasitism' that underpinned important feminist writings such as South African Olive Schreiner's *Woman and Labour*. Schreiner (1855–1920) had used both fiction and polemic to argue for women's freedoms, pacifism and racial equality. Her hugely influential 'feminist bible', *Woman and Labour* was published in 1911. It was a reworked version of an earlier, larger manuscript that had been destroyed during the unrest of the Anglo-Boer War, a loss Schreiner never quite recovered from. The book echoed the commitment to economic independence and fear of 'parasitism' that Charlotte Perkins Gilman had developed in an earlier popular work, *Women and Economics* (1898). Both books were translated and republished all over the world, and established a feminism focused on the decay of the human race. In Schreiner's words:

> the parasitism of the female heralds the decay of a nation or class, and as invariably indicates disease as the pustules of smallpox upon the skin indicate the existence of a purulent virus in the system.[9]

Within the socialist movement, however, Engels's account of patriarchy remained centre stage and worked to absolve men of blame for women's oppression. Engels argued that it was women who brought about the transition to patriarchy as economic conditions shifted to agriculture, by rejecting group marriage in favour of monogamy, due to 'their longing for the right of chastity'. And since patriarchy was assumed by Engels to be an evolutionary way-station on the route to socialist liberation, he judged it best opposed by a united front of men and women organizing against capitalism. This meant that there was no particular recognition or scrutiny of the nature of women's oppression from many leading nineteenth-century socialists; some, such as Pierre-Joseph Proudhon, continued to hold anti-feminist beliefs, for example that women were destined 'by nature and conjugal law' to hold 'purely domestic functions'.

The German socialist August Bebel (1840–1913) took up and popularized the terminology of patriarchy. He perceived it as a powerful means of explaining how women's oppression by men was linked to the rise of private property and appropriation of labour, but without blaming individual men for this structural feature of society. Indeed, patriarchy was just one amongst many characteristic forms of social organization. In *Woman and Socialism* (1885), Bebel insisted that the current women's movement failed to understand this big picture. Feminist reformers were tied to the status quo and could only imagine minor reforms, such as greater access to education or political rights for women. Socialism, in contrast, recognized that marriage itself was sex slavery, and that all women had a common interest in its abolition. For Bebel, this went hand-in-hand with the abolition of 'wage slavery' and private property. He believed that, while 'bourgeois' women did not share this concern, they still could act with working-class women: 'Though they march in separate armies they may strike a united blow.' Under revolutionary conditions, Bebel predicted, all forms of dependency would be abolished, leading to 'complete economic and intellectual independence'.[10]

Bebel's book was a bestseller, hugely influential in aligning socialism with feminism across Europe and, later, Soviet-influenced countries. It inaugurated a tradition of feminist thinking that was deeply focused on the particular exploitation faced by working-class women under capitalism. Clara Zetkin (1857–1933) was a particularly prominent socialist feminist in this tradition, active across France, Britain, Soviet Russia and Germany. Deeply committed to socialist and later Communist revolution, Zetkin was also active in anti-militarist and anti-fascist campaigning. She linked these commitments to socialist organizing as editor of the socialist women's periodical *Die Gleichheit* (*Equality*) from 1892. Zetkin was implacably hostile to what she saw as bourgeois feminism, and, like Engels, she reiterated the powers of working-class women to organize, in unity with working-class men, against capitalism. Where Engels and Bebel, however, had also seen potential for women to unite across class lines, Zetkin was relentless in rejecting this. Despite seeing women as sharing a 'function of bearing, nourishing and rearing new human life', she saw class privilege as preventing any common activism and worked hard to keep socialist feminism distinct from other feminist groupings.[11]

Even those revolutionaries who supported feminism assumed it would be attained as a by-product of socialist revolution. The early writings of Russian revolutionary Alexandra Kollontai echoed Zetkin's reductive, rigid refusal of any possible alliance with 'bourgeois' women. She also asserted the inevitability of women's liberation, echoing the optimism of August Bebel and his followers in the German Social Democratic Party that women's emancipation was, in Bebel's words, a 'great river, whose majestic course can be stopped by no object in nature'.[12]

In this respect, Engels's formulation of patriarchy lacked critical potential for many activists. Numerous women – socialist and of other persuasions – contested the complacent idea of women's emancipation as a side effect. They recognized that patriarchy had its own dynamics and was unlikely to be addressed simply by a socialist revolution. Patriarchy was capable of morphing across time, and even of delivering benefits to some women. It offered advantages to men, the majority of whom benefited very directly from women's labour and political exclusion. This meant that many socialist men who had read their Engels and Bebel still found it hard to perceive their own oppressive behaviour towards women.

The 'Turk Complex'

Patriarchy was understood by its early socialist theorists as a system of distributing property, and thus fundamentally as a form of economic organization. It also had legal and political manifestations, such as in the *Patria Potestad*, the civil code that placed a woman in the permanent legal position of a minor, under the authority of her father or husband, which characterized many Latin American nations. But patriarchy also came to be used by feminists to indicate ways of thinking and seeing – as a set of values that shaped not just law and politics but also culture and social norms.

British activist Eleanor Rathbone (1872–1946) was trying to get at this sense of how patriarchy might infuse the deepest psychological nooks and crannies of men and women when she offered the racially marked idea of the 'Turk complex' to describe male mentalities towards women. It represented for her the practical, material male dominance exerted through their wage advantages, and the egoism and narcissism that accompanied it. Rathbone deployed orientalist language to capture her outrage; it had been a commonplace in many national contexts to imagine 'the East' as a site of women's subordination and confinement by men. The contrast between Muslim and non-Muslim treatment of women had been central to arguments about women's subordination produced in the eighteenth century by figures such as Josefa Amar. The harem, Hindu child brides and immolated widows, clitoridectomy and payment of a bride price, all provided ways of imagining the world based on the powerful contrast of 'East' and 'West', even if this was often vague in geographical and religious terms. This intellectual framing made it hard for many feminists in imperial nations to see women in the Middle East, South and East Asia as potential agents of feminism. As a leading American feminist, Elizabeth Cady Stanton put it:

> In the Turkish Harem where woman is little above the brute of the field, where immortal mind is crushed and soul itself as it were blotted out . . . in those Seraglios where intellect and soul are buried beneath the sensualism and brutality which are the inevitable result of the belief in women's inferiority, even here she is not only satisfied with her position but glories in it.[13]

Through the 'Turk complex', Rathbone wanted to convey the psychological elements of patriarchy, constructed through the intimate worlds of family, the education system and friendship groups. She was a well-connected establishment figure, born into a wealthy ship-owning family in Liverpool, and active in social service. Her work with the wives and mothers of British servicemen during the First World War led her to endorse the payment of state benefits directly to women to reflect their work as mothers – a proposal she termed 'family endowment'. This was deeply unpopular with trade union leaders, who feared it would provide an excuse for employers to cut the wages that they paid male workers. It was to be an important feminist aspiration for those who emphasized women's reproductive needs.

During her years of campaigning across the 1920s and 30s, Rathbone described endowment as a utopian policy – seemingly a minor welfare payment, but in practice a major strike against the way in which men saw themselves as the most powerful figure in the family. If men could no longer claim to be breadwinners, Rathbone hoped, then women could imagine themselves as autonomous individuals in their own right. If wages were equalized, women could aspire to new kinds of careers, and solve their basic problems of poverty. They would also have the opportunity to live without men if they so chose – as Rathbone herself did, in a long-term relationship with another woman. Like many feminists, she used her proposals for change to try to get at her sense of how society was organized in deep structural ways to men's advantage:

> Among the strongest instincts of human nature is the desire of power, of domination, of being looked up to and admired. Through all ages and in all countries . . . men even the humblest and most oppressed have found scope for the satisfaction of this desire in their power over their own wives and children. Even the slave was lord in his hut.[14]

The 'Turk complex' captured Rathbone's sense of male tyranny and selfishness.

This way of thinking encouraged 'Western' women to imagine themselves as saviours of female victims of male aggression, in ways that were often complicit with the violence and brutality of imperial occupation. Rathbone used her prominence as a Member of Parliament in Britain to tour India in 1931 and argue for the enforcement of British legislation on child marriage in India. She had previously formed a 'Committee for the Protection of Coloured Women in the Crown Colonies' to work for feminist goals within the British Parliament by methods that barely consulted the women in question. Rathbone did, however, come to realize that imperial paternalism was the wrong tool, particularly after she encountered Indian women's deep resistance to talk of protection. She began to campaign for the enfranchisement of Indian women, though she was willing to accept a 'special franchise' for wives in India, rather than the full adult suffrage that British women had received in 1928.[15] Rathbone can be seen as one of many 'feminist imperialists' – she was insistently committed to democratic self-determination as the best means of righting wrongs against girls and women, yet also continued to see British control of other nations as a compromise, likely to advance rather than hinder feminist causes.[16]

Rathbone's talk of the 'Turk complex' was not taken up by other feminists, but her fascination with the mental structures and pervasiveness of patriarchy was widely shared. The American Charlotte Perkins Gilman was also fascinated by the mental structures of male oppression, and coined an alternative term to capture societies organized around a gender hierarchy that advantaged men: 'androcentrism', a 'sexuo-economic structure' that she believed had grave implications for humanity. Gilman's thinking on androcentrism or 'the man-made world' drew, like Engels, on the ethnographical work of Lewis Morgan. Gilman accused human societies of obsessing over sexual difference: 'We have been so taken up with the phenomena of masculinity and femininity, that our common humanity has largely escaped notice.' Her feminism was humanist in its terrain though, like Rathbone's, it was always infused with the racial hierarchies of 'civilization'. Despite her humanism, she still maintained that 'the savage who can count a hundred is more human than the savage who can count ten.'[17]

In Gilman's view, androcentricism deformed human evolution, by confining women to 'sex work'. In such societies, 'motherhood is an exchangeable commodity given by women in payment for clothes and food.' Gilman sought to support mothers, but also to prioritize their 'useful working life' that preceded and followed the reproductive period. Unlike feminists more influenced by the individual rights of liberalism, Gilman's critique of androcentrism went with a vision of the collective good of 'the race', and humanity in general: 'Our human-ness is seen to lie not so much in what we are individually, as in our relations to one another.'[18]

Instead of androcentrism, Gilman proposed an economic system based on cooperation. Like the 'utopian' socialists, she envisaged a different socio-economic order, though she did not recommend withdrawal into isolated communes. Instead, she anticipated a wholesale social shift away from privacy, with kitchenless individual homes, shared food production and dining spaces, and professional cleaning services. She was keen to distance herself from the socialist or Communist connotations of such an approach and insisted that it was to be undertaken 'on a business basis to prove a substantial business success'.[19] Where Rathbone had sought state intervention, for Gilman it was the marketplace that could fulfil women's unmet needs for scientific and efficient household organization and, in turn, spark a feminist or 'sexuo-economic' revolution.

Nannü

Gilman's wider evocation of 'the race' was a commonplace rhetorical tactic for gender activists of the late nineteenth century, whose work was rooted in social Darwinist ideas of racial advancement. China, understood through the optic of foot-binding, was imagined by Europeans as a site of women's degradation, as well as being a source of fascination. The South African feminist and novelist Olive Schreiner wrote to her friend Karl Pearson, a British eugenicist, insisting that in relation to the 'woman question' it was 'very important to understand something of the Chinese. A wonderful light might be thrown over our whole subject by studying them.' This sounded promising, but she continued in racially objectifying terms: 'They are almost as distant from us as the Orang from the Gorilla.'[20] Racial science incited sensationalist and casually racist engagement with the ideas and social organization of other cultures. As it grew in influence over the nineteenth century, its tenets infused some versions of feminism with the violence of racial stigma.

But even Schreiner had to admit that China couldn't be so easily pigeon-holed, when it was reported around the world in 1912 that Chinese women in some regions had obtained the vote. It was awkward, to say the least, that this had happened some years or decades ahead of the enfranchisement of many European and American women.[21] Schreiner noted, in typical orientalist terms: 'China is awakening from her long sleep & even the women are ceasing to bind their feet.'[22] But she knew nothing of the active feminist movement that had developed in China, stimulated by the patriotic projects of nation-building and campaigning against the long rule of the Qing dynasty (1633–1912). Most women's suffrage activists of the early twentieth century were allied to Sun Yat-sen's Revolutionary Alliance, and they hoped to achieve both 'women's rights' (*funüjie*) and national advancement under the new Republic of China, established in 1911. As national self-determination became a more prominent project in the twentieth century, feminism frequently became couched in terms of race and nation-building. Chinese political philosopher Liang Qichao, for example, argued in relation to the practice of foot-binding that 'women suffer in plain sight from the bitterness of this terrible poison, but in truth it is our entire race that is left with the greatest injury.'[23]

In relation to ideas of patriarchy, Chinese intellectuals were sometimes deeply influenced by imagined sources of 'Western freedom'. This included the many men active in writing about women's rights in early-twentieth-century China. Jin Tianhe's landmark publication of a republican-feminist essay, *The Women's Bell*, in 1903 was perhaps the most prominent example of this. Jin Tianhe (1873–1947) wrote of his longing for 'the fresh air of European civilization', invoking Enlightenment thinkers such as Rousseau and John Stuart Mill as well as Japanese educators to dispel China's 'slumbering world of darkness'. In keeping with Rousseau's critique of women's love of luxury and immorality, he painted an alternative ideal picture of the liberated woman who was a good educator of her children, a patriot, dressed modestly, and free of superstition. He called for women to 'spread the seeds of freedom from the West' by teaching and public speaking, as well as physical exercise.[24]

The anarchist-influenced feminist He-Yin Zhen (*c.* 1884–*c.* 1920) had little patience with Jin Tianhe's talk of the 'flower-like spirits of all women'. She had participated in the vibrant political circles of Chinese radicals exiled to Japan in the early twentieth century. This led her to co-edit a journal, *Natural*

Justice, published by the Society for the Restoration of Women's Rights in Tokyo (1907–8), as well as contributing to the Paris-based journal *New Century*, published by Chinese exiles. He-Yin took an ambitious approach to theorizing the structural inequalities that characterized women's experiences. She offered a re-reading of a Confucian Mandarin term, *nannü*, to mean a sexed system of social organization. It might be translated as 'sex-gender' or 'patriarchy', though *nannü* is challenging to translate because, unlike 'patriarchy', it also captures a variety of broad oppositions – past and present, China and the world. Formed of *nan* (man) and *nü* (woman), it can be seen as 'the foundation of all patriarchal abstractions and markings of distinction'.[25]

In the early twentieth century, Mandarin was fluid and relatively uncodified, and thus open to the invention of new words and foreign influences. There were a variety of terms for 'women' that emerged in China during the upheavals of this period, as intellectuals brought out different qualities of women. Writers who drew on evolutionary thinking talked of women as *nüxing*, a sexed term that also had connotations of Western modernity. Chinese socialists preferred to identify women as *funü*, a term drawn from the translations of the Marxist work of Bebel and Engels on the 'woman question', which defined 'women' in relation to social production as a 'mass subject'.[26]

He-Yin's writing, rooted in her experiences of Japanese intellectual debates, suggested the impetus that linguistic openness and cosmopolitanism could give to innovative thinking, particularly in a context in which gender did not closely map onto biological ideas of sex. *Nannü* offered a way of linking distinctions of gender to the organization of bodies, labour and power through cultural and economic life. It enabled He-Yin to imagine a world where 'the nouns *nanxing* [male nature] and *nüxing* [female nature] will no longer be necessary'.[27] For her, this implied the end of capitalism, the state, private property, as well as racial and sexual difference.

He-Yin rejected ideas of Western European influence and was critical of the liberal and capitalist underpinnings of ideas of modernization. She drew instead on the anarchist writings of the Russian Peter Kropotkin, and the Japanese anarchist Sentarō Kemuyama. Her 1907 essay 'On the Revenge of Women' laid out the global and transhistorical character of *nannü*:

> I address myself to the women of my country: has it occurred to you that men are our archenemy? . . . This situation is by no means confined to the ancient world and is just as prevalent in the modern world as it was in the past; nor is it a uniquely Chinese situation, since the same thing happens in foreign lands as well.[28]

She traced this system to social institutions such as marriage, as well as to the intellectual traditions of Confucian classical scholarship. Alongside the economic, sexual and psychic patriarchal structures, He-Yin anticipated the emphasis of late-twentieth-century feminists, that patriarchy was embedded in the structure of language. Patriarchy was, for He-Yin, embodied in the very character of Chinese writing; the term *furen* (another term for 'woman') derived from the character *fu*, meaning 'broom', pinning women to household labour.

He-Yin asserted that women faced despotic oppression and objectification as a form of male property. Her 'Feminist Manifesto' (1907) called for the end to the patriarchal renaming of women by their husbands' names. Though she had married, her own name represented her political stance (Zhen stood for 'thunderclap') and included Yin, her mother's maiden name. She sought equal treatment and education of both sexes as part of a wider social revolution. In sexual terms, she demanded the end of monogamous marriage, free divorce, and the abolition of prostitution. In characteristic anarchist terms, all this was to be achieved not by 'reform or boycotting, but by the application of brute force to coerce men into making us equal'.[29]

Despite the revolutionary conditions of the fall of the Qing dynasty in 1911, He-Yin Zhen found it hard to maintain her position as a female intellectual and agitator. When her husband died in 1919, she disappeared from public view, and nothing is known of her subsequent fate. Her brief, brilliant period of activism is testament to both the possibilities and the personal costs of feminist activism.

Women's Liberation and Patriarchy

A number of thinkers in the later nineteenth and early twentieth century were thus thinking ambitiously about how gender informed the structures of society and offered different ways of naming male dominance. Despite these alternatives, it was the idea of patriarchy (sometimes reframed as 'the Patriarchy') that proved most workable for women in the 1960s onwards, though it developed a wider range of meanings than envisaged in its Marxist origins.

The American writer Kate Millett (1934–2017) was prominent in theorizing later versions of patriarchy. She had been raised in Minnesota, and her alcoholic father abandoned the family when Millett was fourteen, leaving her mother to raise her three children alone. By the 1960s, the Oxford-educated Millett was closely involved in the countercultural hippie movement, peace activism and women's arts. She participated in the surrealist-influenced avant-garde in Japan while living there in the early 1960s and was exposed to the deep opposition to the presence of American troops on Japanese soil. For Millett, however, it was the aggressive sexual politics of America and Japan that became her major concern. She was shocked by the Japanese women 'who served us on their knees at the feasts where I [as a foreign artist] was permitted to sit up and chat with the men'.[30] She was also radicalized by the 1965 sexual torture and murder in Indianapolis of sixteen-year-old Sylvia Likens. This crime was carried out by a woman and children, and Millett wanted to understand how distorted social values might make this possible.

Millett saw sexual politics as resting on the psychological power of 'sex-role stereotypes', elaborated through institutions of religion, family and marriage to produce 'a pervasive doctrine of male superiority' that not only caused women's victimization by men, but the overall distortion of values that could lead to abusive behaviour such the Likens murder. She maintained hope that things could be organized differently after a sexual revolution. Her 'manifesto for revolution' in 1968 claimed:

> When one group rules another, the relationship between the two is political. When such an arrangement is carried out over a long period of time it develops an ideology (feudalism, racism, etc). All historical civilizations are patriarchies: their ideology is male supremacy.[31]

Millett approached ideas of patriarchy through a review of literary figures. She pointed to the violence and misogyny of Sigmund Freud, as well as canonical authors of sexually explicit novels, such as D. H. Lawrence and Henry Miller. Millett's development of the idea of 'enforced heterosexuality', later termed 'compulsory heterosexuality' by Adrienne Rich, was to be a powerful influence on lesbian thinking. It helped give rise to the concept of 'heteronormativity' – the idea that opposite sex, gender-binary interactions are socially imposed as the default 'normal' in contemporary Euro-American societies. Ideas of patriarchy thus gave rise to a rich literature which was later to prompt the development of queer theories of sexual fluidity and possibility. With echoes of He-Yin Zhen's dream of transcending sexual difference, Millett predicted that humans would be 'unisex': 'each individual may develop an entire – rather than partial, limited and conformist – personality.' In terms of sexual desire, this would create 'bisex, or the end of enforced perverse heterosexuality'.[32]

Millett's later book-length elaboration, *Sexual Politics* (1970), became a defining influence amongst American and British women's liberationists. Its popularity led to Millett being featured on the front cover of *Time* magazine in 1970, described as 'the Mao Tse-Tung of Women's Liberation'. The magazine was forced to use a drawn portrait, because Millett did not want to be identified as a 'leader' of women's liberation and refused permission for a photograph. Nonetheless, she became one of the most high-profile feminist writers of the early days of women's liberation.

Drawing on French feminist philosopher Simone de Beauvoir, Millett termed patriarchy a deep-rooted 'habit of mind' that allowed men's domination of women, as well as the domination of racial minorities by whites, the young by the old, and women by other women, to seem normal. Her account of patriarchy was supplemented by feminist theologian Mary Daly (1928–2010), who identified the Judeo-Christian tradition as a central institution of patriarchy. Daly argued that

> the image of God as exclusively a father and not a mother, for example, was spawned by the human imagination under the conditions of patriarchal society and sustained as plausible by patriarchy.[33]

Working in American universities, Daly controversially established women-only spaces in the classroom. This practice was later extended to many of the women's centres, bookshops, discos, shelters and discussion groups of women's liberation.

Daly was an important figure in the radical wing of the women's liberation movement, which was characterized by an emphasis on 'women's culture' and separatism. She explored the alternative spiritual universe of women's liberation in her book *Gyn/Ecology* (1978), and linked this to her sense of the environmental degradation that went with 'planetary patriarchy'. Prefiguring the urgency over environmental extinction that has become widespread in the twenty-first century, Daly termed

Gyn/Ecology 'an extremist book, written in a situation of extremity, written on the edge of a culture that is killing itself and all of sentient life'. Daly was more willing than most of her peers to blame individual men for this, describing herself as unashamedly 'anti-male': women, she argued, must have

> the courage [to] admit to ourselves that males and males only are the originators, planners, controllers, and legitimators of patriarchy. Patriarchy is the homeland of males; it is Father Land: and men are its agents.[34]

Daly aimed her anger very directly at men, but like He-Yin Zhen, she also wanted to explore how patriarchy was infused into language itself. Her writing experimented with new modes of expression that attempted to get beyond the ordering of the world into patriarchal categories. This involved the re-appropriation of stigmatized names – hags, witches, harpies, spinsters – and the celebration of women-centred modes of living and creating, through strategies that she termed 'Sparking', 'Spinning' and 'positive paranoia'. Feminism was for Daly

> the a-mazing struggle, which is exorcism, [and] the ecstatic process of Spinsters dis-covering the labyrinth of our own unfolding/becoming . . . into the Otherworld – which is her own time/space.[35]

Her books were not easy to read, and Daly was criticized by the indigenous women's movement for appropriating the symbols and ideas of indigenous cultures while arguably still seeing women of colour as 'less feminine, less human, less spiritual' than white women.[36] For some women, Daly was life-changing. One reviewer in Milwaukee in 1980 described

Gyn/Ecology as 'one of the most eloquent and dangerous books to come out of the feminist movement', that gave women 'the power inherent in our being able to speak and define ourselves'. Reworking language would become a hugely important project for the women's liberation movement, particularly in the United States and France. For some, this was a straightforward matter of challenging the embedded gender stereotypes in language. One 'Non-Sexist Code of Practice for Book Publishing', produced by the Women in Publishing Industry Group in Britain, stated simply:

> Words and images can reinforce the idea that women are lesser beings than men. For instance, the suffix '-ette' when used in words such as 'usherette' does not merely imply the female gender but also implies the lowly yet suggestively cute status that feminine descriptions hold – so that a small kitchen becomes a kitchenette.

They asked designers, copy editors, publishers and illustrators to actively challenge sexist materials: 'the media are particularly effective and insidious vehicles for sexism. They are also, potentially, influential instruments of change.'[37]

Others, in contrast, found language to be less open to direct reform. An interest in the psychic dimensions of language led the Bulgarian-French feminist philosopher Julia Kristeva to theorize a realm before the child learns to speak, where it has a relationship with its mother that is feminine, poetic, rhythmic, musical. Kristeva, heavily influenced by psychoanalysis, labelled this realm the 'semiotic' or 'chora', a place of richness and connection that exists prior to the 'symbolic' world of language. This insight was influential upon French feminist experiments with *écriture féminine* (women's writing). Feminist literary critics such as Hélène Cixous called for women to write themselves and their sexual pleasure in non-linear, subversive writing that moves beyond 'phallocentric' formats:

> Where is the ebullient, infinite woman who, immersed as she was in her naiveté, kept in the dark about herself, led into self-disdain by the great arm of parental–conjugal phallocentrism, hasn't been ashamed of her strength? Who, surprised and horrified by the fantastic tumult of her drives . . . hasn't accused herself of being a monster?[38]

Cixous invited women to write with passion, precision and invention about their bodies and desires, and 'break out of the snare of silence'. 'Phallocentrism' was an alternative means of naming male dominance, but with a particular emphasis on the symbolic realm of the 'phallus' (erect penis). The emphasis on language led some philosophers to talk of 'phallogocentrism' – combining 'phallus' with 'logos' (word or logic) to show the deep infusion of male domination in the symbolic realm of language. Novelists such as Algerian Assia Djebar (1936–2015) took up this challenge of writing in a context of a society shaped by French colonial occupation and Islam, in which 'the masculine public sphere [was] opposed to the intimate, family sphere, the men's spaces different from feminine polyphony – murmurs and whispers . . .'[39]

For all the excitement of reworking language and imagining feminist/female monstrosity, radical feminism in this mode could be unworkable in everyday life. Assia Djebar maintained a complex relationship with feminism, and she was wary of its assertions of commonality between women. Few writers found it easy to express *écriture féminine*, and others complained that it was over-intellectual, or based on an essentialist view of the feminine. Even the popular and widely read Mary Daly, the reviewer in Milwaukee concluded,

> leaves us feeling ready to act but not sure how to proceed or what direction to move in . . . How do we obtain equal rights and reproductive freedom if we don't deal directly with the male power structure?[40]

The problem was that patriarchy or phallocentrism could seem indistinct – Kate Millett's influential account subsumed a ragbag of different intellectual and literary traditions under the single term, and failed to account for meaningful change between different economic or political orders.[41] This lack of precision was embraced as a strength by some, who viewed historical and cross-cultural difference as simply meaningless in the face of women's oppression. An American radical feminist group published a 'Fourth World Manifesto' in 1972, premised on what now reads as a naïve sense of global commonality:

> The repression of female culture is only a question of degree all over the world; the underlying reality is basically the same: the denial of self-determination for women. Women travelling to a foreign country can readily communicate and understand other women in that country because female work and roles (culture) are basically the same all over the world.[42]

This group adopted the term 'colonialism' to capture male hegemony, but this was deeply insensitive to the intersecting oppressions of race, empire and national origin. It proved hard to remain mindful of different women's experiences when using the concept 'patriarchy', and the various movements associated with women's liberation frequently alienated those women who had also been victims of enslavement, class exclusions, colonial violence or racism.

Double Jeopardy

From the start of the powerful upsurge in feminist organizing that followed the anti-colonial, peace movement and civil rights protests of the late 1960s, the interaction of different axes of oppression was visible to many within the women's movement. Frances Beal wrote a pamphlet in 1969 titled *Double Jeopardy: To Be Black and Female* that captured her sense of the interwoven nature of the oppression of black women and men:

> Black women are not resentful of the rise to power of black men. We welcome it. We see in it the eventual liberation of all black people from this corrupt system under which we suffer. Nevertheless, this does not mean that you have to negate one for the other. This kind of thinking is a product of miseducation; that it's either *X* or it's *Y*. It is fallacious reasoning that in order for the black man to be strong, the black woman has to be weak.[43]

Due to their experiences of gender, race and class, African American women had what Beal termed 'very specific problems that have to be spoken to'. Nineteenth-century African American women activists such as Sojourner Truth and Anna Julia Cooper had already written about 'double enslavement' and 'triple exploitation'. These ideas were also developed within the Communist and socialist left through the work of Trinidadian-born Claudia Jones (1915–64). Active in the American Communist and black nationalist movements, Jones was deported to Britain in 1955, where she continued to organize for Communism, anti-colonialism and women's rights. She talked of 'triple exploitation' and highlighted the 'madam–maid' relationship between white and black women that deeply infused their relationships in the United States. For Jones, even well-meant efforts to span these divisions were undercut by employers' habit of

> assuming that the duty of the white progressive employer, is to 'inform' the Negro woman of her exploitation and her oppression which she undoubtedly knows quite intimately.[44]

Frances Beal's formulation of black feminism was urgent, not to be postponed in favour of struggles for racial liberation:

> We must be liberated along with the rest of the population. We cannot wait to start working on those problems until that great day in the future when the revolution somehow miraculously, is accomplished.

Black women could not assume that white feminists would support black women's needs. Like Claudia Jones, Beal termed white women 'economic enemies' of black women: 'If your mother worked in a white woman's kitchen, she knows what I mean.'[45]

Beal had been active within the Student Nonviolent Coordinating Committee in the American civil rights movement, but became frustrated by its increasingly macho Black Power politics. She co-founded the Black Women's Liberation Alliance in 1970, which later became the Third World Women's Alliance, and aimed to put social justice, anti-racism and women's liberation at the heart of its mixed-sex activism. Based in New York, the Third World Women's Alliance later published its periodical under the title *Triple Jeopardy: Racism, Sexism and Imperialism.*

It was helpful to work with this idea of multiple sources of oppression, but in practice the politics that resulted could seem like a competitive totting up of marginality. Chicana feminist Elizabeth Martínez satirically termed this effect the 'oppression Olympics'. In 1988, sociologist Deborah King coined the term 'multiple jeopardy' to indicate 'several, simultaneous oppressions' and the 'multiplicative relationships among them'. She hoped to highlight that the oppressions of black women were not additive, but interactive.[46] Later termed the 'matrix of domination' by sociologist Patricia Hill Collins, or 'intersectionality' by scholar Kimberlé Crenshaw, this concept of interacting oppressions is one of the most important contributions of black feminist theory.[47] It made it possible to refuse to compare and quantify the quality of marginality or oppression, and to demand that activism address simultaneously the exclusions of race, class, gender, ability, and so on.

A key feminist theorist who was educated in racially segregated American schools, bell hooks, was profoundly alert to the ways in which white women tended to see race and class exploitation as

> merely the off-spring of the parent system: patriarchy . . . Within the feminist movement in the West, this has led to

> the assumption that resisting patriarchal domination is a more legitimate feminist action than resisting racism and other forms of domination.

hooks proposed instead that

> to end patriarchal domination should be of primary importance to women and men globally not because it is the foundation of all other oppressive structures but because it is that form of domination we are most likely to encounter in an ongoing way in everyday life.

Her own experiences of her father's authority as more directly threatening on a daily basis than race or class oppression was influential. However, hooks saw this as a historically specific judgement, which could not be extended to an assumption that 'the feminist movement should be *the* central political agenda for females globally'.[48]

Patriarchy and Men's Movements

Since the early days of the 'woman question' and stretching into later phases of women's liberation, many men felt that they must respond to feminism, or possibly even share in the liberation it promised. 'Patriarchy' neatly identified a system that individual men might fight against and repudiate, even if they were beneficiaries of its power structures. Mostly drawn from civil rights and left politics, a rapidly growing pro-feminist anti-sexist men's movement emerged in the 1970s and 80s. Prominent in Australia, Belgium, Britain, Scandinavia and the United States, men who identified with feminist politics joined consciousness-raising groups and women's marches. Their presence was not always welcome, and increasingly in the 1970s most feminist women preferred to explore women's liberation in women-only settings.[49] Not deterred, some men shifted into 'anti-sexist men's groups', and debated the ways in which men could be allies of feminists. Many were convinced that men too suffered from conventional binary gender structures and hierarchies, which locked men into damaging forms of emotional isolation, violence and sexual anxiety. Gay men were particularly alert to ways in which they shared with women the injuries of patriarchal prejudice. Straight anti-sexist men tried to learn to be more in touch with their emotions, their bodies, and to disavow their homophobia. Men tried to take on more responsibility for fathering, and to renounce their male privileges by listening and being accountable to feminists.

The anti-sexist men's movement saw itself as responsive both to women's liberation and to gay men's politics. *XY* magazine in Australia, for example, was edited under the principles 'male-positive, pro-feminist and gay-affirmative'. Men's groups offered alternative versions of patriarchy. The British anti-sexist magazine *Achilles Heel* debated the idea of 'patripsych', developed by therapist John Rowan. 'Patripsych' was intended to name the internal, unconscious structures of the oppression of women which corresponded to external social forms. Just as Eleanor Rathbone had somewhat clumsily tried to map the psyche of male oppression in her idea of the 'Turk complex', anti-sexist men also dwelled on the inner experience of being an oppressor. Men maintained unconscious patterns of aggression, which defended them from awareness of their oppression of women, Rowan asserted. His use of 'patripsych' aimed to open up a discussion of men's self-oppression, and to encourage more positive, emotionally literate forms of masculinity. While feminists welcomed male efforts to stop burdening women with their emotions, 'positive masculinities' remained problematic for many feminists who were alert to benefits all men gained from cultures of male violence, dominance and aggression towards women.

Raewyn W. Connell, an Australian theorist of masculinities, offered more workable resources to male feminists by her open acknowledgement of the violence and inequality associated with contemporary masculinities. As an activist in the 1970s, and prior to her transition to becoming a woman, Connell had joined the early marches and consciousness-raising groups of the Australian men's movement. In its early stages, the thinking about gender within the men's movement was often framed through talk of 'sex roles' and 'men's roles'. A crisis in 'men's roles' might, it was tentatively hoped, bring about the end of patriarchy. The emphasis, however, seemed to be on the crises faced by men, rather than the oppression and trauma faced by women. Connell's later work in the 1980s and 90s focused more helpfully on masculinity as a set of practices configured within the structures of gender relations and historic legacies of empire. She emphasized the enormous power and privilege this offered men, recognizing the naïvety of hopes for men's voluntary renunciation:

> Men's dominant position in the gender order has a material pay-off, and the discussions of masculinity have constantly under-estimated how big it is. In the rich capitalist

> countries, men's average incomes are approximately double the average incomes of women. Men have ten times the political access of women, world-wide . . . Men control the means of violence, in the form of weapons and armed forces. I call these advantages the 'patriarchal dividend' for men, and this dividend is not withering away.[50]

In such an environment, Connell argued, the status quo was barely threatened by men's groups. Any movement of 'oppressors', however well intentioned, would (at best) retreat into a positive, therapeutically oriented form of men's politics that tried to make men feel better about their selves and actions. Many feminist women were unconvinced of the depth of men's commitment to change. There was a persistent suspicion that signing up to feminism was a profoundly limited, half-hearted commitment for many men, or even a means of chatting up or hitting on activist women.

Yet for all their scepticism, the anti-sexist men's movement did produce important new ideas. Connell's key insight was to think in terms of many genders and to identify hegemonic or dominant masculinities, alongside subordinate ones. Men able to earn wages, or practise certain sports, for example, were and are able to enjoy the privileges that unemployed or non-sporty men do not. Male hegemony is never static but always contested; Connell offered in the 1990s a dynamic, historically aware portrait of the gendered power struggles at play that has added new levels of sophistication to theories of patriarchy. Her work on the different kinds of masculinities that might emerge in relation to resources and constraints of class, ethnicity, physical ability and so on resonates strongly with the powerful intellectual resource of feminist accounts of intersectionality.

In the recent era of scandals over male abuse of power, talk of patriarchy has been less prominent than newer terms such as 'toxic masculinity' and 'lad culture'. Understanding the intellectual origins of patriarchy can help explain why it has been eclipsed in recent debates. Its roots in ethnography and Marxist theory gave patriarchy an association with sequential models of human society that left it prone to being understood as a 'passing phase'. This teleology left many thinking that the passage of time was inevitably going to result in more liberal and egalitarian gender politics. It was therefore a surprise when the rhetoric and policies of political leaders such as Donald Trump, Jair Bolsonaro and Rodrigo Duterte in the twenty-first century became so overtly anti-feminist. The threatened or actual removal of rights to abortion, the growing persecution of sexual minorities and the impunity of perpetrators of sexual and gender violence in the courts has focused feminist attention on why change has been so slow or has gone into reverse. In such a climate, the tendency of talk of 'patriarchy' to focus on structural factors and to excuse individual men from blame seems an inadequate response. Much evidence of the deliberate abuse of women and girls and impunity for abusers has come to light in seemingly multiplying scandals spanning business, politics, show business, religion, education and childcare. Ideas of 'toxic masculinities' *can* be understood as systematic, but can also usefully be applied personally, as qualities of individual men.

Meanwhile, patriarchy has become widely co-opted into

contemporary geopolitics in ways that make it less serviceable for feminist ends. There has been a tendency amongst policy makers to demonize radical Islam, particularly since the American invasion of Afghanistan in 2001 and Iraq in 2003. Powerful links have repeatedly been made between the 'war on terror' pursued by Western powers and the status of women. Laura Bush, wife of former US President George W. Bush, argued in 2001 that 'The fight against terrorism is also a fight for the rights and dignity of women.' Her husband, George W. Bush, had similar views, arguing: 'A central goal of the terrorists is the brutal oppression of women, and not only the women of Afghanistan.' The US-based Feminist Majority Foundation endorsed the invasion as a step towards the liberation of Afghan women and girls, though other feminist groups such as Code Pink rejected it. Subsequent interventions by the United States in the Middle East have continued to refer to patriarchal religion as a rationale.

The perceived links between Islam and patriarchy have resulted in widespread debate over the nature of Muslim gender orthodoxies and practices, with a tendency to sweeping generalizations. In 2016, former British Prime Minister David Cameron spoke of 'patriarchal societies' when presenting a policy to enforce English-language classes for Muslim women in Britain. For Cameron, Muslim women were prevented from integrating by 'the menfolk' and he called for 'British values' of liberalism and tolerance to work against extremism. Ironically, the resulting policy threatened those who did not speak English with deportation. This use of patriarchy to criticize specific religious cultures, rather than a wider form of social organization, has made it extremely challenging to identify the existence of Islamic feminism, despite its long-established presence (explored in Chapter 5).

We should not be too ready to discard 'patriarchy', though we might want to put it into dialogue with contending terms such as *nannü* and to recognize its tendency to aggregate important differences between women and men, and between historical periods. Understanding the broad outlines of how societies can be organized to disfavour and dispossess women has been a crucial intellectual move for feminists. This work has helped to resist ideas of a 'sex war' between men and women, and instead to shift the debate onto structural questions of how gender inequities work across language, labour markets, religions, criminal justice systems, the psyche and families. No single idea is likely to be useful in all contexts. But in this chapter we have seen how similar concepts of male dominance have done work across several centuries, inserting feminist concerns into doctrines of socialism, anarchism, nationalism, republicanism and Black Power, as well as developing distinctive forms of activism. The next chapter turns to the spaces of such activism, and the tactics of invasion and occupation that allowed feminists to claim new ground.

CHAPTER 3

Spaces

When Mary Wollstonecraft wrote *A Vindication of the Rights of Woman* (1792), she was living in her own rooms in London's Bloomsbury. Like many writers, she lived in somewhat spartan circumstances. She had dedicated her book to the French diplomat Charles Talleyrand, the man placed in charge of popular education just after the French Revolution. When he visited her in London, she offered him wine, but her poverty meant she could only serve it in a teacup. Nonetheless, the space she could call her own mattered deeply to her. Wollstonecraft (1759–97) lived a peripatetic life, travelling between England, France and Scandinavia. She experienced unhappy love affairs, deep mental anguish and the birth of an illegitimate daughter. In 1797, in a happier phase of her life, she settled into a marriage with the radical philosopher William Godwin. Even after marriage, Wollstonecraft insisted on living in her own house, though she was already pregnant with their daughter. This 'marriage under two roofs' was controversial, both at the time and for more than a century. It meant that Wollstonecraft's reputation for sexual licence and unconventionality eclipsed her intellectual work for much of the nineteenth century – she was labelled a 'hyena in petticoats' by her critics. But her need for her own space was paramount, and suggestive of the deep, persistent concern of feminists with the politics of space.

Wollstonecraft's efforts to entertain her intellectual and political peers in her own place were echoed in the Paris salon of Flora Tristan (1803–44). Tristan, born to a Peruvian aristocratic father and a French mother was, like Wollstonecraft, a writer who inhabited the margins of radical literary and political circles. She wrote about women's and workers' rights in Paris during the revolutionary decades of the 1830s and 40s. Tristan entertained in her small apartment on the Rue du Bac, where her visitors had to climb many flights of stairs. But unlike Wollstonecraft, Tristan could not rent her apartment under her own name; she had been stalked relentlessly by her husband, André Chazal, whom she had married in 1821. Deeply unhappy, she had abandoned the marriage only four years later. Chazal sought custody of their daughter, and eventually tracked Tristan to the Rue du Bac in 1838 and shot her. Tristan survived, and went on to publish the travelogues, *Peregrinations of a Pariah* and *Promenades in London*, which sharply observed the inequalities of gender and class across France, Peru and England. But her vulnerability in her home reminds us that, whether due to lack of money or male harassment, it has not been easy to establish feminist spaces.

Feminists have persistently, creatively and doggedly appropriated spaces for political activism and solace. Some of their interventions were designed to subvert male dominated spaces and make women's absence plain. Suffragist Susan B. Anthony (1820–1906), for example, led attempts to usurp public spaces in the United States such as the polling booth and political rally. In Rochester, New York, she and sixteen other women invaded a polling station and tried to vote for the president in 1872, for which she was arrested. In 1876, Anthony disrupted a large public celebration of the centenary of the American Declaration of Independence by entering the speakers' platform and offering a 'Declaration of the Rights of Women' to the chair.[1]

Later activists used tactics of occupation, in the form of peace camps, sit-ins, marches and strikes. They also turned to new spaces – particularly the intimate spaces of the home – as sites of politics. '*Lasciate la piazze!*' (Leave the piazza!) was the slogan of the small groups of consciousness-raising feminists in Italy, fed up with the crowd dynamics of radical politics and the heroic masculinities that went with them. Instead, they invited women to meet in their own homes and politicize what went on in what had been thought of as the private sphere.[2]

Contestation of space has been central to feminism, though it often proved difficult to maintain a claim on space when faced with hostile and aggressive counteractions. The spaces occupied have sometimes been deeply unpromising or unsought, such as the prison cells experienced by suffrage and feminist activists jailed for their protests all over the world. Other spaces have been commercial, yet still capable of being imbued with feminist potential. The tea shop, for example, gave women a safe place to meet with female friends, and thus became integral to feminist campaigning in the early twentieth century.[3] Sellers of suffrage newspapers were forced off the pavements and into the gutters by prohibitions on street trading. But they took the opportunity to chalk the pavements with slogans and meeting times nonetheless. Similarly, the town square where impromptu political meetings might be hosted, the marketplace where women traders might defend their interests and rights – all provided opportunities for solidarity and resistance amongst women, and ways to make ends meet.

Women have often lacked resources and thus have been confined and constrained in the spaces they could access. 'Marriage under two roofs' or independent living were only available to the relatively privileged. One such woman, the modernist writer Virginia Woolf (1882–1941), called for women to have 'a room of one's own' in 1929. However, she was under no illusions as to the lives of poorer women who would never achieve such spatial autonomy. Three years later, she wrote an introduction to a collection of essays by working-class women, which reflected on her own financial privilege. Woolf was half-fascinated, half-appalled at the muscular arms and large bodies of the women she encountered and was sharply aware of the class gulf between them and her.[4]

Hiratsuka Raichō (1886–1971) had the resources to create a room of her own. She had raided the funds her mother had put aside to pay for Hiratsuka's wedding, and used them in 1911 to found the Japanese feminist group Seitōsha (Bluestockings) and their magazine, *Seitō*. She shocked conventional opinion by living openly with her lover and having two children out of wedlock, before eventually marrying her children's father in 1941, at the age of fifty-seven. As editor of *Seitō*, Hiratsuka claimed her own space, and maintained an office at her home in Akebono-chō, Japan. The room reflected the relationship Japanese women sustained with feminism as a set of ideas many saw as imported from 'the West'. Her space was divided into a 'Western' main portion, with a desk

Figure 3.1
Tokyo members of Seitōsha in 1911. Hiratsuka stands second from the left

and books, facing a Japanese space with incense and mats, which Hiratsuka used for meditation.[5] Space is not a simple resource, and has always been marked by factors such as ethnicity and religion. Hiratsuka had the freedom to draw on what she saw as the best of two cultures. But for many women, their religion, class, ethnicity or race helped define what spaces they could inhabit.

How women inhabit space has also been a feminist concern. In 1974, Rita Mae Brown noted in the feminist periodical *Quest*, 'Women and men are taught to use space quite differently.'[6] As a prominent lesbian-feminist novelist, Brown described how women occupied their own personal space in a way that was structured by their expectations of the male gaze and their reluctance to take up space:

> a basic pose of non-feminism is casting the hip slightly forward in male company. Even while being seductive, the non-feminist is careful never to diminish the male's authority . . . Most non-feminists lower the eyes or look to the side, returning a gaze furtively, even more furtively with men.

She advocated a deeper understanding of how sexism was rooted in women's gestures, facial expressions and posture.

This politicization of posture and personal space became a major theme in women's liberation activism, encouraging feminist art criticism, women's self-defence classes, feminist dance movements and campaigns for women-only spaces on public transport. Drawing on the idea of 'free space' developed by Chude Pamela Allen, a US civil rights and women's liberation activist, there was a prioritization of separatist spaces in women's liberation circles, to develop 'women's culture' and provide safety for straight, lesbian and queer socializing.

In this chapter, I look at the kinds of spaces claimed by feminists, including the workplace, spaces of worship and women-only refuges from violence. I also include a discussion of the efforts made by feminists to use the 'space' of the market to empower themselves. The many feminist criticisms of capitalism can obscure the extent to which making a living has been a powerful feminist concern. Feminist enterprise has historically ranged from the precarious living of market traders to more elaborate and long-lived feminist businesses, such as bookshops and publishers.

Spaces of Labour

In 1859, a wealthy young Lincolnshire woman, Jessie Boucherett (1825–1905), called for the radical rethinking of the labour market, to open up 'honourable' trades and professions to women. She was well aware of male opposition to the entry of women to 'men's jobs'. But she stressed women's want of confidence and ignorance of 'industry'. And while she knew many women had to work for material survival, she stressed as goals the self-respect and higher status that women's work would bring.

Boucherett had been inspired by the 'drawing-room lectures' given by the writer and art historian Anna Jameson (1794–1860) on the position of women in the mid-1850s. Jameson had made an independent income from her writing since the 1820s, and this enabled her to leave an unhappy marriage, travel widely and establish herself as a public intellectual. She used her lectures to call for 'a more enlarged sphere of social work' for women in prisons, hospitals and workhouses. Despite women's financial needs, Jameson preferred to talk of their voluntary labour.[7] Some of her peers were more alert to the economic needs that led women to work for money; Harriet Martineau (1802–76), for example, another self-supporting and famous writer, insisted that 'three millions out of six of adult Englishwomen work for subsistence.'[8] But in these early demands for women's freedom to work, there was often a reticence about why they might want or need to work. Wealthier women were deeply invested in employment as a form of self-cultivation; poorer women sought economic survival. These conflicting interpretations were to set up a division in women's movements across many different nations, and dogged efforts to convince working-class women that feminism could speak to their needs.

The debates over women's work were central to *The English Woman's Journal*, a London periodical founded in 1858 which called for access to the professions for 'educated' women. Not content with polemics, the journal's editors also created their own physical space. They rented a small office to manage the production of the journal, and also provided its readers with a reading room, first in Princes Street and then a larger space nearby in Langham Place. It was within these rooms, decorated with the paintings of editor Barbara Bodichon, that Jessie Boucherett ran the Society for the Promotion of the Employment of Women (SPEW) from 1859. It offered women an employment agency and coordinated other activities, such as training women in book-keeping, telegraphy and paralegal roles. SPEW also established the woman-run Victoria Press which printed *The English*

Woman's Journal. Boucherett recalled later that 'from this small office and humble reading-room have grown almost all the great women's movements of the present day.' SPEW's activists were in lockstep with another powerful claim to public space for women, in the schools and university colleges that emerged in the nineteenth century.

In Britain, Girton College was founded in 1869 through the efforts of Emily Davies (1830–1920). She worked with *English Woman's Journal* editor Barbara Bodichon to create the first British residential higher education institution for women, at Cambridge University. Their welcome at Cambridge was lukewarm, however; women were not given the right to hold a degree from that university until 1948, seventy-nine years after Girton's foundation.

In the British Empire, there were similar developments. In British-ruled Burma, for example, Mya May Hla Oung was a key figure in sponsoring schools and colleges for women and girls. She framed this within a critical account of the impact on Burma of the 'foreign civilisation' of the British, whose 'disintegrating influence' she feared was reducing the gender equality of property and marital rights that characterized Buddhist Burma. 'I would sooner be a Burmese woman than one of . . . the proudest of the Nations of the West,' she declared in a 1903 magazine article.[9] In an ambitious move in 1908, Hla Oung sought to challenge the hegemony of Christianity in Britain, by funding and participating in the first Buddhist mission to Britain. By the time she set up a mission outpost in the London suburb of Penge, British women were already entering new trades in large numbers, including hairdressing, pharmacy, clerical work, printing and the decorative arts. SPEW meanwhile continued to rent offices that hosted women's movement organizations until 1920, providing crucial resources and physical space for those seeking to improve the status of women.[10] The physical location became an iconic site, giving its name to this group, who are remembered as 'the Langham Place feminists'.

The central demand of SPEW – for women's access to workplaces – was to prove divisive and controversial in the years that followed. What the many women who already worked in low-paid and demanding jobs such as agricultural work and domestic service wanted was better pay and more respectful treatment. Those selling sex wanted less police harassment. Working-class British women, whose employment rates in the nineteenth and early twentieth centuries were higher than those of middle-class women, were deeply frustrated at the naïvety of calls for free access to labour markets. Poor female workers who lacked employment rights and worked under conditions of extreme precarity did not often look to employment as a space for self-realization and empowerment. Nor did they seek new careers and qualifications. Instead, many welcomed the efforts of the British state and trade union movement to restrict the hours they could work and to ban certain so-called 'dangerous' trades to women.

Feminists such as Jessie Boucherett were wary of the ways in which women were categorized as weak workers in need of protection alongside children. She suspected that 'protective' legislation to prevent them working at night or giving them rest breaks would lead employers to employ men instead. But for many working-class women, the paternalism of the state was a lifeline, easing their exhausting and dangerous work.

The British women's movement was deeply split over the debates on the workplace. Some feminists had mounted campaigns to prevent what they saw as the state harassment of a series of women workers, including women in the 'dangerous trades' of coal mining, bar work and, perhaps most controversially, prostitution. There were also defenders of protection, many located within the trade union movement and later the British Labour Party. Ethel Snowden, a suffrage and Labour Party activist, argued in 1913 against the figure she termed 'the out and out feminist'. Snowden celebrated that women should be prevented from working at night and after giving birth. But her arguments were dangerously vague on what this might mean, and how much compulsion might be exercised over women's choices. Due to women's motherhood, Snowden noted, 'the woman's body may be requisitioned for [the] special work' of reproduction. It would be better 'if the prospective mother could be . . . kept at home altogether until their children themselves are working for money'.[11] There had been a quick transition in her argument from some form of maternity leave to a *full* exclusion from the labour market for the entire period of raising children to adulthood. The talk of 'requisitioning' women's bodies seemed to echo the earlier attempts to regulate sex work in Britain's Contagious Diseases Acts that had given police powers to detain, examine and forcibly treat any woman they suspected of being a prostitute. Snowden's words also resonated with what would later become fascist commitments to high birth rates.

After the suffrage was awarded to older British women in 1918, the largest British feminist organization, the National Union of Societies for Equal Citizenship (NUSEC) faced major divisions on this question of 'protected' labour. The campaign for the vote had papered over deep divisions around women's employment. At its foundation in 1919, NUSEC had called for 'equal pay for equal work, involving an open field for women in industry and the professions'. But by 1927, NUSEC leader Eleanor Rathbone argued that feminists should approve of protective legislation if 'the well-being of the community' required it or the workers themselves called for it. This prompted a large group of NUSEC's executive committee to resign, fearing that nebulous appeals to 'the race' or 'the community' would banish women from certain jobs. The British feminist journal *Time and Tide* declared that NUSEC was 'no longer a feminist body'. But other women, often those who themselves held down factory jobs, continued to welcome any protection the state could offer.[12]

Similar tensions emerged over the struggle for the Equal Rights Amendment (ERA) in the United States. Championed by the National Women's Party and, from 1966, by the National Organization for Women, this attempt to enact a constitutional amendment dominated post-suffrage activism and became emblematic of the feminist cause in the United States. As in Britain, it caused intense controversy over its likely effect in ruling out forms of 'protective' legislation such as maternity leave and women's minimum wages. Critics argued that women workers required specific protections from the deep exploitation they frequently suffered in labour markets, particularly from low pay and long hours. There was no consensus behind the ERA, and despite a campaign that stretched into the 1980s (and some recent ratifications in Nevada in 2017 and Illinois in 2018), it has so far failed to be ratified by sufficient states to pass into the constitution.

For historian Dorothy Cobble, the ERA struggle has been simply irrelevant to many women's lives. She argues that the momentum of the feminist movement in mid-twentieth-century America shifted away from ERA and the constitution and towards the labour movement.[13] The key feminist spaces became the union and the picket line. Cobble highlights the organizing of activists such as Pan-Africanist Maida Springer Kemp (1910–2005) and Jewish Lithuanian Pauline Newman (1887–1986). Springer Kemp and Newman both helped organize female garment workers in New York. Springer Kemp became a leading figure in the International Ladies' Garment Workers' Union, and by the 1950s was working to extend union rights in Liberia, Tanzania, Kenya and Ghana. Pan-Africanism informed her politics alongside feminism, and she was deeply concerned with equal pay and childcare for women workers.[14] Newman worked for the Women's Trade Union League (WTUL), and lived in an intimate relationship with another feminist trade unionist, Frieda Miller, who in 1944 became director of the US Women's Bureau. Cobble terms them 'social justice feminists'.

This was a significant period of reorientation of trade union activism to better represent women's needs. The huge growth of women working in clerical, light industry, teaching and retail jobs made them a prominent new constituency for union organizing. Maida Springer Kemp identified her union as having 'an outstanding record in raising the status of women', though she was one of its very few visible female leaders. Despite being made up mostly of women members,

Figure 3.2
Maida Springer Kemp (centre, standing) visits garment workers at a factory in Bristol, England, 1936

the International Ladies' Garment Workers' Union was led by men and maintained a gender-blind 'non-discrimination' policy rather than a more active analysis of gender disadvantage. Union loyalists Springer Kemp and Newman both stressed that union bargaining rather than legislation was the best route to equal pay for women, and they opposed the Equal Rights Amendment. They also insisted that the needs of mothers and children be incorporated into employer provision, a hugely important demand as the baby boom of the 1940s and 50s saw more women workers juggling the demands of birth, breastfeeding and childcare. Their case by case, gradualist approach could be criticized for failing to challenge the wider gender order; this became the complaint of women's liberationists, frustrated by the compromises women trade unionists had made within a highly unequal status quo. Nevertheless, it is important to acknowledge the existence of a 'social justice' tradition within the feminist movement, where working-class, migrant and black women have been prominent and effective.

It was activists within the labour movement who introduced repeated versions of an alternative to the ERA – a Women's Status Bill, first presented to Congress in 1947. Where the ERA proposed strict legal equality, the social justice feminists associated with the labour movement preferred that women workers be treated according to their situation. Pauline Newman called ERA supporters 'selfish careerists'; in turn, ERA supporters saw their opponents as dupes of male-dominated unions. These challenges were starkly illustrated in the fraught debates over the Equal Pay Act in the United States in 1963. Where social justice feminists had hoped for equal pay for *comparable* work, Republican congresswoman and ERA supporter Katharine St John aligned herself with 'equality feminism' and insisted that the legislation must guarantee equal pay for the same work. In the highly gender-segregated US labour market, this ensured that the resulting legislation would only apply to the small range of occupations where men and women were hired in exactly the same roles.

The competing interpretations of what paid employment meant to women lay at the heart of the disputes between these different varieties of feminism. Those who chose to work with labour unions often found both resources and opposition to women's claims and needs. Women's demands for better wages and conditions sometimes mirrored those of male workers, but most disputes that involved women also threw up questions of the specific kinds of marginalization faced by women workers, including maternity issues and sexual harassment at work. Male-dominated unions were slow to recognize these issues, and to place women in leadership roles. Nonetheless, the labour movement has been an important ally and resource for those attempting to make the workplace a space of women's empowerment.

The Marketplace

Feminists working in the labour movement positioned themselves in opposition to 'bosses' and were often critical of the whole system of capitalism and how it treated workers. Yet the women's movement has not always and everywhere been opposed to the world of enterprise and commerce. Across many different economies in the nineteenth century we can see patterns of everyday mobilization around petty trading amongst women living precarious lives. Lacking alternatives, poor women were often forced to take up casual and ad hoc work as laundresses, market traders and sex workers. These activities allowed for scraping by, through clandestine selling and trading, with a constant battle to evade authorities' attempts to license and regulate their lives. Maria Odila Silva Dias's study of working women, free and enslaved, during the nineteenth century in São Paolo, Brazil, exemplifies this precarity and empowerment through trading. In the years prior to the abolition of slavery in 1888, Brazil was a country where manual labour was culturally devalued. As 'combative women', free and enslaved working women found sources of solidarity amongst other women traders, and resistance to attempts by the government to control and tax their economic activities.[15] Their resistance was often based on what has been termed the 'weapons of the weak' – rumours, stalling, manipulation and evasion.

Occasionally, women's strategies of evasion or stalling were insufficient, and they turned instead to overt forms of organizing and resistance. In British-governed Nigeria, for example, village women were key producers and traders of palm oil. Amongst the Igbo people of the Niger Delta area, women exercised considerable power in public roles such as the *omu*, controlling women's market activities, alongside the male equivalent office of *obi*. British colonial interventions in this division of power worked to fortify the male *obi*, while attempting to sideline the female *omu*. However, in the 1920s, British demands for higher 'hut taxes', imposed through British-appointed 'warrant chiefs', overstepped the perceived authority of the chief system and its ability to compel payment from women. Women had powers of collective insult, known as 'sitting on' men, and in 1929 these strategies were used to contest excessive taxation and political marginalization. Over 10,000 women joined together in protest. They used traditional forms of insult such as women's nakedness to defy the governance of indigenous and British elites.[16] These protests drew on vernacular traditions of dancing and spirit possession, as well as the moral authority derived from Igbo divisions of labour around trade. One source noted that the market women were 'nearly naked wearing only wreaths of grass round their heads, waist and knees and some were wearing tails of grass . . .'[17] Women mocked the authority of warrant chiefs by throwing sand – barren earth – at their 'rulers', and demanding that they give up their caps of office to women. Their protest meetings ended in barrages of insults. Carrying machetes, the women faced down both British and indigenous soldiers in a rebellion sometimes termed 'the women's war'.

This militancy led eventually to the use of lethal force by troops, who fired on women protestors, killing twenty-one, in December 1929. In the context of attempts to mechanize agriculture and control trade that tended to give greater power to men, as well as colonial administrative structures that also privileged male powerholders, these ritualized forms of disorder show the importance of the marketplace as a site of women's activism, but also the high costs access to it sometimes carried.

The memorable protests of 1929 can be read as a contribution to the anti-colonial movements that resulted in the eventual ejection of British rulers in 1960. But it remained a women-led action, defending the spaces of the marketplace that afforded Igbo women some freedom to determine their economic status, and premised on female solidarity and agency. At a historic period where most self-described feminist activities centred on access to the professions, to the vote and to equal pay, it cannot be termed a feminist action. The women's protests were rooted in traditional Igbo moral economy and insult traditions rather than a recognizably feminist repertoire. Nonetheless, the women's leadership and solidarity resonated with feminist approaches, and have made the protests important to later Nigerian activists.

The 'women's war' helped inspire the bold claims on market rights amongst the women of the Nigerian town of Abeokuta, led by the charismatic Funmilayo Ransome-Kuti (1900–1978). Educated in Nigeria and Britain, she had been a member in the 1940s of the Abeokuta Ladies Club, a paternalistic welfare organization aiming to 'raise the standard of womanhood'. Ransome-Kuti expanded it to include literacy work amongst market women and through this came to understand better their precarious livelihoods. Women complained of unfair taxes and being compulsorily stripped naked by inspectors to judge their age and thus their taxable status. The Ladies Club changed its name to the Abeokuta Women's Union in 1946, and Ransome-Kuti adopted the print-wrapper clothing of market women. She organized them into tax resistance, terming her demonstrations 'picnics'. Some lasted forty-eight hours, during which women refused to work and instead sang songs – over 200 were composed during the 'picnics' and protests in late 1946. The protestors defied both colonial authorities and the local Ogboni warrant chiefs, refusing to honour male-only ritual objects and seeking global publicity to protest police use of tear gas

Figure 3.3
Funmilayo Ransome-Kuti, Nigerian activist for women's rights, socialism and Pan-Africanism. Ransome-Kuti deliberately adopted the dress of women market traders as a mark of respect for their concerns

and arrests. As historian Cheryl Johnson-Odim has argued, Ransome-Kuti was to become a significant Pan-Africanist and democratic socialist, who travelled to China, Moscow, Ghana and Sierra Leone to protest colonialism and injustice against women. Though wary of Communism, she aligned with the Women's International Democratic Federation, an umbrella organization which sponsored women's activism across the Communist sphere of influence. She was also a critic of the military rulers of Nigeria from 1966 and was harassed by police. A raid on the home of her son, musician Fela Kuti, led to her injury and death in 1978.[18]

Ransome-Kuti's legacy in Nigeria, as in many other African nations, has been to maintain a strong awareness of the needs of working-class and rural women. While some African commentators have been sceptical that feminism could ever be distinguished from its perceived Western imperial origins, Ransome-Kuti was clear that women disproportionately bore the painful costs of colonial occupation. She clarified the case for women's liberation being threaded into the 'liberation of the oppressed and poor majority of the people in Nigeria'.[19] This statement formed the mission statement of Women in Nigeria (WIN), established in 1983 to highlight the negative effects of the oil economy, inflation and externally imposed structural adjustment policies on Nigerian women. Economic hardship had come increasingly to the fore, and again the costs had fallen disproportionately on women. The military governments ruling Nigeria at this time had curbed dissent and protest.[20] Aiming to enlarge the public sphere of debate, WIN raised women's issues such as access to water, forced marriages, protection of sex workers, and girls' access to education.

This work required coalitions with market women, university students, sex workers and women farmers, and sensitive navigation of the diverse ethnicities and religions of Nigeria. WIN insisted on a non-doctrinaire approach that included men as members and, at times, beneficiaries of their actions. Despite some precedents for male involvement in feminism, WIN's willingness to accept and integrate men into feminist activism remains unusual. It was underpinned by a commitment to sharing the burden of the transformation of gender relations. Women, encumbered by their domestic labour and economic marginalization, had limited time and resources. WIN not only welcomed men's contributions to their work but also celebrated and demanded men's involvement. It represented not only practically a source of energy and resources but also, WIN argued, a fundamental reorientation of men's consciousness. Men were often drawn to WIN by its involvement in social justice struggles that spanned the sexes; in turn, WIN hoped that men would gain a deeper commitment to feminist goals.[21]

The inclusion of men was also a stance that responded to a very specific challenge of this time and place. It reflected a resistance to the growing religious fundamentalism that characterized Islamic and Christian Nigeria in the 1980s and 90s. Faith leaders had begun to seek single-sex forms of worship and association, and, it was important to WIN as a secular organization, that they provide a model of cooperation between the sexes and mixed-sex spaces. Their openness to all – no criteria were attached to membership – created tensions over conflicting goals and priorities. But this spurred internal efforts to build coalitions across divides. WIN provided an answer to the perennial question of who could be a feminist by experimenting with an entirely open-door policy.

Feminist Businesses

Women living precarious lives as market traders were often just getting by in economic terms. They drew on each other for solidarity and had a strong sense of their rights. However, they rarely had the resources to be able to campaign over a longer time period or establish their own spaces and institutions. But there have been historical moments where explicitly feminist initiatives have built up resources and been able to fund spaces that were dedicated to women's empowerment. In Detroit, for example, members of the women's movement were able in 1976 to purchase and renovate a prestigious central Detroit building, the former Women's City Club, and open it up as a hub for feminist socializing, business start-ups and campaigning.

The women in Detroit were building on the existence of a wave of feminist small businesses catalysed by the women's liberation movement of the 1970s. In the United States, an entrepreneurial culture was well entrenched, and it is no surprise that many American women, inspired by the talk of autonomy and control within the feminist movement, opted to found their own businesses. Many were critical of larger capitalist corporations and wanted a more ethical alternative. They also saw businesses such as bookshops, legal practices, women's health centres and publishers as key to spreading the feminist message. They developed feminist products that were controversial – an apron emblazoned with 'Fuck housework' produced by the New York-based Liberation Enterprises was rejected as an advertisement even by the tolerant counter-cultural newspaper *Village Voice*. Nonetheless, feminist entrepreneurs found a ready market for politicized trading.

They also drew on a prior tradition well established amongst lesbian women of setting up bars and cafes that could be safe, tolerant spaces for sexual minorities. Lesbians had often faced discrimination over their appearance and sexual choices and were deeply aware of the need for women's autonomous space.[22] Their campaigns for 'woman space' sometimes equivocated between feminist and lesbian emphases, but as historian Alexandra Ketchum has argued in relation to Ontario's cafes and restaurants, it was often possible to appeal to both constituencies. Unaccompanied women in Canada had found it difficult to enter spaces where alcohol was served due to its prohibition traditions; bars were stigmatized or hostile spaces. By creating spaces as 'women's clubs' on a membership basis, it was possible to guarantee a women-only environment such as that of the Three Cups coffee shop in Toronto which provided a women's dance space from 1975. Lack of finance meant that this project never attained its own premises but was forced to improvise. The attempt to carve out a 'woman space' was a symbolic battle that shifted across the city as existing social spaces were temporarily occupied.[23]

Whatever their sexuality and political leanings, most women-run businesses found difficulties accessing the capital they needed to buy stock, rent premises and hire workers. Banks were unwilling to lend to women, particularly if they were married. Mortgages and credit cards were routinely refused or required a husband as guarantor, and women of colour were particularly barred from sources of finance. As historian Joshua Clark Davis has shown, the problems of finance led to the establishment of feminist credit unions and banks, such as Detroit's Feminist Federal Credit Union (FFCU), founded in 1973.[24] Its founders were looking to expand their Women's Health workshop, but soon realized that there was a national appetite for feminist lending and borrowing. An early leaflet invited women supporters to 'invest our savings in loans to our sisters instead of in male owned and controlled banking institutions with sexist lending policies and employment practices'. The FFCU was female-run and described itself as 'like a women's center . . . with bulletin boards and posters about Feminist news and activities'.[25] They opened branches all over Michigan, and the model spread to other states. Assets from feminist credit unions totalled around $1.5 million nationally by 1975. These unprecedented sums, for the usually poorly funded women's movement, created opportunities for wider investments.

After much debate, the credit unions set up FEN – the Feminist Economic Network – to coordinate their activities. The ambitious founders of the Detroit FFCU proposed that FEN buy and renovate the former Women's City Club in their city. Some feminists were deeply suspicious, fearful that a rich organization could end up taking control of a grassroots, flat-hierarchy women's movement. Even though the FFCU operated on a not-for-profit basis, its critics still saw feminist businesses as 'hopelessly enmeshed in a larger economic system which understood one thing – profit'.[26]

FEN went ahead nonetheless, employing local active feminists to clean and repair the building. The intensity of work required – long days, low pay and poor conditions – was immediately controversial, and women workers talked ominously of going on strike to protest. The opening went ahead in April 1976, offering a hotel and swimming pool for women, bars and a nightclub. The nationally famous activist Gloria Steinem cut a ribbon made out of dollar bills at the opening to symbolize a feminist commitment to enriching women. But this glitzy launch was ill-fated. Membership to the club cost $100 annually, a sum far beyond most women in Detroit. The operating costs were crippling, and the wider women's movement was ambivalent about the whole project. The premises were shut after only five months.

This was a major blow to the vision of feminist space within a capitalist marketplace. FEN's meteoric rise and fall should not however be seen as representative of all feminist businesses. At the very local level, lesbian-feminist bars and cafes continued to thrive, as did businesses such as artisan jewellery-making and feminist hairdressers. Despite criticism of the beauty industry and its impossible demands on women, it proved possible for women's salons to provide important spaces for feminist and anti-racist solidarity and networking. In Britain, for example, the Manchester black women's cooperative, founded in 1975 and renamed Abasindi in 1980, offered hairdressing spaces for black women. Co-op members recognized that black women's hair had been devalued in a white-oriented beauty culture.[27]

Feminist presses were another means for women to carve out space in the marketplace, and to occupy the 'cultural space' of publishing. Projects such as Kali for Women in India, Virago Press in Britain and Asmita Women's Publishing

House in Nepal were longer lived than the Detroit Women's City Club; some have survived well into the twenty-first century and are still thriving, as we will see in Chapter 4. They produced books for perhaps the most iconic and recognizable form of feminist space – the women's bookshop. Such spaces permitted campaigning, quiet reflection, intellectual inspiration and debate, eating and socializing. They have attempted to span enterprise and politics, though with varying levels of success. Bookshops such as the Women's Press in London (1907), Women and Children First in Chicago (1967), the Shokado Women's Bookstore in Kyoto, Japan (1975), the Libreria delle Donne di Milano (1975), Streelekha in India (1984) and Binti Legacy in Nairobi (1996) have formed a powerful network for the distribution of feminist ideas. Crucially, these commercial spaces have been open to women of all classes, and most have also welcomed men to at least some of their spaces. They have helped stake a claim for feminism within the everyday settings of high streets and have provided very visible reminders of the feminist promise of change.

Streelekha, a feminist bookshop in Bangalore, was established in 1984 as 'above all, a meeting place for women'. It offered literary readings, counselling, legal advice, and a mail order service that aimed to reach a wider audience in India with feminist books. Its founders noted that 'women's movements in the third world are not isolated from the other movements for social change', so the shop would also stock books on 'peace, development, ecology and movements of workers, Dalits [low-caste "untouchables"], peasants'.[28] Committed to providing the 'theoretical ballast for feminist action', the Streelekha collective were concerned about affordability. They were well aware that most Indian women could not afford expensive feminist books, and that their commercial prospects were precarious. In order to build resilience, they twinned their bookshop with the Toronto Women's Bookstore in Canada and New Words Bookstore in Massachusetts, USA. This led to the exchange of books, periodicals and bookselling expertise in both directions. The Streelekha *Feminist Daybook*, for example, was sold in the twinned North American shops, where fundraisers were held to support Streelekha in its plans to open up a book van, and to provide a lending library, Kavya for Women.[29] Streelekha was a site of alliance building, both with other radical protest movements that intersected with feminism, but also with the well-established international networks of the feminist book trade. Its members were determined to use commerce to support themselves, their premises, feminist presses and authors – though they were also deeply critical of the global capitalist book trade that resulted in unaffordable prices for booksellers in poorer countries and the manipulation of prices by powerful publishers. For all the awkwardness of their alliance, the commercial enterprise could also be a community space, and feminist entrepreneurs were alert to the limits of empowerment possible within the marketplace.

Spaces of Worship

Previous historians of feminism have sometimes portrayed the movement as a rebellion against religion. Faith has been widely associated with fundamentalist efforts to control women's worship and dress. Jewish atheist Ernestine Rose had long rejected religion as a major source of social and sexual inequality. Suffragist Elizabeth Cady Stanton also took issue with conventional religion and issued a clarion call for an 'entire revolution' based on a critical re-reading of the Christian Bible. She declared that

> The Bible teaches that woman brought sin and death into the world, that she precipitated the fall of the race, that she was arraigned before the judgment seat of Heaven, tried, condemned and sentenced.

This doctrine meant for Christian women that

> Marriage for her was to be a condition of bondage, maternity a period of suffering and anguish, and in silence and subjection, she was to play the role of a dependent on man's bounty for all her material wants.[30]

Stanton wanted to keep the Christian faith, but without this emphasis on women's subordination. She drew together an international committee of women in the controversial project of re-reading the Bible from a feminist perspective. Many women she approached refused, but a group of twenty-six were finally assembled, including Finnish activist Alexandra Gripenberg, Austrian Irma von Troll-Borostyáni and French social reformer Isabelle Bogelot. Stanton published their collective commentaries on the position of women in the Old and New Testaments as *The Woman's Bible* in 1895 and 1898. Arguing that prayers should be jointly addressed to a Heavenly Mother and Father, Stanton's text became an immediate bestseller, though it was immensely notorious amongst other suffragists and wider publics.

Such works remind us that feminism has been no secular

movement. Stanton had become interested in the spiritualist movement in the 1860s, and many feminists found both orthodox and unorthodox faiths to be inspirations. Religions have also provided important, if often improvised, spaces for women such as Violet Johnson (1870–1939), an African American domestic servant and Baptist lay leader who worked in suburban New Jersey. Rather than Stanton's overt feminism, Johnson was motivated by spiritual commitments to morality and justice. These principles, however, carried political implications of social justice and claiming spaces that were profoundly gendered. Lacking the resources that feminist activists such as Jessie Boucherett had used to claim public rights and space, Johnson was nonetheless able to create physical spaces, of the most modest kind, that reveal how women's activism could be pursued at the grassroots.

As a domestic servant, Violet Johnson's access to space of her own was limited. Servants were deeply aware that the bedrooms, kitchens and sculleries they slept and laboured in were someone else's property. Employers had a legal right to enter these rooms, inspect belongings and bodies, and govern comings and goings. Servants were subject to dismissal for trivial or imagined offences, and this could be sudden and hard to contest for these workers with few resources. Between jobs, they could often only turn to boarding houses or temporary accommodation with kin. This made the demarcation and control of space a powerful concern. Servants often had little but the space in their personal trunk or box where their privacy could be respected. Perhaps this sense of the intrusion of employers onto her intimate spaces made the creation of a meeting place for Bible study particularly important to Violet Johnson. As historian Betty Livingston Adams has documented, having rented a commercial laundry in 1898, Johnson transformed it into a sacred space, eventually to become the Fountain Baptist Church in Summit, New Jersey. Its founding eight congregation members were all female African American domestic servants.[31]

While the nineteenth-century Baptist Church welcomed the establishment of African American-led churches, it nonetheless had a long-standing tendency to treat them with paternalism. In frustration, African American male ministers organized their own conventions and congregations in the 1870s and 80s, aiming to highlight their respectability and autonomy. But this proved an exclusionary move for the women worshippers who had often taken very prominent roles as spiritual leaders. African American Baptist churches came to regard women's religious ministry and preaching with caution, denying women leadership roles despite their preeminence in sustaining and funding congregations. Women who felt a strong sense of religious mission were feared as dangerous to the precarious social respectability African American churches sought. Violet Johnson's Fountain congregation in Summit, New Jersey, was female-dominated, but its male pastor, Edward McDaniels, retained formal powers of leadership.

The original laundry quickly became too small for the Fountain Baptist Church, and the congregation committed itself to building new premises. Without resources amongst its members, it was forced to turn to external donors, whose motives were not just philanthropic. Money was provided through the appeal of Pastor McDaniels, who stressed to donors the problems that the growing numbers of female 'Southern Negroes' would pose as they entered domestic service in New Jersey.[32] African American women were associated with sexual licence and fecundity; a church would help regulate their behaviour, McDaniels implied to white and black middle-class supporters. The sacred space Violet Johnson had sought was thus in practice not always one of liberation. It was a site of mixed messages, where women's voices and agency were simultaneously supported but also denied.

Whatever the rationale, the resources to provide services of any kind to African American congregations were meagre. In Summit, donors were able to afford the construction only of a basement to the envisaged new church. It was completed, with a temporary roof, in 1908, and immediately occupied for services. By 1912, repeated flooding had forced the congregation out. Eager for more substantial and habitable space, the church proposed instead an ambitious plan to buy the disused Summit City Hall. This attempt to occupy a prestigious civic space pushed at the limits of what was acceptable for a female-dominated African American congregation. White residents campaigned against the sale, arguing that it would lead to the ruin of businesses and threaten property values. Incendiary talk of a 'colony' of 'negroes' in the suburb made clear the profound importance of preserving 'white space'.[33]

The widening colour bar within New Jersey in the early twentieth century had made the promise of sacred space that might serve the black community, or even transcend racial divides, unrealizable. The Fountain Baptist Church ended up occupying a modest building funded by white donors who were motivated by their desire to keep this congregation out of more high-profile sites. White trustees held the deeds to the building and controlled the hiring of pastors.[34] The attainment of a useable space had come at the high cost of a substantial loss of control over its uses.

Despite the problems of the physical quality of the spaces available to her, and the contests over how and by whom they should be occupied, Violet Johnson continued to prioritize the creation of spaces dedicated to women's needs. In 1918, during the disruptions of war work, she took on an apartment that she personally occupied, but which she also termed the Industrial Home for Working Girls, or the 'Home away from Home'. She aimed to provide a dedicated space for 'colored girls' working in wartime industrial production that would be 'homey and pleasant'.[35] This was a competitor to the larger initiatives dominated by white women in the Young Women's Christian Association (YWCA). Johnson's small home provided space and support for over 800 young women during the First World War and after. The YWCA, glad to avoid the tricky question of how to accommodate black women's expertise and leadership within their own spaces, supported Johnson's project. It offered her residents access to YWCA facilities – but only on a racially segregated basis.

In the context of the tightening of forms of segregation and violence in the northern states of America, African American communities were increasingly beleaguered in the early decades of the twentieth century. It became harder to form multiracial spaces, particularly as the economic pain of the Depression in the 1930s made the lives of working-class and ethnic-minority women materially tough. Nonetheless, Johnson's 'Home' continued to provide space, allowing young women to run clubs exploring African American literature and history in the 1920s and 30s.

Despite the complex power-play between men and women, and the racist response of white residents of Summit and the local YWCA, the Fountain Baptist Church and other women's spaces still gave Violet Johnson and her female peers opportunities to engage in reform. They were prominent in the temperance activities of the Women's Christian Temperance Union, and in women's suffrage campaigning. Johnson also became involved in anti-lynching activities, as did union activist Maida Springer Kemp. For Johnson, this issue not only raised the need to protect African American men, but also illustrated African American women's vulnerability to rape and pregnancy by white men. She wrote to President Woodrow Wilson in 1919: 'the story of the assaults white men have made on colored women's honor is written on the faces of our race.'[36]

Violet Johnson pursued justice at the intersection of race and gender, and despite being located in the New Jersey suburbs and thus far from sites of state power, she did not hesitate to address the president. Her work was scaled up from the grassroots level through her participation in bodies such as the National Association of Colored Women and the State Colored Women's Republican Club. But attempts to lobby at the national legislative level raised difficult choices for her. Black women were forced to choose whether to ally with white women in causes such as alcohol control, or to remain loyal to organizations of racial justice such as the National Association for the Advancement of Colored People (NAACP), who opposed bans on alcohol sales and prioritized racial justice. In 1922, Violet Johnson joined white women in supporting a prohibition candidate. In 1924, she broke with white women to support an anti-lynching candidate. Her support for women's needs was not pursued in the name of feminism, though she consistently worked to advance women's needs and interests in many settings. But feminism was an inadequate term to capture the intersecting oppressions of race, class and gender that shaped Johnson's activism at this historical moment. In any case, her preference for 'women's Christian mission' as an alternative way of making sense of her work should be respected. Her work for social justice had shared concerns and tactics with feminists; but during her life it was frequently the case that working-class and black women did not find their concerns treated respectfully within the feminist movements they encountered.

Johnson died in her 'Home away from Home' in 1939. Fittingly, her funeral was conducted in the Fountain Baptist Church she had founded. But even in death, the limits of space for African American working-class women were still evident: Johnson was buried in an unmarked grave, in the plot of her white former domestic service employers.[37]

Autonomous Spaces

Violet Johnson's use of her own apartment to provide a safe space for African American working girls was a tactic that would have been familiar to later generations. The 1970s and 80s saw an explosion of feminist shelters, refuges and places of safety, mostly focused on what was increasingly named as 'domestic violence', as well as rape and sexual assault. Where previous debates had talked of wife-beating, the new terminology stressed both how serious and pervasive violence was, and that its effects stretched beyond wives to encompass children, girlfriends and other relatives.

In Australia, the women's refuge movement had been established through largely church-run shelters, founded by women using similar tactics to Violet Johnson. But in the 1970s, the powerful idea of patriarchy (see Chapter 2) came to inform a feminist approach and inspired women to set up some very different spaces. Replacing a focus on *individual* experiences of violent partners, where the blame had often been laid on women for eliciting violence, feminists offered an alternative analysis. They explained male violence towards women not as an individual pathological event but as a structural feature of patriarchy that preserved the stability of the status quo.

Recognizing the scale and centrality of male violence against women made it urgent to find new spaces where it could be resisted. Shelters such as the Halfway House in the state of Victoria were opened in the early 1970s. They aimed to give women a safe place in which they could reassess their lives, experience respite, and explore what it could feel like to exert control over their circumstances. The spaces offered were heavily used, and often very overcrowded. Cooking space was minimal, and mattresses were squeezed into every possible space. The shelters were run by a mixture of paid staff, residents and volunteers. The involvement of residents was particularly crucial in decision-making and everyday labour, as a means of drawing them into feminist debate and preventing a top-down 'rescue' approach. In the early days, shelters were improvised – rooms in the houses of feminist activists, or squatted buildings. Nonetheless, they provided a crucial service at a time when police and welfare services were, at best, often uninterested in supporting women living with violent partners.

In Australia, state funding was provided unusually early for refuges, with money for a national women's refuge programme available from 1975. The Australian women's movement had been more willing than women in other countries to see the state as a useful ally. This created opportunities, expanding and equipping the spaces available to women. But it also posed the problem of co-option, summed up in the coining of the term 'femocrat' – a feminist bureaucrat. It left Australian feminist institutions reliant on funding that could be withdrawn when hostile governments were elected. And it tended to privilege the leadership of educated and white women who had the confidence and knowledge to navigate state bureaucracies.[38]

The alliance with the state raised particularly acute tensions for Australian Aboriginal women and left them enormously suspicious of whether feminist spaces were welcoming and safe for them. The legacies of Aboriginal disenfranchisement, forced adoptions and child removal programmes, sterilization and welfare surveillance meant that public institutions were deeply problematic for Aboriginal Australians. Some women's organizations, such as the Union of Australian Women, had attempted to include Aboriginal women and their concerns in their campaigning of the 1950s and 60s. Affiliated to the left feminist Women's International Democratic Federation, the Union of Australian Women reported regularly on Aboriginal struggles against dispossession. The women's liberation movement of the 1970s was however less rooted in the struggles of working-class and racially marginalized women. Tikka Jan Wilson, a refuge worker, wrote an account in 1996 of how an Australian feminist refuge became polarized between white and Koori Aboriginal women. Despite its policies talking about anti-racism, the refuge's white workers tended to judge Koori workers as 'lazy'. They had little awareness of how this might be a cultural stereotype, nor how the refuge might be experienced as a 'white' space in its racial codes and cultural values. White feminists sought to treat refuge users as 'women', erasing the specific disadvantages that Aboriginal women experienced in accessing their services. Their narrative of sisterhood was naïve or forgetful in the face of a long history of white racist aggression and sexual violence. White women had been deeply implicated in the welfare services that had sought to control Aboriginal communities in the nineteenth and twentieth centuries, and these practices were sometimes replicated in the feminist shelters.[39]

Similarly, immigrant Australian women experienced problems of exclusion in a system where there was little understanding of their specific needs and few resources for translation services. Refuge workers were often unwilling to give immigrant women space in the refuge because they considered them unlikely to leave violent partners. One recalled that her peers 'saw migrant women as difficult and believed that efforts to support and empower migrant women were wasted, as they tended to go back home to an abusive partner'.[40] Ethnicity was casually blamed as a cause of violence, rather than the wider structural factors of isolation and poverty that made some groups more likely to experience abuse and less able to contest it. Refuges run by white Australian women also proved on occasion unwilling to challenge racist assumptions that immigrant women were dirty or required special accommodation for diet or religion. This meant that some imposed informal bans on migrants. As one worker recalled, 'Not a week went by where you didn't have at least two or three refuges saying, no Vietnamese women, no Turkish women, no Aboriginal women, no Arabic women.'[41] As a result, specialist refuges were formed that could accommodate immigrant or indigenous women, such as that set up in 1975 by the Italian migrant support group Co As It in Carlton, Melbourne. State funding was offered – but, tellingly, at a lower rate than for 'mainstream' women's refuges. The dominance of what has been termed 'white' or 'Anglo' values within the Australian refuge movement left the feminist spaces developed only partially available to immigrant and Aboriginal women.

Claiming and creating spaces has been a core feminist activity, though the spaces that resulted have not been free of boundary work and policing. Those without the privileges of class or racial advantages have sometimes struggled to access the overtly feminist spaces of women's centres, refuges and bookshops. Building spaces through state funding or joint work with social workers or police have created dilemmas for feminists. The abusive state, complicit in controlling, imprisoning and deporting poor, disabled or queer people, migrants and people of colour, has forced feminists, on occasion, to keep their distance.

Some feminist places have been highly provisional, or not fully under women's control; some have thrived even in unexpected spaces such as in the congregations of a male-led church or the small business start-up. Feminists have not always been invested in building long-lasting or elaborate spaces; the newsletters and zines of the late twentieth century were sometimes deliberately amateurish and fleeting. Feminist ambitions have on occasion been directed towards control of the microspaces of women's bodies, and how they are positioned in space. Small and intimate spaces and ephemeral media have however proved as important as vehicles of feminist dreams as the larger and more lasting spaces and places – a place in the constitution, a harassment-free workplace, or the women's centres, archives, libraries and bookshops that made up the concrete infrastructure of modern feminisms.

We turn now to an ephemeral object that introduces the 'things' populating feminism, with the invention of the first women's rights postal mailing label in the revolutionary 1840s.

CHAPTER 4

Objects

Anne Knight (1786–1862) was an English Quaker active in the campaign against slavery in the 1820s. She came from a modest family in Chelmsford, Essex, and like many Quakers she was well educated and familiar with radical political debates. She had been a member of the Chelmsford Ladies' Anti-Slavery Society when they toured Europe in 1825, connecting with abolitionists across the continent. But like so many other radical women involved in the movement, she was shocked by her treatment at the 1840 World Anti-Slavery Convention in London.

Women had played a leading role in the movement – one contemporary described them as forming 'the cement of the whole Antislavery building'.[1] And yet the Convention's male organizers were determined that women should occupy neither the platform nor the main hall. The American delegation were particularly angry at this, and the issue dominated the entire first day of the Convention. In the end, women were allowed to watch from the spectators' gallery, but had no further input. Some of their male supporters joined them in the gallery in an act of solidarity. The controversy inspired American delegates Lucretia Mott and Elizabeth Cady Stanton to hold their own women's rights convention, which took place in 1848 at Seneca Falls, New York.

Anne Knight was inspired to campaign for women's rights in Britain; she wrote to a friend in 1840, 'We are not the same beings as fifty years ago, no longer "sit by the fire and spin" or distil rosemary and lavender for poor neighbours.'[2] She raised the question of women's rights within the British Chartist movement and became deeply involved with the French women's movement. Knight joined the 1848 revolutions in Paris that followed the overthrow of the monarchy and attempts by workers to form a radical government. She allied herself to the socialist feminist Jeanne Deroin (1805–94), a seamstress and follower of Charles Fourier, who had demanded women's suffrage and rights during the revolution through a series of periodicals – *Voix des Femmes*, *Politique des Femmes*, *Opinion des Femmes*. On her return to Britain, Knight formed the first British women's suffrage association, the Sheffield Female Political Association, in 1851. This was a deeply controversial move – Deroin had been jailed for her feminist activism by the increasingly repressive French government. Nonetheless, Knight's group managed to get a petition for all adults to have the vote on equal terms presented to the House of Lords.

Knight was a globally connected, articulate woman who called for the 'equalization of human privilege'. She probably authored the anonymous pamphlet that circulated in Britain in 1847, which claimed, 'Never will the nations of the earth be well governed, until both sexes, as well as all parties, are fully represented and have an influence, a voice, and a hand in the enactment and administration of the laws.' As she kept up correspondences with other supporters of women's rights all over the world, she was unusually innovative in using her

Figure 4.1
Anne Knight holding a sign that reads 'By tortured millions, By the Divine Redeemer, Enfranchise Humanity, Bid the Outraged World, BE FREE'

letter-writing as a vehicle for a novel political tool – that of creating a recognizable 'brand' to support her message. Knight had designed 'labels printed in bright yellow, green and pink', which quoted her views on women's suffrage. She attached these to her letters, creating what may have been the first feminist colour scheme. As historian Bonnie Anderson describes it, 'these miniature broadsides crammed lines of tiny type into a two- by three-inch rectangle and ensured that a single missive could proselytize many.'[3] However, not all were convinced of this message. Anne Knight's cousin refused the labels Anne had sent her, commenting stiffly,

> I do not quite see the propriety of sticking them on all our Letters. I think the way in which truth is conveyed to the mind is very material, and we are cautioned not to cast pearls before swine.[4]

In modern history, women have often been closely associated with consumption. This has varied from the association between women and luxuries in the eighteenth century – the fripperies of fashion and jewellery – to the more mundane domestic consumption that became central to femininity in the nineteenth century, as the housewife became an established figure. In the twentieth century, the rise of mass capitalism led to an avalanche of commercial consumption for both sexes, but women largely retained their pre-eminent place as the consumers of fashion, household goods and food. The embedding of femininity in consumption has been a source of feminist frustration. Activists have sometimes preferred the realm of ideas and dreams and have tried to shake off the stereotypes of shopper and housewife.

Shopping, some argued, roots women in the grasping world of pleasure. But feminists have not just sought to transcend material culture; objects have helped to make political points, to communicate feminist ideas, to identify other feminists and to promote feminist dreams. They have been appropriated and produced by feminists, and have circulated within the movement and across national borders. Retail and shopping have turned out to be, in some circumstances, feminist activities.

This reflection on the *material* ways in which feminist ideas might circulate or be represented has become an important concern of historians. If feminism is a mosaic, what materials are its patterns formed from? New scholarship has looked at the uses of objects by campaigners and seeks to understand better how our sensory engagement with the world can infuse politics and ideas. Our ability to touch, taste and wear feminist objects can be a powerful means to support or contest the movement. Anne Knight's cousin may have felt that this was casting 'pearls before swine', but for generations of women who have worn suffrage colours, sashes and women's liberation badges, this has felt like an empowering move. Creative feminist reuse of 'things' has been widespread. Greenham Common Peace Camp in Britain saw chain letters inviting women around the country to bring personal items such as clothes and photographs to cover the fence during the blockade of 1982. Candles, nappies, sanitary pads, sketches and coloured wool were used to make the fence a focal point of life versus death. And despite the swift destruction of their work by soldiers, women at Greenham continued to 'darn' the fence; as one recalled:

> Never have I seen such beautiful, meticulous darning . . . Huge areas of the hideous fence soon started to look like beautiful tapestries . . . It all turned into one lovely smooth surface, for they sewed it with such ingenuity and care.[5]

Circumstances could make the most unlikely object a feminist item. In Britain, the pint glass became an icon of women's right to leisure space and alcohol when a woman who was refused a pint of beer in a pub in Cardiff took a private legal case against the publican in 1980. He had begun limiting women to half pints in 1972, when two lesbians had ordered pints at his bar: 'They were making their affection for each other clear to see, so I decided to ban pints for ladies.' Eight years later, the judge ruled this homophobic action illegal. But it must have taken the edge off the feminist pints that were raised in celebration when his judgement made clear that he was less motivated by women's equality than by fear of male violence: 'If you refuse to serve a young lady a pint glass of beer it could possibly lead to a male companion becoming quite disorderly.'[6]

Scholars Alison Bartlett and Margaret Henderson have recently written about the 'feminist things' of the Australian women's movement. They have usefully divided their approach to 'things' into categories that include corporeal things such as clothing and body accessories; 'world-making' things such as films and books; and protest things such as banners. They remind us that some objects only become 'feminist' when taken from an everyday context. Bolt-cutters in DIY shops, for example, were bought by Greenham Peace Camp protestors and 'became our favourite tool; little and big pieces of fence started to decorate cars and ears and clothes and walls at home', one protestor recalled. Such objects might become iconic and fêted. At the Pine Gap Women's Peace Camp in Australia, for example, a banner featuring bolt-cutters that had been made at the British Greenham Peace Camp was proudly displayed, alongside a 'hanging of [Greenham] fence wire'.[7] Henderson and Bartlett conclude that 'activist objects . . . make feminist things happen.'[8] By infusing feminist culture into material things, objects concretize it, making it more durable and leaving a legacy that later generations can claim or transform. In this chapter, we will see how objects have been making feminist things happen over the last two centuries.

Branding Feminism

The colours chosen by Anne Knight – pink, green and yellow – may simply have been intended to catch readers' attention. But by the early twentieth century, the British women's suffrage movement had adopted recognizable colour schemes – red and white for the National Union of Women's Suffrage Societies (NUWSS, established in 1897), to which green was later added in reference to the colours of the Italian Risorgimento (the movement for the reunification of Italy). The romantic republican nationalism of the Italian movement, led by Giuseppe Mazzini and Giuseppe Garibaldi, was a powerful influence on British radicals such as Charlotte Despard and Emmeline Pankhurst. Pankhurst argued, 'Just as Italy was kept down by the strong hand, so women are kept in subjection by the strong hand.'[9] Nonetheless, she wanted to distinguish her own Women's Social and Political Union (WSPU, established in 1903) from the competitor NUWSS.

Her organization adopted for its colours purple, white and green – representing dignity, purity and hope respectively.

These colours might be displayed through sashes, typically worn over an all-white dress, or sported in hats, accessories or the dress itself. Wearing the colours provided the opportunity to recognize other activists, but perhaps more importantly, to join events of mass spectacle, creating a sense of irresistible mass support for women's enfranchisement by thousands of women parading through sites such as Hyde Park and Trafalgar Square in London, and Princes Street in Edinburgh. The women who joined the NUWSS 1913 pilgrimage to London marched across Britain wearing raffia cockades, sashes of red, white and green, and matching haversacks.[10] Other suffrage organizations also chose colours – the Men's League for Women's Suffrage chose what they perhaps hoped was the dashing colour scheme of black and gold. The International Woman Suffrage Alliance took white and gold, while the Tax Resistance League adopted the sober colour scheme of black, white and grey.[11]

In the WSPU, Emmeline Pethick-Lawrence told supporters, 'each one of you can become a subvendor of the colours' in choosing what to wear in daily life.[12] Department stores advertised in the suffrage journals, and suffragists who could afford it wore smart dresses and hats with pleasure. Historians have charted a close and commercially savvy relationship between fashion retailers and the suffrage movement. Selfridges advertised 'Suffrage Dorothy Bags of soft kid' in the journal *Votes for Women* in 1910, featuring a drawcord of white, green and purple leather. You could also order ribbon in the WSPU colours at 1 shilling a yard, as well as buy suffrage stationery advertised as 'smooth, tough paper': 'The design is a purple diamond enclosed in a green wreath with the words "Votes for Women" inscribed in the centre.' The WSPU had 'approved' laundries, hairdressers, drapers and restaurants. Nevertheless, when suffrage supporters in Britain opted to break windows to protest their disenfranchisement, they chose to break the windows of the massive department stores in central London that sold these items alongside those of government and parliamentary offices. On a memorable day in March 1912, relays of women appeared every fifteen minutes to throw stones through the windows of prestigious shops on Haymarket, Piccadilly and Oxford Circus, breaking around 400 windows, at a cost of over £5,000. More than 100 women were arrested for this action.

This willingness to target the windows of department stores made the political point that no institution was excluded from feminist action. Yet the WSPU also ran their own retail outlets, which designed and sold items such as button badges featuring photographs of leading members, calendars with inspirational quotes from famous women and bespoke paper napkins celebrating key parades or the imprisonment of high-profile figures. Their design and creation of badges to mark prison service rooted the suffrage movement in cultures of craft and silversmithing. And in a nod to their male supporters, they also sold a tobacco pouch, as well as many items themed to the celebrity personalities of the organization, such as 'Emmeline' bags, cards, photographs and posters. The shops of the WSPU were widely distributed across the country in 1910, when they had over thirty branches. Their shop windows offered visible sites, open around the clock, for publicizing their campaigns. Located on high streets, they encouraged other women to volunteer, raised funds for the WSPU, and made a decisive claim for feminist politics in the commercial public sphere.

Suffrage shops and offices also sponsored the careers of small businesswomen who were often committed suffrage supporters, and who designed craft or fashion items to express their sentiments. Clara Strong (1858–1938) was one such. A suffragette milliner and honorary secretary of the Clapham WSPU branch, Strong offered readers of *Votes for Women* fashionable hats that included 'motor bonnets, with veil'. Roberta Mills (1870–1928) advertised belts and other leather items in the colours of all the different suffrage societies, claiming that there was 'nothing like leather for suffragettes' wear'. Mills sold leather goods through the WSPU headquarters in Clements Inn in central London, alongside costumiers who offered 'artistic garments' of loose robes, embroidered collars and trimmings of flowers and foliage in suffrage colours for processions.[13] Another supporter advertised sweet pea seeds in white, green and purple, bringing feminist visual culture to British gardens.

In the United States, there were similar close relationships between commerce and the suffrage movement that gave rise to a range of feminist objects. The California State Suffrage Association, for example, had adopted yellow as its colour, following the precedent of the first Kansas 'Sunflower State' women's suffrage campaign of 1867, and the successful Washington State campaign of 1910. Californian suffrage offices were dominated by yellow chrysanthemums, banners and posters. In San Francisco during the campaign that led to women being awarded the vote in 1911, activists appealed to merchants to set up yellow window exhibits. More than fifty shops did so during the campaign, as historian Jenny Sewell notes, 'The city wore the color that was soon to be the color of success.' The Californian suffragists also adopted a specific retail item to symbolize their cause, by selling and serving 'Equality Tea' in offices, fairs and department stores. In bespoke packaging, and perhaps nodding to the inspirational British suffrage movement by choosing a bracing English Breakfast blend, this item was not a random choice of commodity. Instead, Equality Tea symbolized the determination to root out the evils of alcohol by a feminist movement that was strongly associated with temperance. It was this controversial emphasis that saw the 1911 suffrage campaign defeated in San Francisco, where it had been opposed by bar and saloon owners, though it was won across California through the support of rural voters.[14]

Historian Margaret Finnegan has documented the attempts by American suffragists to use techniques of mass advertising, by commissioning huge posters, signs on streetcars, sandwich boards and electric signs. When denied space to advertise on New York's subways by an anti-suffrage company, suffragists turned instead to women's own bodies. They organized teams of women to ride the subway holding 'lapboards' that spelled out their message: 'One million women in New York want the vote'. They commissioned and sold or gave away feminist objects that included veil pins, cuff links, pennants, playing cards, fly-swatters, matchbooks, yellow streamers, doilies, horns and balloons. The 1915 New

Figure 4.2
Equality Brand Tea, produced in 1917 for the campaign for women's suffrage in California

York State campaign saw 1 million suffrage buttons distributed, alongside baby rattles and 35,000 fans that declared 'Keep cool! There will be nothing to worry about after we get Votes for Women.'[15]

While cultivating a world of feminist objects, the suffrage movement also sometimes renounced consumption as a fundraising tactic. The British movement hosted regular 'self denial' fundraising drives, probably copied from the Salvation Army, where members were invited to give up on minor luxuries – flowers, cocoa, butter, bus fares. Money released from these uses would be sent to the suffrage societies and raised substantial sums each year in 'self denial' weeks. A similar appeal was made for selfless donations at mass suffrage meetings such as that held in London's Albert Hall in October 1908. On this occasion, with the WSPU leaders Christabel and Emmeline Pankhurst in jail, Emmeline Pethick-Lawrence called for women in the audience to renounce their worldly comforts. This led to supporters not only promising money but stripping off their watches and jewellery, which were ostentatiously carried to the stage by young women in white dresses with purple and green belts, and the value totted up on a blackboard.[16]

Though some poorer women responded to the calls for self-denial and sent in their pennies, it was clear that talk of giving up flowers and butter, or dressing in suffrage colours, was mostly aimed at wealthier women. American suffragists noted that reaching working-class women was 'the despair of our workers, because they are so hard to get at'. In 1910, Brooklyn suffragists found a means to get their propaganda into the hands of poorer women by printing 30,000 paper bags with suffrage slogans calling for 'lower taxes, less rent, a clean and happy city, and full-time school for every child'. The bags were distributed for free use by sympathetic grocers, aiming to reach 'the faithful mothers, sisters and aunts who are to be found working in the kitchens'.[17] What those in the kitchens thought of the campaign and its paper bags that promised so much is not recorded, but the bags were a deliberately ephemeral object of everyday use, enrolled into the suffrage campaign.

Suffragists sometimes feared that their political message was trivialized by its widespread hitching to forms of cheap or disposable consumption which might preclude deeper forms of commitment. This was particularly problematic when manufacturers latched on to the potential of suffrage as a promotional 'bait'. There was extensive production of suffrage-branded objects that had no connection to the women's movement, such as the Johnson Educator Food Company's Suffragette Cracker. In 1911, suffragist Mary Ware Dennett had become cynical about seeing yet another such object, which claimed '"All women vote for?" what? I'm sure I don't remember. It may have been a cereal, a tooth-paste, a carpet-sweeper, or anything else . . .'[18] Dennett's discomfort with the encroachment of capitalist consumption was shared and amplified by later generations of women's liberationists who were deeply committed to escaping the capitalist compulsion to consume.

Feminist Bodies

In a context of anti-capitalism, punk and grassroots activism, it was perhaps no surprise that the British women's liberation movement of the 1970s was reluctant to embrace the politicized consumption of their suffrage forebears. They preferred the low-key, low-capital world of feminist craft businesses such as Marged Shoes, which described itself as 'A women's collective making shoes for women' in Tregaron, Wales. There was nothing like the early-twentieth-century explosion of colour-themed mass retail, but instead a turn to 'world-making' and protest objects. The London feminist bookshop Sisterwrite included alongside their books a range of objects for sale, mostly posters, badges and records. Perhaps more controversially, Sisterwrite also sold speculums, which became appropriated as unlikely feminist objects.

Women's groups in the 1970s had sharply criticized the medical technologies, often designed and wielded by men, which surveilled and controlled women's bodies. The cold metal speculum had been imposed on women by gynaecologists, often with little attempt to consult and include women in their healthcare. It had been developed by the American physician James Marion Sims, a slave owner in Alabama who used it on enslaved women in the 1840s without their consent. It was soon used aggressively against prostitutes by police in France and its colonial territories during forcible examinations for sexually transmitted diseases, a use which stretched into late-twentieth-century techniques of police harassment of sex workers across many locations. Victorian feminists such as Josephine Butler proclaimed the forced inspection of prostitutes, using speculums, 'instrumental rape'. Radical feminist Andrea Dworkin (1966–2005) described how medical doctors used it against her when she was arrested in the mid-1960s in a Vietnam War protest: 'They pretty much tore me up inside with a steel speculum and had themselves a fine old time verbally tormenting me as well.'[19] It therefore seems an unlikely feminist object. Nonetheless, the speculum was capable of being recuperated and reclaimed. The Detroit Women's City Club opened in 1977 by the Feminist Economic Network had plans for a speculum factory within the building. In London, Sisterwrite sold cheap plastic versions, warmer than the metal implements preferred by medics, and with very different uses in mind.

The feminist appropriation of the speculum invited women to use them to see their own bodies, hoping to overcome any disgust or shame they might feel about their own vaginas, previously seen as hidden or 'dirty'. Adrienne Sallay recalled a meeting of her women's group in Sydney, Australia:

> We removed our knickers and lay down on the floor in a circle, feet towards the centre, clutching our mirrors. I can still recall the smell of the new carpet, the feel of the cushion at my back, the serious way we approached our biology, the classic array of mirrors. There were hand mirrors with long elegant handles, curved magnifying (!) mirrors, unframed pocket mirrors, tiny mirrors from lipstick containers and my gold compact mirror. At first we adopted very serious faces as we peeked and peered at ourselves, holding our mirrors and long arms and tilting them at our unsuspecting vaginas.

Eventually, however,

> the solemnity of the occasion became disrupted. Someone looked up from her mirror at all our legs waving in the air, at our flushed faces, at our discarded knickers, and soon

Figure 4.3
Wonder Woman wields a speculum on the July 1973 cover of *Sister*, the newspaper of the Los Angeles Women's Center

> we were all laughing at the poses we had adopted, at the discoveries we had made, and at the pleasure we had felt.[20]

The emphasis on self-revelation empowered women to re-visualize and learn to love their own bodies. It also helped foster autonomy from the male-dominated, hierarchical health professions. The speculum thus became a symbol of reclaiming women's medical empowerment, captured in the Wonder Woman cartoon that was reproduced by *Sister*, the journal of the Los Angeles Women's Center in 1973. Seizing a speculum from a cowering doctor, Wonder Woman declares, 'With my *speculum*, I *am* strong! I *can* fight!' But for feminist philosopher Donna Haraway, the choice of Wonder Woman was revealing of a white ethnocentricism and lack of sensitivity to wider health issues. The speculum, she argued, was a visual technology that risked replicating the colonial gaze and its invasive technologies. The appropriation of women's bodies, even if by a speculum in their own hands, paralleled the appropriation of land and indigenous bodies by many centuries of conquerors. For Haraway, the speculum could still be a feminist technology, but by understanding it not as an object but a way of seeing the big picture. For her, this big picture encompassed not just the relatively privileged women in the self-help groups of the global North, but also the global poor who needed not just reproductive freedoms but basic healthcare. A speculum could thus be a 'freedom- and justice-oriented policy formation' rather than just an object. This, she argued, represented a new 'civil rights' focus for feminist movements.[21]

Haraway provided a compelling picture of health inequalities, the toll of toxic work conditions and absent healthcare that mostly non-white women bore across the global North and South. But her reading of feminist health activism was perhaps too pessimistic. Much of it had stemmed from the very groups she had identified – the poor, the uninsured, the undocumented and migrant women. Women's groups were sites where material concerns over bodies and health were widely discussed, often with a deep awareness of how global structures were at play in the distribution of healthcare. The health manual *Our Bodies, Ourselves*, a publishing phenomenon of the 1970s onwards which originated in Boston and circulated around the globe, was a key element in feminist healthcare activism. Translated into many languages and formats, as scholar Kathy Davis has shown, it allowed feminist health activism to be tailored to the diverse settings in which feminisms emerged. Numerous local editions of *Our Bodies, Ourselves* adapted feminist health politics according to local conditions.[22] Despite the US origins of the original collective, Davis argues that it was not imposed as 'cultural imperialism' on women in other locations, but was reworked to reflect the embodied knowledge of its local adapters.

The Bulgarian translators, for example, preferred to foreground the empowerment of individual women in relation to their bodies in their 2001 edition. Bulgaria's transition away from socialist government in 1989 had left little appetite for an emphasis on groups and communities. The Bulgarian edition treated abortion in a straightforward manner, reflecting its legal and uncontroversial status within Bulgaria, and tweaked the title to read *Nasheto Tyalo, Nie Samite* (*Our Body, Ourselves*) to reflect an individualist approach. This was reversed in Latin America, where translators of *Our Bodies, Ourselves* preferred to stress the role of women's health as understood within families, health movements, traditional healing practices and communities. Very different versions, with different illustrations, testimonies and emphases, produced *Our Bodies, Ourselves* as a 'feminist' object that bridged localities but responded to local concerns. One such concern was the significance of 'feminism' as a label, which was unpopular with Bulgarian women because it had connotations of the collectivist propaganda of Marxism and Leninism. In Latin American editions, however, it was the term *auto ayuda* (self-help) that was unacceptable. As a Cuban editor explained,

> nobody takes care of themselves by themselves . . . it's your relationships that keep you well and it's in relationships that you gain all the things that make you well, including the energy for collective action, which is part of health.[23]

Determination to challenge coercive or commercial elements of women's bodily experiences led to the invention of some innovative 'feminist things'. Activist Susanne Gannon recalled the 'mind-blowing' discovery of how to make tampons out of sea sponges and cotton when at university in Melbourne in the 1970s. There had long been a tradition of feminist activism over the costs women bore due to menstruation, particularly over the taxes levied on menstrual products. There were red-caped 'menstrual avengers' at Australian feminist marches, and protestors at government offices in

Canberra wearing t-shirts that warned legislators, 'I bleed and I vote'.[24] Tampons, where available, could represent women's liberation from cumbersome pads or rags. They allowed for more physical freedom, ongoing attendance at school, and discretion about bodily cycles. The British magazine *Spare Rib* alleged the misery of Chinese women using 'rough brown paper' in 1980. A delegation of British visitors demonstrated the properties of tampons in the teacups of their Women's Association of China hosts in Nanjing in 1980, presenting them as an object of liberation.[25] But real liberation came not just from access to a commercial product, some argued, but from making your own. The Bristol Free Sanitary Protection Group, for example, manufactured their own tampons as part of a street theatre performance in 1977, and gave them away to the audience. A woman in Salem, Oregon, published her directions for rolling her own tampons in the Michigan journal *Lesbian Connection* in 1986. Stressing natural components, her tampons included '¼ cup small pieces of sponge, virgin wool and shredded cotton. A tsp of dried bits of seaweed (laminaria) or dried bits of leather (for added absorbency).' Her method required ironing cotton and darning the removal string, but gave her 'comfort and choice . . . It can be spendy (about twice as much as store bought) and time consuming, but it's worth it!'[26]

Tampons remained tabooed objects in many parts of the world, where women found touching their genitals problematic, or where there was a social requirement to preserve young women's hymens to prove virginity, or where they were simply not available. And even in places where tampons were routine for many women, their use was still subject to extreme discretion. Their tabooed nature was demonstrated by their power to shock when worn by punks as fashion items, or featured in feminist fancy dress. And there were constant feminist efforts to highlight their negatives – non-recyclable applicators, toxic shock associations, unaffordability for many women. The efforts by large companies such as Playtex to market tampons in deodorized formats were resisted for the implication that women's genitals were offensive-smelling. And the link between synthetic materials in tampons and toxic shock syndrome caused extensive debate amongst feminists, concerned at the lack of transparency and accountability of tampon manufacturers when faced with the deaths of scores of women.

There was, then something of a love–hate relationship between feminists and tampons in the global North, and a search for alternatives. The sea sponge was 'environmentally friendly, cheap and reusable, less festooned with images of discretion and shame than other products designed to make menstruation invisible'.[27] Many feminists liked the association with the 'natural', and the turn away from profit-making corporations. Natural sea sponges were advertised in the British feminist press, and a women's liberation group in Sheffield reported that a sponge was 'more efficient, feels more natural, more comfortable, and is certainly much CHEAPER'.[28] A community pharmacy in Madison, Wisconsin, advertised 'natural brown sea sponges' to readers of the feminist journal *Bread and Roses*: 'We sell sea sponges and encourage women to share their comments. More importantly, we encourage you to seek a peace with your body that is your own.'[29] The Melbourne women's refuge, Matilda, called its newsletter the *Sea Sponge Monthly*, a playful reference to alternative menstrual culture and a metaphor for 'the way womyn were soaking up information and devising new ways of living our lives'.[30] The body proved a site of feminist creative energy, spiritual connection and spark for the invention or repurposing of feminist 'things'.

African Alternatives

The playful and radical reworkings of the tampon amongst feminists in the global North contrasted with the relative absence of adequate sanitary products in much of the global South. In the 2010s, this has led to campaigns around 'period poverty', pushing for more provision for women forced to miss school or work due to menstruation. Forty years earlier, however, many Euro-American feminists did not perceive women in Africa as sharing their need for dignity and safe provision during menstruation. Such concerns were eclipsed by a focus on women's genitals as the site of male religious or cultural violence through practices of cutting that became termed 'female genital mutilation'. Campaigns against these practices have been led by many African women, but have also been the site of tensions when framed insensitively in terms of 'barbarism'. This has led to a complex reception for feminism and women's liberation in sub-Saharan Africa. Many African women did not identify with a political movement they felt to be dominated by white women and colonial mindsets. But there was interest amongst women involved in nationalist liberation movements in exploring women's place in the nation and the gendering of ideas of 'negritude' developed by scholars such as Aimé Césaire and Frantz Fanon.

Empire had not only unleashed violence, radical scholars argued, but had also instilled inferiority complexes and other psychic traumas amongst colonized peoples. These ideas were explored by Senegalese-born, French-educated writer Awa Thiam. Her collection of first-person testimony from women in West Africa was published in France as *La Parole aux Négresses* in 1978, and translated into English as *Black Sisters, Speak Out* in 1986. Thiam was disappointed that struggles for national liberation had often delivered little for women in the newly independent countries such as Senegal and Côte d'Ivoire. But she was also frustrated that women themselves seemed to be complicit in patriarchy. Her transcribed conversations with groups of men and women often included silences from women where Thiam was expecting vigorous debate. She characterized many African women as 'in thrall, as passive victims'. For Thiam, their use of skin lighteners and hair straightening showed women's complicity with colonial and patriarchal cultures.

The testimonies Thiam collected, however, were at odds with ideas of victimhood and complicity. The women she spoke to described using traditional and Islamic religious structures to gain divorces when their marriages were unhappy. A Senegalese woman identified as 'Médina' described adopting an informal hunger strike and sex strike when she was married without her consent to a cousin she had never met. Médina had been brought up in Saint-Louis, the cosmopolitan former colonial capital of Senegal. She describes having fallen in love with a young man she had met at school; her account strongly conveys her sense of choice and rebellion against family constraints. In another striking testimony, a

Nigerian female teacher describes sharing the care of her five children with her husband: 'he was quite ready to change the babies' nappies or bath them if I was busy with something else.' She and her husband had both studied abroad, but encountered criticisms of their habits from their families:

> 'The wife must work her fingers to the bone for her husband if she hopes to go to paradise,' they say, adding, 'it's written in the Koran.' I was often tempted to retort, 'Crap! Mind your own business!'

These were the voices of assertive, educated and sometimes globally well-connected West African women who were far from passive in reshaping their relationships with men.

Though Awa Thiam was aware of the problems of using 'feminist' in an African context, and seemed to overlook the forceful women whose testimony she published, she nonetheless embraced the idea of a black African feminist movement. Thiam had criticized white feminists such as Kate Millett for erasing black women and orienting feminism silently to white women's needs. Her alternative feminist inspiration was drawn from the iconic anti-colonial struggles of women she celebrated in Algeria, Vietnam and Zimbabwe. She envisaged a celebration of African women's culture, and a feminism that could work in alliance with African men. She experimented with this as a member of the Coordination des Femmes Noires (Black Women's Coordination), founded in France in 1976 to contest racism and sexism. Inserting such concerns into the existing women's movement was not easy. *Black Sisters, Speak Out* offered a short reading list that showed an awkward combination of canonical readings.

Feminist texts such as Benoîte Groult's *Ainsi Soit-Elle* (*As She Is*), Simone de Beauvoir's *The Second Sex* and Shulamith Firestone's *The Dialectic of Sex* sat alongside anti-colonial and countercultural authors (Fanon, Wilhelm Reich) and anthropological studies of Africa. There was little black feminist literature or African women's literature that could inform and bolster Thiam's call for an African feminism. Texts such as *As She Is* did not help. Written by Benoîte Groult (1920–2016), a white upper-class Frenchwoman, *As She Is* controversially foregrounded African culture as deeply violent towards women, centred on practices of clitoridectomy and infibulation (cutting the labia and clitoris and sewing the vulva). This set the stage for Thiam's book, which was widely cited in France to reinforce ideas of African women as uniquely oppressed. Thiam's accounts of polygamy, clitoridectomy and forced marriage were divorced from the accounts of resistance and alternative and cosmopolitan gender orders that were also visible in the book.[31] She was criticized by women such as Aissatou Diallo, editor of *Amina* magazine, for her naïve presentation of African womanhood as rooted in rural and religious oppression. *Amina*, a Paris/Dakar production aimed at women in Francophone Africa and the African diaspora, by contrast reflected the concerns of urban and educated African women and helped disperse paternalistic accounts of African women's victimhood.

Intense debates continued as to the relevance of feminism in African contexts. Some countries saw state-sponsored women's movements, such as the Organization of Mozambican Women, founded by the Frente de Libertação de Moçambique (Mozambican Liberation Movement, Frelimo) in 1972.

Frelimo had already denounced polygamy and the payment of 'bride price' at its second Party Congress in 1968. After it came to power in Mozambique in 1975, the ruling party positioned women's liberation, in President Samora Machel's words, as 'the fundamental necessity for the revolution'. In practice, Frelimo's orthodox Marxism and centralizing tendencies left little space for women to find autonomy and voice within its 'state feminist' initiatives. Frelimo's women's literacy and production drives were materially grounded in the provision of objects such as the tractor and the pen. Yet women did not always gain access to such things. Frelimo's policies often proceeded with little consultation with women themselves, and were inattentive to the reproductive and domestic labour women were also asked to do. The use of tractors remained dominated by men and illiteracy remained high amongst Mozambican women (around 70 per cent in 2005, compared to 40 per cent of men).[32]

Neither racialized European feminisms nor state-sponsored alternatives offered much creativity or political momentum for African feminisms. However, in the 1980s and 90s, scholars such as Ifi Amadiume and Oyèrónkẹ́ Oyěwùmí foregrounded the diversity of gender in many African societies. They highlighted non-binary forms of gender that intersected with age to produce complicated opportunities for women and non-binary people to exercise power in precolonial and colonial Africa.[33] This work resonated with the fluid and non-binary accounts of gender which had begun to be developed by other feminist theorists in this period and suggested how African perspectives might be innovative and influential. The African Feminist Forum began to meet regularly to reflect

African culture and world views in feminist campaigning. Established in Ghana in 2006 and represented nationally by organizations such as the Liberian Feminist Forum, the founding charter of the African Feminist Forum stated:

> As we invoke the memory of those women whose names are hardly ever recorded in any history books, we insist that it is a profound insult to claim that feminism was imported into Africa from the West. We reclaim and assert the long and rich tradition of African women's resistance to patriarchy in Africa. We henceforth claim the right to theorise for ourselves, write for ourselves, strategise for ourselves and speak for ourselves as African feminists.[34]

A hundred and twenty years previously, the anonymous Ghanaian letter-writer cited at the outset of this book who satirized white male 'Just Ass' might well have agreed.

Protest and 'World-Making' Things

The powerful words of the African Feminist Forum were themselves a material object when printed as a 'thing' of ink on paper. Books, pamphlets and magazines have been amongst the most attractive, visible and portable elements of feminisms. They have conveyed the deep feelings discussed in Chapter 6. As one Australian feminist recalled of the writing produced in the 'initial exhilarating flush of feminism' in the 1970s, 'the emotion rises like steam from the page: exhilaration, elation, bonding, sisterhood.'[35] Writing and reading have been so central to feminism that, for some scholars, 'the women's movement appears to have written itself into being.'[36]

This sense of the power of writing led to experimentation

with branded feminist pens. The Women's Suffrage Party of New York, for example, produced a specially inscribed dip pen in their colours – black and yellow – imprinted with 'Votes for Women'. The Women's Social and Political Union in Britain also offered an inscribed pen, sales of which would help the feminist cause. The pen can of course also be used for other purposes, including anti-feminist writing. But the special relationship between feminism and the written word makes the pen a powerful feminist object.

For much of the past two centuries, the power of the pen has been amplified by the technologies of printing and bookbinding, and the growing means to distribute print around the globe. The printed word has been a crucial inspiration for the circulation of feminist dreams and ideas, whether in hardback, ephemeral pamphlet, newsprint or DIY zine. Much of this print production has happened outside of formal publishing houses, with small groups issuing books and pamphlets when resources permit. The *mini-komi* informal newsletters of the 1970s Japanese women's liberation movement, or the zines of the riot grrrl movement in the 1990s, were produced on shoestring budgets, without technology or distribution networks. Feminist print culture has sometimes been sponsored by publishing houses that do not directly identify as feminist but where women have been prominent as authors or partners, for example Zimbabwe's Baobab Books or Morocco's Le Fennec. At other times, feminist writing has been deliberately commissioned and encouraged by the founding of publishers such as Kali for Women in India. Founded by Ritu Menon and Urvashi Butalia in 1984, this project built on the experience of running the Indian feminist English-language magazine *Manushi* in 1978. The founders were determined to amplify Indian feminist knowledge production, to counter the dominance of book publishing by visitors and scholars from the global North and to make books cheaper for Indian readers. One of their best-known books was *Sharir ki Jaankari* (*About the Body*). With a print run of thousands, it was never on sale in a bookshop but was distributed at cost price to rural women. It was originally written through rural village workshops in Rajasthan that addressed women's health concerns. The first version was written collectively by more than a hundred women and produced by hand. With something of the feeling of *Our Bodies, Ourselves*, it was intended to empower and educate rural women to resist issues such as rape within marriage and foetal sex selection. But the illustrations of naked bodies proved unwelcome in subsequent workshops, with villagers protesting that naked bodies did not feature in their everyday environments. Kali for Women reworked the book to include clothed bodies, but with lift-up panels that allow bodies to be viewed more intimately. The male print firm refused to print even this version, and Kali for Women shifted their trade to an all-women print collective in Delhi. They continued to use hand production for the binding, allowing for the production of a tangible, useable, locally-responsive feminist book.[37]

Other feminist publishers have established a professional, visual style that has created an instantly recognizable feminist book aesthetic. Virago Press was launched in London in 1973 by Carmen Callil, an Australian working on the countercultural periodicals *Ink* and *Oz*. Callil and her team were deeply committed to recovering the out-of-print work of women's writers through their Modern Classics series, and the green spines of their books created a distinctive feminist aesthetic. As one American visitor noted of the bookshop in London, 'what is awesome about the Virago bookshop is walking in and being greeted, face to face, with every Virago title in print. A sea of green books . . .'[38]

The green resonated with an earlier Irish women-only publishing project, described by writer James Joyce as producing books in 'calf covers of pissedon green'. Cuala Press, run by Elizabeth and Susan Yeats from 1902 in Churchtown, near Dublin, never declared itself feminist; it published many more men than women in its luxury, hand-produced Arts and Crafts books. As the sisters of Irish poet W. B. Yeats, the Yeats' contributions were often overshadowed by their more famous older brother. But as Simone Murray has argued, the unmarried Yeats sisters supported their male relatives and trained their all-female workforce in composition and typography over four decades as Ireland moved from British rule through revolution and civil war to independence. They stressed women's need for economic autonomy and access to labour markets, along similar lines to the arguments made by the Victoria Press pioneers in the 1860s (see Chapter 3). Indeed, it was the Victoria Press founders who had offered training in printing to Elizabeth Yeats through the London-based Women's Printing Society.[39] The infrastructure of initiatives to support women's employment produced a tangible legacy of women's and feminist print production across time and space.

In sum, the production of books and magazines has its own world of material culture, rooted in mundane processes of production, through writing, bookbinding and the

Figure 4.4
Elizabeth Yeats working the hand-press in the Dun Emer (later Cuala) press room, c. 1903

manipulation and inking of print presses. Even in the later twentieth century, when first broadcast media and then digital media have seemed to displace print, the role of a tangible paper-based record of feminist activism has remained crucial. As the Filipina activist Anna Leah Sarabia noted, despite her production of thousands of hours of radio and television content, what mattered was 'a track record in hard paper copy, whether this be in the form of photocopied leaflets and newspapers, difficult-to-read mimeographed monographs, or compilations of work already published several times over'. Sarabia co-produced a book on Filipina experiences, *Telling Lives*, that was marketed at the 1992 International Feminist Bookfair in Amsterdam, and she has continued to publish books subsequently.[40]

Spanning the simple pencil, pen and scissors, the Albion hand-press and 14-point moveable type used by the Yeats sisters, the Gestetner and Roneo machines that transformed feminist knowledge production in the twentieth century by allowing for cheap reproduction of newsletters and pamphlets, the growing sophistication of tools such as the IBM golfball typewriter and the later technologies of word processing and digital publishing, these changing communications technologies of the past two hundred years have been central to the materializing of feminist ideas and creative energy.

While there have been periodic dramatic, revolutionary feminist experiences of barricades, high emotions and militancy, the everyday labour, financing and sale of feminist things have been equally significant. This chapter has revealed a rich selection of objects bought and sold, refashioned and subverted, which have given feminists ways in which they could tangibly touch, wear or purchase feminisms. Ranging from the temporary iconicity of a pint glass wielded by a woman drinker to the role of 'feminist companion species' taken on (perhaps unwillingly) by the sea sponge, objects have been enrolled into feminist movements, repurposed, cut up, painted, gifted, sold and treasured.

The idea that feminism could be commodified has created controversy; critics have been fearful that it draws a radical political movement into the world of profit and production. Opportunistic businesses have sometimes tried to commodify feminist creativity. But making money has sometimes been a useful goal for activist women, as we saw in Chapter 3. Political movements need resources, as early-twentieth-century women's suffragists were well aware. Women could use bookshops, editing, design and printing to help support themselves, and make other kinds of activism possible. Historian Joan Marie Johnson has argued that 'money was an effective means to force change in a society that was highly patriarchal.'[41] The spaces created within the marketplace could provide entry points for all kinds of women for whom a consciousness-raising group was a scary prospect. And similarly, the magazines, badges, pens, scarves and posters of feminism could allow women to tentatively explore feminist affiliation, or to playfully display their politics.

In the next chapter, I turn to feminist fashion. But I'll end with this irresistible hymn to feminist material culture from Australian feminist Deni Fuller, writing of the 'woman' symbol:

We made the symbol in paper, tin, calico, paint, timber, print, sequins, silver, cardboard, linen, wool, canvas, denim, chalk, texta, Letraset, porcelain, batik, leadlight, tattoo, thread, clay, crystal, sand, beads, glitter and gum leaves. We waved it, we wore it, we painted and graffitied it, silk-screened and laminated and embroidered it, and wrought it in earrings and pendants and rings. We put a fist in it for determination. We linked two together for sexuality and solidarity. We mass-produced it in kitchens and on back verandas and we plastered city lamp posts and the sides of shops with it, we distributed it through the mail and by hand on the streets. We loved it and it loved us back.[42]

Figure 4.5
The 'woman' symbol on Women's Liberation badges of the 1970s and 1980s from France, Britain and Italy

CHAPTER 5

Looks

Since the global Women's March of 2017, a 'feminist look' has become widely recognizable through the invention of the 'pussy hat': a knitted or crocheted pink hat with two corner 'peaks' that resemble small ears – or it could be a female vulva. The adoption of the hat by thousands of women and non-binary people on the march and around the world subsequently has provided a visual statement of mass protest. Its handmade status speaks to a long history of women's craft skills, and its name contests and de-stigmatizes Donald Trump's comments about 'grabbing women by the pussy' which were widely reported during his presidential campaign. Yet fashion has long been a particularly loaded and contested site of feminist 'things'. Women's bodies have been physically and symbolically injured and constrained by forms of dress designed to immobilize, to please men and objectify female sexual attributes, or to demonstrate women's purity and modesty. From 'rational dress' to pussy hats, clothing has been a site of feminist challenge and subversion.

> When I would play with the little boys in Bryant Park
> although you said it was rough and unladylike, that was
> feminism. When I took off my veil or gloves whenever

> your back was turned or when I stayed in my room for two days rather than put on stays [a tight-fitting corset], that was feminism. When I got out of paying calls to go riding or sailing, that was feminism. When I would go to college, in spite of your protests, that was feminism. When I kept to regular hours of work in spite of protests that I was 'selfish', that was feminism. When I had a baby when I wanted one, in spite of protests that I was not selfish enough, that was feminism.[1]

This was how American ethnographer and anthropologist Elsie Clews Parsons (1875–1941) recounted answering her mother's pained question 'What *is* feminism?' Parsons made her adolescent protests at stays, gloves and veil centre stage in her acts of rebellion, alongside education, meaningful work and reproductive freedom.

The image of the trousered, hatless or braless woman has long been centre stage in the visual imagery of 'the feminist'. Figures such as the French writer George Sand (1804–76) captured public notoriety by adopting male dress, claiming it was both economic and practical. From 1800, Parisian women had to apply for a police permit to wear men's clothes, making Sand's choice of dress subversive. Sand had no permit, but was widely ridiculed for her cross-dressing. Her fellow author Victor Hugo commented satirically, 'George Sand cannot determine whether she is male or female. I entertain a high regard for all my colleagues, but it is not my place to decide whether she is my sister or my brother.'[2]

For Elsie Parsons, it was not only her resistance to

conventional fashion but also a visible act of consumption – smoking a cigarette – that carried the strongest connotations of how it felt and looked to be a feminist. George Sand had controversially combined smoking (in her case, cigars and a hookah) with her rebellion against feminine dress. In the twentieth century, Parsons also encountered a hostile environment. Her *Journal of a Feminist*, penned in the 1910s but unpublished until 1994, described again and again her efforts to smoke in American restaurants, stations and train carriages. She was frequently forbidden, but nonetheless found that as a college-educated white woman she had considerable freedoms. Parsons was able to smoke, wear trousers and roam the American South-West, recording Native American folklore. Her anthropological observations led her to see social conventions as malleable and externally imposed. Daringly, she extended this to her own gender: 'this morning perhaps I may feel like a male; let me act like one. This afternoon I may feel like a female; let me act like one. At midday or midnight I may feel sexless; let me therefore act sexlessly.' Clearly, the twenty-first century 'discovery' of gender fluidity has resonances in the past, even if naming it as 'trans' is relatively recent.

In this chapter, I will explore the role of fashion and bodies within feminist activism. Twenty-first-century controversies over the veil and 'burkini', as well as the obsessive media scrutiny of the clothes of public figures such as Hillary Clinton, reminds us of the central place of women's clothes in delineating their 'place' in society. Choosing to look different is an act of revolutionary potential. In addition to subverting dress norms, feminists have also problematized ideas of who is doing the 'looking'. In the 1970s, activists identified the 'male gaze' as a major oppressive feature of art, culture and social life, and adopted their own practices of subversive looking. In 1986, feminist scholar Chandra Talpade Mohanty took this concept further when she authored a powerful critique of the failure of 'Western' feminism to understand and respond to the power inequalities faced by Third World women, titled 'Under Western Eyes'.[3] The idea of 'a look' can thus take many forms and touches on some critical elements to feminist thinking and practice.

We start by focusing on the rise of the 'new woman' in the late nineteenth century, a self-supporting, confident woman whose search for selfhood took her beyond the family and into realms of the workplace, street and legislature. This iconic figure – short-haired and strong-minded – was popularized across the world, as British, Japanese, Chinese, New Zealand and Russian women, to name just a selection, explored 'modern' ways of being. The 'new woman' was closely associated with dress reform and iconoclasm in terms of the management of her hair and body. As we'll see, the activists of women's liberation in the 1970s and 80s also adopted a 'feminist look', associated with dressing for their own or other women's pleasure.

We then turn to another form of dress – the deeply contested act of veiling, spanning different cultural and religious traditions. Despite divisions over its meaning, I argue that coverings such as the veil, headscarf or *chador* are capable of being both empowering and constraining for women. Finally, I reflect on the problems dress reform has posed in fuelling stereotypes of 'mannish' or doctrinaire feminists, creating cliques and insider groups, and giving expression to the exclusions of class and race that have sometimes emerged in the wake of a 'feminist look'.

Beauty, Fashion and Politics

To be fashionable or beautiful has often been a tool for women seeking to exercise power. Feminists have faced dilemmas over whether to gain the social advantages of dress conformity or risk the losses of refusing to look like everyone else. In the Philippines, for example, the experience of Spanish colonial settlement (1521–1898) and American colonial rule (1898–1946) created a complex environment for feminists in which fashion took centre stage. There were calls for Filipina women's enfranchisement from the late nineteenth century, though most women active in public life preferred to organize through the socially conservative 'club movement' where suffrage was low profile. The political practices of the 'clubwomen' were characterized by conservative norms of domesticated femininity and modest dress. Clubwomen found it useful to present themselves as conventionally maternal, respectable and feminine in appearance, to aid their campaigns to support women's health and diet during pregnancy, and to lower child mortality. In this context, the colonial Spanish celebration of motherhood as central to femininity was powerful even amongst educated and active women who were seeking new roles.

Despite Filipina women's political experience and seriousness, the public careers of women were frequently established through their looks. Beauty contests were an important means by which Filipina women gained public profile. Many suffragists, clubwomen and journalists were declared Carnival Queens, and posed in glamorous costumes.[4] The ability to adopt conventional feminine beauty was a powerful means of gaining civic prominence for women.

The replacement of Spanish by American rule in 1898 brought calls for modernization of the Philippines, through women's greater access to education and their eventual suffrage. Like many colonial powers, however, the Americans found it hard to imagine a world in which Filipina women voted before American women. While some white American women were enfranchised in frontier and Western territories such as Wyoming, Colorado and Utah in the late nineteenth century, adult women were not fully enfranchised in the United States until 1920, and racist Jim Crow legislation after this date limited the voting rights of African American and Native American women and men. This may explain why a Filipina campaign for suffrage only emerged in an organized form after 1918, when the American women's suffrage movement had achieved victory in many states and was confident of overall success. For Filipina women, asking for the vote posed a complex choice since women's suffrage was often voiced in terms of Western women's rights and thus risked labelling Filipina women as cooperators with the colonial power. The nationalist movement was reluctant to prioritize women's suffrage, and some key figures opposed it entirely, preferring to associate women with motherhood and the home. This was not an easy landscape to navigate for feminists, and personal appearance remained a key resource.

Female activists in this national context had to make choices about their dress, as well as decide their stance on

Figure 5.1
Filipina suffragist, diplomat and philanthropist Trinidad Fernandez Legarda as Queen of the Manila Carnival, 1924

dress reform. Male politicians in the Philippines, as in many other colonial settings, found it expedient to adopt mostly 'Western' dress, while women active in public life were often expected to wear 'traditional' or folk attire. In the Philippines, there was much feminist resistance to the cumbersome colonial Spanish traditions of blouse (*camisa*), shawl (*pañuelo*) and tunic (*terno*), which featured impractical starched butterfly sleeves. This so-called 'Maria Clara' dress, it was argued, was likely to cause accidents in workplaces and schools, and prevented women from taking part in sport. It also had a tendency to collapse into a sodden mess in the rain. Nonetheless, Filipina feminists such as Pilar Hidalgo Lim (1893–1973) and Trinidad Fernandez Legarda (1899–1998) were aware of the need to distance themselves from the 'Western' connotations of feminism, and they consistently adopted this dress for public events. They were highly critical of 'Maria Clara's' connotations of domestic obedience and confinement but were careful not to appear too American or too transgressive in their 'new womanhood'. This pragmatic choice limited the extent to which they could subvert conservative norms about women's 'natural' place in the world but did ensure resolution of the tensions between colonial and nationalist versions of Filipina feminism. Women's suffrage became a key feminist goal and was achieved through a resounding endorsement in a national referendum in 1937.

Rational Dress and Fashion Heterodoxy

Filipina strategies of cautious conventionality were echoed in other contexts. In the United States, the dress reformer and journalist Amelia Bloomer (1818–94) began a controversial campaign for women to wear loose-fitting trousers under a knee-length skirt in 1849, a year after women all over the world had participated enthusiastically in the revolutionary anti-monarchy struggles of 1848 and American women had met to discuss suffrage at Seneca Falls. Bloomer managed to convince some women that for practical and health reasons wearing the Victorian narrow-waisted dress, long petticoats and boned corset should be abandoned. Her patterns, published in her journal *The Lily*, were in high demand, and shops began to stock 'rational' outfits. Some activists of this period, however, believed that Bloomer's engagement with the world of fashion could not be combined with serious political commitments to reform. Women's rights activist Angelina Grimké (1805–79), who shared Bloomer's commitments to abolitionism and women's rights, opted for 'plain' dressing, refusing frills and silk stockings due to her understanding of Biblical sanctions on fashion: 'My friends tell me that I render myself ridiculous,' she wrote in her diary, but she remained convinced of her 'high and holy calling'.[5] For others, the enormous public outcry over Bloomer's new look became a distraction and media frenzy. Suffragist and abolitionist Mrs Paulina Kellogg Wright Davis (1813–76) consciously dressed to 'remove the idea that all women's rights women are horrid old frights with beards and mustaches'. She had been caricatured as monstrous when she became involved in women's rights conventions in the 1850s. She noted that her audiences were expecting 'a coarse, masculine, overbearing, disagreeable person; with a dirty house, a neglected family and a hen-pecked husband'. They were surprised at her being a 'fair, delicate-looking woman, with gentle manners, and a low voice'.[6]

Figure 5.2
Lithograph of 'The Bloomer Costume', 1851

Nonetheless, Bloomer's calls for change, in the name of health and hygiene, were to have a long shelf life, particularly when the global transmission of feminist ideas brought them into dialogue with alterative dress traditions. In 1902, Japanese journalist Hani Motoko (1873–1957) contributed two articles to the *Fujin shinpō* (*Women's Herald*), a periodical published by the Japanese branch of the Women's Christian Temperance Union (WCTU). Motoko focused on hygiene in relation to women's clothing; she promoted 'reformed' clothing, which combined the Japanese kimono with elements of Western clothing to allow women more physical movement.

The WCTU was dominated by European and North American activists, who were posted overseas to promote ideas of moral purity and women's moral leadership. Alongside control of alcohol, they foregrounded women's social service, and also worked to control and prevent prostitution. This meshed well with the Meiji-era Japanese state's goals to 'modernize' Japan, with a particular focus on modern and efficient motherhood. The WCTU widely promoted comfortable alternatives to the stiff, cumbersome kimono and obi (belt). But there were limits to how far women could be included in Meiji reform. An early Meiji regulation in the year of Motoko's birth had forbidden Japanese women to cut their hair short, and there was always tension between the desire to embrace new fashions and the need for women to personify and embody Japanese traditions.

Motoko's interest in new forms of clothing was mirrored around the world, with dress-reform campaigners arguing that women no longer needed to wear long and bulky skirts, starched collars, gloves and hats. Instead, they embraced

Figure 5.3
Māori dress reformers in rational dress, c. 1906

knickerbockers, split-toed socks, and divided or ankle-length skirts. In New Zealand, women had been given the national parliamentary vote in 1893; the following year, the New Zealand Rational Dress Association was formed, demanding that women be permitted to abandon the corsets that constricted their movement and breathing. Of course, working-class women had never adopted items such as corsets to the same extent as middle- and upper-class women. Yet it was mostly richer or socially powerful women – who could afford to be seen as unrespectable – who championed new dress formats. In New Zealand, this extended to the Māori community, where elite women also embraced rational dress on occasion. While some saw these measures as straightforward health reforms, others linked them to women's wider demands for freedom to move freely in public spaces, to bicycle and to play sport. The New Zealand branch of the WCTU supported rational dress, though some of the controversial trouser-outfits adopted by the most liberated clashed with the WCTU commitment to modesty and purity.

The dress reformers were highly visible in the global imagining of the 'new woman', a potent symbol of social change and gender disorder in the late nineteenth and early twentieth centuries. 'New women' were constantly caricatured in the press as unfashionable, bloomer-wearing bicyclists. But by the 1920s, what had been a 'feminist look' had become more prominent in mainstream culture. Where earlier 'new women' had been laughed at for tweed knickerbockers and uncorseted bosoms, by the 1920s shorter skirts, simpler underwear and short hair had become much more widely adopted by women who enjoyed the new physical freedoms offered by such fashions. For interwar 'new women', self-expression was achieved not only through traditional modes of activism such as joining political associations, but also through consumption of the resources offered by popular culture that moved relatively easily across national borders – cinema, radio, dancing and magazines. Japanese 'new women' and 'modern girls' for example, combined ambitious self-cultivation through their increasing access to education with new accessories of selfhood: the cloche hat, one-piece dress and face powder associated with Western consumerism.[7] In other settings, more hybrid versions of 'modern womanhood' emerged, which used fashion to make a claim to freedoms and agency. Historian Dorothy Ko has described the adoption of Western-style high heels in 1920s Shanghai, worn with the body-hugging, high-collared *qipao* dress. Some Chinese women of the early republic designed shoes that could accommodate and make attractive recently unbound feet.[8] 'New women' were imagined as mobile, on streets and in shops, or gaining independence through paid employment.

The 'new woman' and 'modern girl' phenomena raise important questions about how far these new developments can be linked to feminisms. Certainly, not all interwar women with bobbed hair should be read as making a political statement, and some feminists were critical of the hedonism and narcissism they associated with new fashions. Nonetheless, to associate feminists with the clichés of 'bluestockings' – ill-dressed and sexually unfulfilled – is to ignore the rich experiments with dress and self-presentation that marked the empowerment of women around the world.

Dress could also have more direct political uses. Suffrage

activists deployed what historian Carol Mattingly has termed a 'rhetoric of dress' in adopting colours and styles that had political meanings. Suffrage activists sometimes also selected clothing for its protective and practical properties; padded dresses and robust hats prevented the assaults of policemen and onlookers. Hat pins and fans might form weapons of defence; low-heeled shoes made swift escapes more feasible. Arrested suffragists in Britain were quick to use their clothing to subvert prosecution. Women being held in custody exchanged clothing in order to make it impossible to tally police testimony – which relied heavily on the visual description of clothes – to the individual in the dock. Moreover, the class advantages of fashionable dress sometimes provided protection from arrest, allowing militant women to move into and out of the sites of their protests due to police unwillingness to confront conventionally dressed middle- and upper-class women. Suffrage activists sought to maintain respectability by being 'dainty and precise' in their dress, and to politicize qualities of conventional femininity.[9]

The Look of Liberation

Some of the strategies of early-twentieth-century activists were repeated many decades later. The Turkish feminist Gul Ozyegin recalled her efforts with other feminists in giving out lapel pins decorated with large purple beads in 1980s Ankara. Recalling the offensive properties of suffragist hat pins and fans, these pins were intended for use by women against men seeking to touch their bodies on public transport. Joining a strong tradition of women's self-defence activism, the lapel pin provided a meaningful, useable and visible marker of defiance for Turkish women.[10] It could also evoke recognition and community-building amongst feminists, as a colour-coded signal of membership of the women's movement.

However, many feminist activists of the later twentieth century were sceptical about the strategies and choices made by earlier feminists. One of the areas of conflict was over the dress code of feminism. Early-twentieth-century suffragists, with their strategic adoption of conventional femininity and often bourgeois or traditional dress, seemed unwilling to challenge male power to impose uncomfortable fashions and physical limitations on women. The everyday subversions of the mid-nineteenth-century dress-reform movement were closer in spirit to the women's liberation determination to discard all that was conventionally feminine.

Marie-Thérèse McGivern, a Belfast-based feminist, recalled that in the 1970s:

> We didn't wear make-up, that was kind of seen as, that was the patriarchy forcing us to wear make-up. We didn't wear high heels, so good sensible shoes, always kind of good flat shoes, no high heels in those days . . . We weren't wearing tight fitting clothes and we were wearing comfortable clothes, we weren't dressing for men any more.

McGivern was quick to stress that this did not mean looking masculine: 'we were stylish because in a sense we were women, so the earrings were, you know, got more and more ornate, you know, the hair got more and more punked up and red.'[11] The DIY ethos of punk in the 1970s suited the women's movement, and could be combined with the recovery of women's traditional crafts such as knitting and patchwork.

McGivern recalled wearing 'padded jackets made of quite bright fabrics, often patchworked . . . they were lovely jackets, but again very boxy, they weren't kind of fitted or anything.' These jackets referenced the visual aesthetic of Maoist China, in a deliberate nod to the importance of socialist traditions to the women's liberation movement. Mao had written in 1961:

> China's daughters have high aspiring minds
> They love their uniforms not silks and satins.[12]

The Chinese cotton jacket was borrowed and reworked to become, a 'feminist look' for women in Belfast, and a statement of refusing to present female bodies for male approval.

Women's liberation activists juxtaposed styles, creating subversive looks by placing work boots alongside dresses. Their clothes featured slogans; the t-shirts worn by the Dartmouth College Pyrofeminist Group in the late-1970s United States featured the slogan BTMFD – 'burn the motherfucker down'.[13] Sue Katz, a member of the Boston-based working-class lesbian group, Stick-It-In-The-Wall-Motherfucker Collective, recalls wearing leathers, and desperately desiring the transgressive potential offered by a pvc mini-skirt.[14] Many active in the women's liberation movements found new dress options a powerful means of signalling rebellion in their everyday lives, and for some this included the gender non-conformity of cross-dressing, cultivation of body hair, and breast binding. Women commented on how satisfying it was to dress to please themselves, or to please other women, rather than following conventional or male-defined fashions. In Australia, Alison Bartlett recalled: 'It was a relief not to wear bras. It was sensuous, and it was liberating in a functional way . . . And it saved money.' At a memorable 'Reclaim the Night' march in Brisbane, Australia, one marcher recalled a spontaneous, proud removal of shirts and t-shirts:

> as the collective effect grew others were moved to strip to the waist and parade proudly through the city streets and over [Victoria] bridge. Old and young, gross and scrawny; breasts were swinging and floating, sitting up and looking out, falling languorously and jostling excitedly . . . The police looked more vulnerable in their protective clothing and weaponry, as if they themselves might be in need of protection from the naked breasts unleashed in the street.

For her, this act was 'luxurious, and subversive, and kind of sexy,' leaving the police riot gear looking absurd.[15] The 'feminist look', then, was not just a new wardrobe, but extended to thinking about women's uses of body posture, and placing oneself in physical or public space.

At the Greenham Common Peace Camp in the 1980s, British women developed a characteristic style 'that was colorful, practical, and creative – close-cropped hair tied with colorful ribbons, layered loose clothing that included colorful scarves, boots, and slickers . . .' On occasion, this feminist aesthetic was abandoned in order to bypass security measures. Wearing conventional dresses and skirts, two Greenham women gained access to the base, and enjoyed watching television in a recreation room for military families. Without their ribbons and long jumpers, they were not identified as activists until they left the camp by the front gate.[16]

Women nearer the seats of power were similarly strategic

about what they wore. The British local government politician Valerie Wise, who channelled millions of pounds of public funding to women's groups in the 1980s, rejected dungarees in favour of a conventional skirt suit. At a time when women's liberationists were defying fashion conventions, discarding bras and refusing to shave their body hair, Wise found it 'a huge plunge' just to cut her hair short. But she was clear that conventional clothing gave her more impact as a politician: 'I wanted people to listen to what I said rather than spend ages about what I was wearing, because, you know, I didn't want the distraction of my clothes. I wasn't like a pin-up model.'[17] Sara Dowse, head of the Office of Women's Affairs in the Australian civil service in the 1970s, similarly described wearing 'nothing too flash, but nothing too trendy either'. On appointment her 'look' had moved from jeans to a long denim skirt. But she noticed in the 1980s that codes had changed for 'femocrats', who now wore power suits and shoulder pads: 'the jacket was often red, red in many cultures being associated with power as well as sexuality. And equally significant . . . in its intricate, conflicted blend of power and sexuality, was the reappearance of heels.'[18]

The cultivation of a 'feminist look' was a visible, accessible way of creating a new community. For feminists in Belfast, fashion provided a sense of belonging by adopting a recognizable look: McGivern noted the key role played by dungarees, though she emphasized the problems of supply in 1970s Belfast. She visited New York in the late 1970s and ordered identical dungarees for the women she lived with in a collective, creating a uniformity of dress that went with her collective's ethos of self-sufficiency and sharing all resources.

Policing Dress

The politics of the 'women's liberation look' was not only about pleasing oneself but also, in some cases, about judging other women. Determined to protest sexual objectification, women's liberation movement activists targeted beauty contests across the world – the very sites that Filipina women had used to find entry points into politics. Famously, women interrupted and protested at high-profile competitions, such as the Miss America contest. In 1968, the feminist group New York Radical Women organized a picket of the pageant and performed theatrical stunts – parading sheep, for example, in protest at models being 'judged like animals at a county fair'. They refused to talk to male reporters, forcing newspapers to call in women reporters from their usual ghettos of the women's pages to cover the protest. Famously, protestors set up a 'Freedom Trash Can' full of bras, false eyelashes and copies of magazines such as *Playboy* and the *Ladies Home Journal*; though contrary to popular myth, they did not burn these items.[19] This action spread to Britain, where activists threw flour bombs and disrupted proceedings with football rattles at the 1970 Miss World contest;[20] to New Zealand, where activists cut the power to the 1971 Miss New Zealand contest; and to Peru, where ALIMUPER (Action for the Liberation of Peruvian Women) demonstrated against the 1973 Miss Peru contest in Lima. At the local level, women also took action at countless minor contests. In Scotland, Sandie Wyles, studying for a degree at Aberdeen University, applied for a beauty contest held within the university, along with others from her women's group, as their first political action in 1975:

> So we filled out the form, and I don't think they really knew what had hit them, because we all arrived in this big group, and at that time there was quite a few of them wearing dungarees, even in those days, and no make-up . . . These stewards were saying, 'Oh no, no, you can't come in, you can't come in, you've got to come in one at a time.' And we say, 'No, we're all coming in together.'[21]

Despite the strong opposition of non-feminist women at the contest, described by Wyles as 'really abusive', her women's group made their protest, were written up in a local newspaper, and went on to be active in abortion rights and 'Reclaim the Night' protests in Aberdeen. However, these iconic protests could also be seen as directed against the female models and damaging to ideas of sisterhood. Many models were working-class, and saw success in beauty contests as a source of both self-respect and access to prize money or social status. There were long-standing traditions of beauty pageants within Britain's black community, sponsored by West Indian activist Claudia Jones in London's early Notting Hill carnivals. Women's liberation protests tended to run roughshod over these dynamics of race and class. Their protests also gave credence to the idea of feminists as being against (heterosexual) eroticism and pleasure, and seeking to police other women's bodies by their own standards of acceptable behaviour. The reputation for judgementalism and rigid moralism that resulted became an obstacle to reaching wider audiences. And the compulsory dungarees or Mao-style jackets could be a confining dress code that made it harder to imagine forms of sisterhood and solidarity between women who dressed differently.

Subversive Self-Fashioning and Tensions of Class

The classed nature of clothing had been a long-standing source of tension and power-play within the women's movement. Strategies of hyper-conventionality amongst Edwardian suffrage activists proved problematic for those whose material resources did not allow for elaborate hats and dresses. The relative exclusion of working-class women from protests where fashionable clothing was required meant that many of the most visible actions of the Women's Social and Political Union were dominated by middle- and upper-class women. Nonetheless, working-class women found opportunities to join parades, sometimes dressed in recognizable clothing of their trade, such as the 'mill girl' outfit of shawl and clogs adopted on occasion by suffrage leader Annie Kenney, or the parades featuring midwives and nurses in uniform. But working-class garb was sometimes adopted as disguise or for pleasure. The well-educated and well-connected suffragist Barbara Ayrton Gould (1886–1950) adopted the dress of a 'fisher girl' in order to represent the heroic, life-saving lighthouse-keeper's daughter Grace Darling at the Women's Exhibition in 1909. There is often a sense that middle- and upper-class women enjoyed dressing up as working-class. With more serious intent, however, the aristocrat Lady Constance Lytton (1869–1923) impersonated an imaginary working-class woman, 'Jane Warton'. Lytton was frustrated at being let out of prison after her arrests in 1909, and suspected that her social rank was to blame, though the prison authorities claimed it was due to her heart condition.

Figure 5.4
Suffragist Constance Lytton disguised as 'Jane Warton', a working-class seamstress, *c.* 1914

When she was arrested as the dowdy Jane Warton in 1910 she was wearing

> A tweed hat, a long green cloth coat, which I purchased for 8*s*. 6*d*., a woollen scarf and woollen gloves, a white silk neck-kerchief, a pair of pince-nez spectacles, a purse, a net-bag to contain some of my papers.[22]

In this outfit, she was given a sentence of hard labour and, without medical inspection, was force-fed eight times. The heart condition was genuine, and Lytton suffered a heart attack from which she never fully recovered. The power of clothes to shore up class inequities in Edwardian Britain was clearly demonstrated and understood by suffragists. But the women's suffrage movement remained in many ways unwilling to challenge the conventionalities of dress. Later generations were much more iconoclastic, though issues of class continued to pervade the question of what feminists should wear.

In the late twentieth century, as women's liberation and lesbian groups developed characteristic looks, social class gave clothes cultures very different meanings to different women. Australian feminist Lekkie Hopkins recalled wearing blue and khaki overalls, which for her had strong connotations of physical autonomy: 'We had commandeered the working man's garb, indicating that our bodies were our own, to be used for our own pleasures, not for sale nor for plunder.'[23] But this may not have been so different from the earlier insensitive dressing up by privileged suffragists. The different class backgrounds of women made the class politics of the 'feminist look' painful for some. One activist in the North American feminist bookstore movement, Nett Hart, noted, 'Not all have the economic options to say "no" when faced with coercive gendered dress codes.' Hart argued that feminist efforts to look different in 'denims and flannels' could mean simply that 'middle- and upper-class women dressed the way that working and poor women have always dressed.'[24] For Sue Katz, the experiments with collective ownership of clothing in her Boston collective proved problematic. Coming from an impoverished background, Katz noted that working-class and black women might have a very different relationship to clothes that made collective ownership difficult:

> Many working-class white and black kids had been strictly brought up to be clean and neat and ironed – in lieu of being expensive and trendy and cosseted. Some of us had precious pieces of clothing we had saved for or splurged to buy and didn't really want to share . . .
>
> I never wanted to share clothes. As a child growing up, virtually all my clothes were hand-me-downs . . . People who had nice new stuff all their childhoods surely didn't have the same relationship to clothes. They were cavalier about stuff knowing mommy and daddy would buy them more. The piles in the middle of the room seemed like a fun grab-bag to them.[25]

Frances Beal's pamphlet *Double Jeopardy* (1969) also noted these tensions. She was aware that there was a long history of feminist opposition to the fashionable woman, whom she memorably described as 'spending idle hours primping and preening, obsessed with conspicuous consumption, and limiting life's functions to simply a sex role'. But Beal found no resonance with this ideal within the lives of black women:

> It is idle dreaming to think of black women simply caring for their homes and children like the middle-class white model. Most black women have to work to help house, feed and clothe their families. Black women make up a substantial percentage of the black working force and this is true for the poorest black family as well as the so-called 'middle-class' family. Black women were never afforded any such phony luxuries.

Beal's insights were resonant with earlier racial exclusions. The former slave and abolitionist Sojourner Truth complained that participants at an 1870 suffrage convention were so fashionably dressed that they could not be taken seriously. 'What kind of reformers be you, with goose wings on your heads, as if you were going to fly, and dressed in such ridiculous fashion, talking about reform and women's rights?'[26] But white suffragists were not willing to be criticized by a former slave for their appearance. Truth, who often adopted plain Quaker dress, was personally attacked for her own appearance in the suffrage *Woman's Journal*.

Feminists, in sum, were divided over whether fashion was damaging and patriarchal or an expressive realm of pleasure, and these debates stretch back over many decades. Dress was a cultural site that many working-class and black women did not choose to politicize. As Nett Hart concluded,

> women [should be allowed] the self-definition and self-determination of our own bodies. But we must be aware that the first to use that privilege will be those that are most familiar with privilege.[27]

Men in Skirts

While women's clothing has been subject to enormous scrutiny, commercial pressure and political debate, men's dress codes have also been subject to a feminist gaze. When Elizabeth Cady Stanton addressed the pioneering Seneca Falls congress on women's rights in 1848, she knew that the stereotype of women in trousers would be used to mock and diminish her words. She had supported the campaign for uncorseted, comfortable women's clothing, but did not want to adopt masculine styles: 'As to their costume the gentlemen need feel no fear of our imitating that for we regard it in violation of every principle of beauty, taste and dignity.' She defended the 'loose flowing garments' of rational dress, and could not resist a further satirical comment aimed at men in authority:

> all the Bishops, Priests, Judges, Barristers, and Lord Mayors of the first nation of the globe and the Pope of Rome too, when officiating in their highest offices, they all wear the loose flowing robes, thus tacitly acknowledging that the ordinary male attire is neither dignified nor imposing.[28]

The same accusation was made by Virginia Woolf, who was so amused at the pompous nature of the British male establishment that she published photographs of judges and clerics in wigs, robes and furs in her 1938 polemic *Three Guineas*.

> Your clothes in the first place make us gape with astonishment. How many, how splendid, how extremely ornate they are – the clothes worn by the educated man

> in his public capacity! Now you dress in violet: a jewelled crucifix swings on your breast; now your shoulders are covered with lace; now furred with ermine . . .[29]

Woolf linked the elaborations of masculine dress to the pursuit of war, with military uniform as the ultimate example of how men's dress was a dangerous tool of social status, violence and hierarchy. Using the racist optic of civilization and savagery that so pervaded her era, Woolf argued:

> To express worth of any kind, whether intellectual or moral, by wearing pieces of metal, or ribbon, coloured hoods or gowns, is a barbarity which deserves the ridicule we bestow upon the rites of savages.[30]

Not all men, however, sought to maintain the conventional dress codes of masculinity. Some attempted to diversify what men could wear, or subvert the norms, with the poet and radical Edward Carpenter (1844–1929) terming men's shoes 'leather coffins'. Instead, Carpenter, who identified as a 'third sex' individual, adopted sandals that he made himself, modelled on a pair he had been sent from India.

Carpenter produced sandals for his radical friends, but was widely regarded in the early twentieth century as a crank for his dress unorthodoxy. The project of subverting male dress only took on more mainstream prominence during the later twentieth century, as movements including hippies, beatniks, punk, glam rock and women's liberation challenged conventional fashion codes. For some men, this started with the small rebellion of wearing feminist and anti-sexist badges, with slogans such as 'just another man' or 'celibacy is subversive'.

Others went for a fuller transformation: Welsh anti-sexist activist Pete Six attended men's groups in the 1980s wearing a black cape, red clogs and what he termed 'paint-on trousers'. Influenced by punk, he knitted his own pink and red jumpers, shaved the sides of his head and sported a tight, plaited ponytail in an effort to develop an alternative anti-sexist men's fashion culture.[31] Commentators were not always impressed; a *Guardian* journalist sarcastically noted:

> New man stepped out of a traditional stereotype and immediately found himself another. With his pleated trousers, voluminous shirts, Chinese slippers and self-effacing manner, he labours under a most crippling burden; no one really takes him seriously.[32]

Nonetheless, the *Guardian* had co-sponsored a photo competition, 'The New Man of 1985', with the company Aramis Menswear. They awarded a prize to John Colvin for his designs of men's dresses, which John had worn as a member of Bristol anti-sexist men's groups in the 1980s.[33]

Just as hierarchies of class and race had complicated feminist efforts to reform fashion, so race and ethnicity proved a minefield for anti-sexist men. Colvin, a dancer, had been inspired by the sense of physical wholeness which he perceived amongst African Caribbean and African men. In a later interview he reflected:

> I think many of us would accept the stereotype that if we are men of a West Indian or black African cultural background we have a greater awareness of our body movements and a greater fluidity than most men of

> Western cultural origin, but I have yet to see this sense of body movement exposed or exploited in the fashion industry.

John's careless 'we' and evocation of non-white men as closer to their bodies was an unfortunate choice of inspiration and highlighted the lack of engagement within the British anti-sexist men's movement with black and Asian men.

In practice, it did not prove easy to reform men's dress. John Colvin was surprised at the level of sexual harassment he received from men, recalling having men put their hands up his skirt. For a man in a skirt, he reflected:

> the reality of dressing in the streets is, it's risky. It's a political act every time. You have to feel confident, you have to have your wits about you, you get harassed, you get abused, mainly, I never got abused by a woman, but I got abuse from men.[34]

Experiments by some anti-sexist men with androgyny or cross-dressing were motivated by their alliance and affiliation with the women's movement. Others wore skirts, dresses and bras because they wanted to express queer or gay sexuality. Still others had feelings of being the wrong gender. The attempts by all these different groups to subvert male dress powerfully demonstrate how hard it has been for both sexes to self-present in ways that contradict gender norms. Men who wore women's clothes or 'alternative' fashions often found this to be unsafe. They rarely acknowledged, however, that women and non-binary people suffered similar forms of harassment on a daily basis, compounded by legal institutions that refused to prosecute for rape or assault if women dressed 'provocatively' in short skirts.

Hijabistas

Women's clothes have often deliberately provided a refuge from street and workplace abuse through devices of veiling and cloaking the body. These strategies of self-protection have had feminist potential despite often being read as a form of oppression. When the French-Peruvian writer Flora Tristan travelled to Peru in 1833–4, she encountered women in Lima who wore the *saya* and *manto* – garments that veiled their upper bodies and heads. The *manto*, a black cloak, covered the upper body, while the *saya* covered women's heads, mouths and one eye, an arrangement that Tristan described as 'being at once economical, very neat, convenient, and always ready without ever needing the least care'.

Tristan was emphatic that this dress gave women the power and freedom of disguise:

> The woman of Lima, whatever her position in life, is always *herself*; never is she subject to constraint. As a young girl, she escapes from the domination of her parents through the freedom given by her costume. When she marries, she does not take her husband's name but keeps her own, and always remains her own mistress.

Peruvian women, Tristan reported, were free to move around the streets of Lima, talk and flirt with men:

> These ladies go alone to the theatre, to bull fights, to public meetings, balls, promenades, churches, go visiting, and are

Figure 5.5
Woman wearing *saya* and *manto*, Lima, c. 1860–80

> much seen everywhere. If they meet people with whom they want to chat, they speak to them, leave them, and remain free and independent in the midst of the crowd, much more so than the men, whose faces are uncovered.

For all her enthusiasm, Tristan maintained familiar ideas of the hierarchy of civilization that gave Europe precedence over the rest of the world. She believed that Peruvian women were 'inferior in moral concerns [compared] to European women': 'The stage of civilization that these people have attained is still far removed from ours in Europe. In Peru there is no institution for the education of either sex . . .' Tristan posed women's freedom in Lima as a kind of moral infancy. She may also have been naïve to think that freedom could be attained through a simple veil. Peru's legal system did not recognize women as citizens, and society was dominated by socially conservative institutions and large landowners. This was not an environment where women were already liberated, as Peruvian feminist demands of the early twentieth century revealed. The Peruvian feminist activist María Jesus Alvarado Rivera (1878–1971), for example, was jailed in 1924 for her agitation for women's rights and was subsequently forced into exile. Nonetheless, Tristan's observations are of interest because of the deep controversies that have long been associated with practices of veiling – frequently understood as a tool of patriarchy. These debates have been particularly prominent in relation to Islamic practices. Indeed, Tristan was alert to the similarity between Peruvian customs and the veil worn in many Muslim countries. She concluded that in Peru: 'all the women wear it, no matter what their rank; it is respected and is a part of the country's customs, like the veil of Moslem women in the Orient.'[35]

Tristan's comments echoed those of an earlier traveller, the English aristocratic letter writer Lady Mary Wortley Montagu (1689–1762). As the wife of the British Ambassador to Turkey, Lady Mary observed the lives of women of the Ottoman Empire. She sought to counter the myths that circulated amongst Europeans concerning the low status of Muslim women, such as the idea that, for Muslims, women did not have souls. She was also a proponent of veiling, both through observations of Muslim women and her own practice. In similar terms to Tristan, Lady Mary regarded the veil as a welcome source of anonymity for women.[36] Later campaigns also welcomed the freedoms of Middle Eastern fashions. When Amelia Bloomer celebrated her designs for trousers, she argued that they were 'Moslem' in inspiration. A San Francisco newspaper described an American follower of Bloomer in 1851 as 'magnificently arrayed in a black satin skirt, very short, with flowing red satin trousers, a splendid yellow crape shawl and a silk turban, *a la Turque*'.[37]

Despite these sympathetic accounts of Islamic dress, the lives of Muslim women have often been characterized by non-Muslim observers as lives of oppression. Across the nineteenth and twentieth centuries, many Western commentators had seen the harem and the headscarf as symbolic of the need for secular feminist 'rescue'. Muslim women themselves were also sometimes critical of dress codes, though others found Islamic dress to be a source of empowerment. The controversial politics of veiling in Egypt and other Muslim countries sheds light on why head covering has caused dilemmas for many decades.

Veiling, Nationalism and the Colonial Gaze

The debates over the 'woman question' at the Rasheed Women's Conference in 1799 suggest a long history of interrogating gender in Egypt. This was a process often dominated by wealthy and upper-class women. Egypt witnessed flourishing women's literary and cultural salons in the nineteenth and early twentieth centuries, such as those hosted by Princess Nazli Fazil (1853–1913) and the Lebanese Mayy Ziyadah (1886–1941). Their salons offered space for direct intellectual exchanges between women and men about social, political, cultural and gender issues, which were tentatively extended to wider circles. In Cairo in 1914, the Women's Educational Association was formed, offering public lectures for women about women's issues. This was a response to women being prevented from attending the Egyptian University, established in 1908. Moreover, women were entering the public sphere through their involvement in charity organizations, established and run by upper-middle-class women and funded by women of the Egyptian aristocracy. These offered medical services, shelters and orphanages to poor women and children. Although these activities were largely philanthropic rather than directly feminist, they played an important role in expanding women's involvement in public life. They allowed some women a degree of mobility across the gender-restricted lines separating the ostensibly private sphere of the domestic from realms of civic and commercial activity. Although most of the roles taken up by women seemed related to the domestic sphere of nurturing and caring for others, they also involved breaking out of the confines of the home and engaging with social problems. Elite Egyptian women's active work in social and political issues was reflected in their efforts to include women's rights in the 1923 constitution, after the 1919 revolution had led to Egypt declaring itself an independent state. There was, however, no constitutional guarantee of gender equality until the overthrow of the monarchy in 1952.

The Egyptian activist Huda Sha'arawi (1879–1947) was born into an upper-class family that practised the seclusion and veiling of women; she was married to a cousin at the age of thirteen. Nonetheless, Sha'arawi did not live a life of confinement. She accessed formal education in her own right, wrote and published in French and Arabic, organized girls' education, and regularly lived apart from her husband. Her political activism was rooted in nationalism, and she took a leading role in organizing women in the 1919 anti-British protests that led to semi-independence as the Kingdom of Egypt. In 1922, Sha'arawi's husband died, and she began to reject the seclusion of the *hijab*. Notoriously, with fellow traveller Saiza Nabarawi, she deliberately unveiled her face at Cairo's train station when returning from the meeting of the International Woman Suffrage Alliance (IWSA) in Rome in 1923.

This unveiling was celebrated by Sha'arawi's European contemporaries as an important step forward for Egyptian women, even though most rural and working-class Egyptian women did not wear any kind of veil in the early twentieth century. For Sha'arawi herself, unveiling was a minor issue, and an article published shortly afterwards in the

International Woman Suffrage News did not even mention it. Instead, she foregrounded the organization she had founded in 1923, the Egyptian Feminist Union.[38] Sha'arawi brought out the feminist magazines *L'Egyptienne* and *el-Masreyyah* and concentrated her campaigning on reform of family law and women's access to education. She worked closely with international women's organizations such as the IWSA, a powerful network founded in Berlin in 1904 to push for women's suffrage globally. By 1929, the IWSA had affiliated representatives from fifty-one nations. Its regular congresses debated issues of economic, educational, moral and political rights for women, and tried to show how enfranchisement could be linked to wider emancipation for women. Its monthly journal, *Jus Suffragii* (*The Right to Vote*), documented the women's movement across the world, in English and French versions. Through this international network as well as her domestic actions, Huda Sha'arawi became a very high-profile representative of Egyptian feminists. Her prolonged efforts to gain women freedom and rights were documented in her memoir, *Mudhakkirātī* (*My Memoir*). In contrast, when translated into English, the book was given the orientalizing title *Harem Years: The Memoirs of an Egyptian Feminist*. It was still hard for Anglophone audiences to imagine women in Muslim countries without recourse to images of seclusion and veiling, despite Sha'arawi's extensive and public feminist activism. Mocking the Western obsession with the veil, Sha'arawi herself described 'the veil of ignorance' which obscured Western women's views on Egyptian women.

Veiling may not have been Sha'arawi's main target, but it remained an important concern for many Muslim women.

Nazira Zain al-Din (1908–76) was a born into an intellectual Lebanese family and educated in both Muslim and Catholic settings. She spoke out against the veiling practices called for by some Islamic authorities in the 1920s, while she was still in her teens. Her 1928 book, *Veiling and Unveiling*, challenged Syrian clerics who were arguing for what Zain al-Din termed 'the black all-enveloping cloth and the face veil'. She linked dress restrictions to other physical constraints Muslim women faced, arguing that Islamic clerics 'wanted the veils to be the walls of the boudoirs, to be left only for the grave'. In her interpretation, Islamic scripture was perfectly compatible with women's freedoms. It was premised on ideas of natural freedom of will and thought, possessed by both men and women; she found no mention of facial covering in the Qur'an. Zain al-Din argued for the enhanced role for mothers in Islam, and highlighted the Qur'an's defence of women's property rights, rights to divorce, and forbidding of female infanticide. Like many other feminist polemics of her time and earlier, *Veiling and Unveiling* positioned women as innately possessed of reason, and blamed women's failings on their lack of access to education. And like many nationalists of her period, Zain al-Din regarded nations that confined women as necessarily weakened in the struggle to compete with other nations and secure independence.

In the colonial settings that nurtured the activism of women such as Zain al-Din and Sha'arawi, it was hard to find a way of advocating women's freedoms without posing the problem in colonial terms, as a question of the 'primitive backwardness' of the colonized. Feminism seemed to be invested in modernizing the nation on Western terms. Zain al-Din's opponents accused her of having allowed missionaries to dictate the contents of her book. Though she published a refutation of such criticism in 1929, titled *The Girl and the Shaikhs*, she did not publish further.

The veil remains a complex symbol. For some women, it was a cultural and spiritual practice that was compatible with women's public organizing – indeed, it was embraced as a practice that enabled such organizing. Egyptians such as the well-educated Zainab al-Ghazali (1917–2005) organized Egyptian women under the banner of radical Islam and social justice. Al-Ghazali had been a member of Sha'arawi's Egyptian Feminist Union. Motivated by her sense of the strong family rights granted to women by Islam, she created the Muslim Women's Society in the 1930s, later transformed into the Muslim Sisters.[39] Her organizations campaigned for recognition of the spiritual equality of the sexes within Islam, though she was also committed to precepts on women's obedience to men. This did not prevent her from lecturing to mass audiences and publishing widely. Al-Ghazali was to spend long periods in jail as a result of her activism, which unsettled the secular-nationalist Egyptian authorities both for its Islamic content and its feminism.

Under Gamal Abdel Nasser's constitution of 1956, Egyptian women were enfranchised and guaranteed equality. Their status became part of Nasser's Pan-Arabist secular modernization project in a shift to 'state feminism' underpinned by ideas of 'national uplift'. The veil was discouraged in this version of nationalist modernity, and women's participation in waged labour was prioritized as a key route to nation-building.[40] Nonetheless, there was no consensus in Egyptian society as to what role faith would play in women's lives, and by the 1970s a resurgent Islamic movement began to promote what was termed an 'authentic' rather than 'Westernized' Islam. Larger numbers of Egyptian women embraced the *hijab* in the 1970s and 80s, particularly younger women on university campuses. Similar trends were witnessed in Indonesia, where versions of the fitted headscarf, the *jilbab* were adopted by women, spurred by the rise of Islamic student activism that contested the secularist, militarized 'New Order' regime of President Suharto that ruled Indonesia from 1966 to 1998.[41] A proliferation of 'modest' Islamic fashion, termed *busana Muslimah*, replaced prior commitments to austere piety. Local styles developed in dialogue with the latest look in Cairo or Jeddah. Wearing the flowing trousers, tunics and changing forms of head-covering that make up *busana Muslimah* could express both nationalist and religious sentiments through the cultivation of pious fashion.[42]

In Iran, there was a similar backlash against the forbidding of women's head-coverings in 1936 by the brutal Western-backed dictator Reza Shah Pahlavi. Wearing a headscarf could be a means for Iranian women to indicate their support for the revolution of 1979 and to demand the right to choose their 'look' in a new articulation of 'Islamic modernity'. It quickly became apparent, however, that the Islamic revolutionary authorities in Iran were opposed to women's presence in public life and used the imposition of the veil to violently impose gender segregation and remove women from public life. In Pakistan, similar coercive Islamicization measures under the military regime of General Zia saw deep challenges to the legal rights of women to work and inhabit public space after

1977. In 1987, a group of women within the Pakistani Women's Action Forum had become incensed by the state's distribution of *chadors* (scarves) and *dupattas* (shawls). They had been active since 1981 in campaigns to uphold women's rights under family law, particularly to contest the arrests and detentions under charges of *zina* (adultery), widely exploited by relatives to control women's behaviour. One of their members, Lala Rukh, recalled how fond she was of wearing the 'beautiful' *chador*, but she refused to be forced to wear it. The group set their head-coverings on fire as a protest against a regime that brutally enforced a hostile legal and cultural environment for Pakistani women.[43] 1987 also saw the assassination in Pakistan of the founder of the Revolutionary Association of the Women of Afghanistan, Meena Keshwar Kamal (1956–87). RAWA members had been working since 1977 on women's literacy and employment projects in Kabul, and campaigning against domestic violence. RAWA had found the whole-body covering of the *burqa* a useful means of smuggling cameras and their mimeographed journal *Payam-e-Zan* (*Women's Message*) in the dangerous, unstable Afghan environment. Their anti-fundamentalist, pro-democracy feminist politics set them against both Soviet occupiers and jihadi resisters, at a deadly cost. Meena's exile in Pakistan had done little to protect her from what was probably state-sponsored assassination.[44]

While some Islamists were actively opposed to feminism, labelling it a mark of the corruption of 'the West', others echoed al-Ghazali in basing their feminism on the Qur'an, as well as within their everyday experiences of empowerment through Islamic institutions.[45] Like all major world religions,

Figure 5.6
Afghan feminist Meena Keshwar Kamal speaking in 1982

Islam sustains a range of interpretations in different locations and historical moments. In Iran's Islamic Republic, despite the rhetoric and legal reforms aiming to confine and veil women after the 1979 revolution, there has been an increasing presence of women in public and cultural life. Ziba Mir-Hosseini has argued that wearing a veil has allowed Iranian women to enter a wider variety of areas in public life. She points to the gradual dismantling of bans, undertaken in the early days of the revolution, on women serving as judges and studying subjects such as engineering. Instead, there has been a reinterpretation of sharia law in the 1990s to encompass feminist principles of women's autonomy, protection from violence and access to the public sphere.[46] From the 1980s, designers and manufacturers began to offer fashionable versions of women's Islamic dress, embraced by some women as an attractive 'look' and marking the rise of Islam as a more powerful political and cultural force.

'Liberating women' has continued to be a widely stated motive for Islamophobic actions, such as the banning of veils and the harassment of veiled women in public places over the past decade in France, Holland, Belgium, Austria, Denmark and New Zealand. The symbolic and actual violence of these bans was demonstrated on French beaches in 2015, when armed police were called to enforce the municipal ban on the 'burkini', a body-covering swimsuit adopted by some Muslim women. Heavy-handed police interventions that led to Muslim women on beaches being forced to remove their modest clothes did not sit comfortably with claims of feminist motivation for the ban. The controversial upholding of the ban on face coverings in France despite the mandatory wearing of facemasks during the Covid-19 crisis has also illustrated the punitive discrimination faced by Muslim women.

The veil continues to be a rallying point for those determined to align Islamophobia with feminism, drawing power from what bell hooks identified as 'the imperial gaze – the look that seeks to dominate, subjugate, and colonize'.[47] Despite long-standing claims that religion is necessarily patriarchal, feminism has never been a uniquely secular movement when viewed in global perspective, and religious motivations have a long history of sparking feminist activism.

Islamic feminism has a long heritage, with strong support for women's rights and education developing amongst Muslims in the Middle East, South and South-East Asia in the late nineteenth century. To understand Muslim women in headscarves or veils as necessarily impelled by male subjection, as so many critics have done, ignores their own sense of choice and complex reasons for covering their heads. It ascribes a monolithic patriarchal stance to Islam in ways that past commentators would not have recognized. Indeed, for many campaigners of the nineteenth and twentieth centuries, it was not Islam but other religious traditions that mistreated women, with particularly strong feelings against the practices of Hindus, Sikhs and Roman Catholics. At other moments, it has not been religions but nations that have been generalized as anti-feminist. In 1917, as the United States entered the First World War against Germany, the *New York Times* published a headline claiming 'Germany Hates Feminism'. The editors presented the United States, in contrast, as 'the land of feminism, the land of privileged womanhood'.[48] There has been enormous historical variability in which religions or nations might be depicted as feminist or anti-feminist, and no such claims can be taken at face value. But the growing momentum behind the Western portrayal since the late 1970s of Islam as, in its essence, fundamentalist and anti-feminist makes it important to foreground the historical presence of Islamic feminism, and the variable ways in which headscarves and veils have been claimed and rejected by Muslim women.

Across the globe, women have had to tread carefully in choosing and challenging how they look. Suffrage activists trod a fine line between enjoying the 'freedom suits' advocated by American dress reformers from the 1840s and staying within conventional boundaries of self-presentation in order to amplify their voices. The suffrage orator Susan B. Anthony noted that when she wore shortened skirts, 'The attention of my audience was fixed upon my clothes instead of my words.'[49] She opted to wear long skirts, despite their dragging constraint on her movements. Dress reform remained popular amongst radical women, but for those nearer to conventional seats of power, it proved distracting and risky.

The experiences of Hillary Clinton in the presidential contest of 2016 remind us that women's dress continues to gain unwelcome attention in the twenty-first century. Clinton appropriated 'pant suits', arguing that 'they make me feel professional and ready to go.' She was also keen to adopt a 'uniform' look that would discourage reporters from being distracted from the content of her speeches and rule out the darker practice of 'up-skirting'. Nonetheless, the coverage Clinton received was relentlessly critical of her clothing choices, whether for looking too male or spending too freely on herself.

Despite the hostile environment faced by women in public life, it has still proved possible for women to make their voices heard, sometimes in highly unlikely surroundings. Women's liberation activists had largely written off beauty contestants as victims of patriarchy, portraying them as sheep or cows. But in November 2017, models competing for the Miss Peru contest approached the microphone in glittering gold dresses. One by one, they announced their names and regions, and their 'statistics'. Replacing the usual bust and waist size, each one announced a headline figure – the number of femicides, assaults on children, and rates of domestic violence in their regions and cities. The protest was inspired by the wider hashtag-led protest #NiUnaMenos (Not One Less), which has highlighted the epidemic of domestic violence and killings suffered by Latin American women and has led to huge protest marches. The juxtaposition of young women's bodies seemingly tailored to the male gaze in the beauty contest setting and the gruesome lists of assaults was controversial. For some activists, it was an unacceptable coupling of feminism with the commercialized and corporate world of beauty contests. But it is the very juxtaposition, and the voices of the often mute or disregarded models, that give this action force. It provides a striking reminder that feminism can adopt many different platforms and voices, and a 'feminist look' can span the beauty contest tiara, the headscarf and the 'freedom suit'.

CHAPTER 6

Feelings

Emotions have long been part of the warp and weft of attempts to rethink the gender order and convey the urgency of feminisms. When I first encountered a book published by the feminist publishing house Virago, with its recognizable green spine, I was probably around fifteen. It was Miles (Stella) Franklin's *My Brilliant Career*, an account of an Australian rebel who defied conventions and drudgery to insist on her right to write. Published in 1901, under a male pseudonym, the author herself was only sixteen. Her refusal of the path of heterosexual romance spoke powerfully to my own emotions across the thousands of miles and many decades that separated us. A couple of years later, I was equally gripped by Simone de Beauvoir's *The Mandarins*, written in the 1950s, which charted her tense, awkward love affair spanning Chicago and Paris. Found by chance in a library in Southern Africa, the book transported me emotionally into a world of intensely serious scrutiny of relations between the sexes. These were the texts that helped me, as a teenager, forge an emotional connection to feminism, even if, when one of my teachers asked me if I was a 'bra burner', I had no idea what he meant.

Looking back historically, it is characteristic of feminist

demands that they have not only provoked strong feelings but have also included a politics of emotion. Josefa Amar's 1786 *Discurso*, written to claim women as rational, had also boldly claimed that women had a right to happiness. Amar may have been influenced by the claiming of happiness as a human right in the American Declaration of Independence. Emotions were central to late-eighteenth-century politics, and a wide spectrum of feelings could be openly expressed in public life by both sexes. Though the following century saw a closing down of publicly acceptable emotions, feelings remained politically important. The absence of happiness had become a characteristic sign of nineteenth-century women's oppression. Henrik Ibsen's heroine Nora claimed she had been only merry, not happy, when dwelling in the houses of her father and husband. Her willingness to walk away from her infantilizing 'merry' marriage, depicted in the Norwegian author's 1879 play, *A Doll's House*, proved one of the most enduring images of women's freedom for late-nineteenth-century thinkers, and continued to resonate into the twentieth. Ibsen's play was the first text translated into Japanese by the editors of *Seitō (Bluestocking)* magazine in 1911. It had been published in Spanish in 1892, was later translated into Chinese in 1918, Bengali and Gujarati in 1923, and Hindi in 1938. *A Doll's House* and Nora's rebellion became a persistent global totem, used around the world to formulate female emancipation as a claim for happiness and self-fulfilment.

Later versions of feminism also maintained emotions as their political terrain. Chude Pamela Allen, of the San Francisco-based group Sudsofloppen wrote in 1968:

> Our society alienates us from our feelings . . . It is imperative for our understanding of ourselves and for our mental health that we maintain and deepen contact with our feelings. Our first concern must not be whether these feelings are good or bad, but what they are. Feelings are a reality. To deny their existence does not get rid of them. Rather, it is through admitting them that one can begin to deal with her feelings.[1]

Sudsofloppen – a nonsense name chosen to make it hard to pigeon-hole participants – recommended that liberation was best undertaken in small meetings. In these settings, women could reveal their experiences and share 'descriptions of the forms oppression has taken in each individual's life'. This 'consciousness-raising' or '*autocoscienza*' model has long been associated with Italian and American women's liberation, but there was also an alternative source of inspiration in the Maoist practice of 'speaking bitterness'. Linked to Mao's well-known saying, 'Women hold up half the sky' (*fùnǚ néng dǐng bànbiāntiān*), this model prioritized voicing one's oppression, to be followed by collective action. Maoists sometimes termed the process 'speak pains to recall pains.'

The idea of women in Communist China and Vietnam as liberated and empowered through such methods became inspirational to feminists in the 1960s and 70s in Australia, Cuba, France and West Germany. The visits made by activist women to China produced important texts such as Claudie Broyelle's *Half the Sky* (*La Moitié du Ciel*), published in France in 1973. This bestseller was quickly translated into German,

Spanish and English, and was influential across Europe, and Central and Latin America. Broyelle stressed Communist women's autonomy to voice and to act on their emotions, and heralded these techniques as a global feminist practice.[2] The American activist Carol Hanisch was deeply influenced by this, relating it to the Black Power concept of 'telling it like it is'. She pithily summed this up in 1970 by coining the feminist slogan 'the personal is political'.[3]

Such methods were never meant to focus on individual emotions at the expense of a wider critique; instead, emotions were a key to clarifying the structural nature of women's oppression, and the urgency of their liberation. For Sudsofloppen, through consciousness-raising,

> we understand *in our gut* something we used to give only lip service to: that there is no personal solution to being a woman in this society. We have realized that if we do not work to change the society it will in the end destroy us.[4]

This chapter explores the gut feelings that underlay feminist engagement and the political demands for new 'ways of feeling'. There has been new attentiveness amongst historians of feminisms to the deep importance of the emotions of activism. Feminism has been described as a 'passionate politics' linked to a sense of anger – a strong emotion which became central to feminist activism. Anger could connote crude stereotypes of activist women, and was on occasion a deeply disruptive, painful personal experience. But to highlight anger alone would be to miss an equally important feminist feeling – that of love. For some, the pre-eminent site of love and care was motherhood, providing a uniquely feminine site of emotional commitment that could take centre stage in feminist campaigning. For others, feminism represented warmth, friendship, trust and desire between women, all of which acted as crucial vectors of feminist change.

Feminist Anger

In Japan, a twenty-year-old woman took to a public platform in Ōtsu on 12 October 1883, to give voice to her anger at women's confinement. Kishida Toshiko (1863–1901) had the social status to make her voice heard in public. Her Kyoto family were well-connected and, working as a tutor, she had been close to the Empress in the Meiji-era Japanese court. Kishida began to make speeches demanding women's rights during the political upheavals of the Meiji period (1868–1912). The government had begun to move away from the isolationism and rigid social hierarchies of earlier periods, giving hope to many 'modernizing' factions that Japan was entering a period of change. Kishida memorably talked of women's lives as lived in 'boxes', created by the demands of absolute obedience to parents and confinement in the home. Raising a daughter under such conditions, Kishida declared, was like trying to grow flowers in salt. This bleak metaphor conveyed the depth of her anger at women's subordination, as daughters, wives and concubines.

Kishida's speech was too much for the authorities; indeed, we only know the content of her speech because it was recorded by a police informer. Kishida was arrested for speaking without a permit and spent eight days in prison. The Meiji government cracked down on its critics, and despite hopes for change, new legislation after 1890 excluded women from any kind of political participation. Women were not permitted to attend political meetings in Japan until 1922. Even after the end of the ban, the anger that greeted women's public interventions was deep and took violent forms. Itō Noe (1895–1923), heavily involved in publishing Japanese feminist thought between 1911 and 1916 as an editor of *Seitō* magazine, was strangled by a policeman after her arrest in 1923.

'Flowers in salt' was a powerful, painful image; later Japanese feminists continued to use strong metaphors to convey their outrage. Tanaka Mitsu, a prominent participant in the *ūman ribu* (women's liberation) movement in Japan, circulated an early manifesto titled 'Liberation from the Toilet' in August 1970. The manifesto, handwritten, was delivered at the Asian Women against Discrimination conference held in Tokyo. It forcefully declared that women would no longer serve men's sexual needs as if they were degraded receptacles such as toilets. Mitsu had been influenced by Black Power writers such as Angela Davis, and in similar terms to the 'Black is beautiful' movement, she attempted to reappropriate the abject figure of the *onna* (a sexually active or sluttish woman) by declaring '*onna* is beautiful'. Her writing also drew on popular ideas of sexual emancipation voiced by Wilhelm Reich, and foregrounded women's bodies as sites of oppression *and* liberation. Feminism should be based on 'truth spoken from the vagina', Mitsu argued, and she identified women's wombs as 'bearing grudges'. Her anger at the everyday acceptance of women and girls as objects of male desire was not couched in talk of women as peace-loving. Instead, Mitsu, a survivor of sexual abuse herself, opened up a space for women to express the violence and anger of 'a womb that thinks for itself, that screams and stamps its revenge in the blood of its own child'.[5]

The gut feeling of anger was a powerful motivator, invoked around the world by women's liberation activists. It also sparked debate about whether violence could be a legitimate form of feminist protest, a concrete means of expressing anger. In the early 1970s, Japan had been convulsed by the scandal surrounding the actions of a small terrorist sect, the United Red Army. Hiroko Nagata, a leader of this group, took part in a violent purge of its members in February 1972, leading to the deaths of twelve individuals. She was arrested, demonized in the media, and convicted of murder. Her actions posed questions for the *ūman ribu* movement about the limits of political violence. Tanaka Mitsu offered Nagata her support, despite disgust at her actions. She was outraged by the media coverage of Nagata, who was widely portrayed as a monster, while the male leader of the United Red Army was read more sympathetically, as ideologically motivated. Nagata was *onna*, an abject woman, and should be offered solidarity by women, all of whom were capable of violence, Mitsu reasoned.

This argument led the *ribu* movement to offer solidarity to the controversial and tragic cases of women who killed their own children, an issue that gained considerable coverage in Japan in the 1970s. They noted that fathers who killed children were portrayed less negatively than mothers and explained maternal violence as due to a social system that trapped women in dependency.[6] Like many within the women's movement, the Japanese *ribu* were not themselves willing to use violence. In contrast to the feminist terrorists whom we will meet in Chapter 7, their actions went no further than symbolic violence. In 1974, for example, feminists sprayed the (glass-covered) *Mona Lisa* portrait with red paint when it went on display at the Tokyo National Museum, in protest at the exclusion of the disabled and those carrying babies from the exhibition.

Anger was not only experienced on Mitsu's terms, as a force for challenging men and patriarchy. It was also an emotion that erupted between feminists. There were many prompts for such feelings, but one that was to prove persistent in the late twentieth century was the marginalization of lesbian women when faced with a largely heterosexual movement. Women's liberationists in the United States had recognized the divisions and conflicts between women relatively early, and held a 'Congress to Unite Women' in 1969 that hoped to heal them. Their hopes for reconciliation were perhaps naïve. Lesbian women had reacted with deep anger to the homophobia of Betty Friedan (1921–2006), founder of the National Organization for Women. Friedan had described lesbian women as a 'lavender menace' and considered them a threat to the unity and public acceptability of the women's movement. In inflammatory rhetoric, she termed them *agents provocateurs*, 'fomenting disruption and extremism, fanning the divisive note of sexual politics – "down with men, childbearing, and motherhood!"' Friedan saw lesbians as diverting 'energies from the political mainstream' in their 'attempt to make a political ideology out of a sexual preference'.[7]

Lesbians were not willing to accept such stereotyping in the interests of unity, nor to maintain a low profile to avoid shocking the mainstream media. It was no accident that the second Congress to Unite Women in 1970 was targeted for a lesbian counter-campaign. The Radicalesbians collective, wearing purple t-shirts emblazoned with 'Lavender Menace', took over the conference hall and plunged it into darkness. They mounted a dramatic stage takeover, and on turning the lights back on, called for women delegates to join them. They also distributed a manifesto, 'The Woman-Identified Woman'. This text captured something of their feelings, and the centrality of anger to their actions:

> What is a lesbian? A lesbian is the rage of all women condensed to the point of explosion. She is a woman who, often beginning at an extremely early age, acts in accordance with her inner compulsion to be a more complete and freer human being than her society cares to allow her. These needs and actions, over a period of years, bring her into painful conflict with people, situations, the accepted ways of thinking, feeling and behaving, until she is in a state of continual war with everything around her, and usually with her self.[8]

Despite the context of their very publicly expressed anger at Friedan and her followers, the emphasis here was on the insidious ways in which *self*-hatred worked within women, 'beneath the edge of her consciousness, poisoning her existence, keeping her alienated from herself, her own needs, and rendering her a stranger to other women'.

Socialization had long worked against the expression of anger by women, making it a difficult tool for some to wield. It was an attempt to normalize anger that led a group of lesbians, some of whom had been involved in the 1970 'Lavender Takeover', to form a collective in Washington DC in 1971

Figure 6.1
Three participants in the Lavender Menace action at the second Congress to Unite Women, 1970

named 'The Furies', after the Greek goddesses of vengeance. They produced a periodical until 1973 and explored ideas of separatism as a means of resolving disputes both with men and with other women, thus limiting the damage anger could inflict. The Furies declared:

> Man-hating is damaging on an individual level because a woman dissipates her energy in hating men . . . Who wants to spend their life operating out of anger, unhappiness, revenge?[9]

Some feminists wanted separatism to be more widely incorporated into the movement and developed the idea of 'political lesbianism' as a necessary position for all women. CLIT (Collective Lesbian International Terrors) were a group of women in New York who published an explosive challenge to 'straight' women in the feminist periodical *off our backs* (*oob*) in 1974:

> the danger of straight women is their disguise. they look like women. and sometimes remnants of the infant women they once were cut loose for a fleeting instant. but that passes and they quickly become again what detestable daddy programmed them to be, and perhaps by this time, after millennia of selection by males for qualities of smallness and stupidity, they genetically are: the mirror of the man . . . they are males in disguise.[10]

For some radical or revolutionary feminists, heterosexuality was a 'choice' defined by patriarchy. While not all women were expected to feel sexual desire for other women, all women could refuse to 'fuck men'.[11] The resulting debates amongst feminists were fraught; many women felt emotionally and sexually unable to withdraw from men. The *oob* editorial collective wrote of their 'internal anguish' after reading CLIT, and feared that 'the fierce anger within [the CLIT statement] would raise a barrier to readers' struggle to hear this message'.[12] Others found the evolution of feminist dyke culture liberating and welcomed the chance to explore their sexualities with new confidence. Lynn Alderson, founder of the London feminist bookshop Sisterwrite, recalled,

> it was to do with the whole of your life, every choice you made was a political decision. It wasn't an intellectual thing, it was emotional and sexual, it was your entire life that felt like it was on the line, you had to change everything.[13]

Beyond Europe and North America, however, the CLIT statement and ideas of political lesbianism sometimes had little resonance. Lesbianism was a major source of division at the landmark 1975 Mexico City World Conference on Women; many global South participants did not prioritize issues of sexuality. As Naisargi Dave has documented in India, there was resistance to the adoption of the language of lesbianism, widely viewed as a Western import until a more open same-sex movement emerged in the 1990s.[14] Indian women in same-sex relationships had previously preferred silence or the label '*ekal aurat*' (single women). After the founding of the Delhi-based lesbian support network Sakhi in 1991, followed in 1995 by Women to Women in Mumbai, there was a wider turn in India towards 'lesbian' as a label. This had been supported by the involvement of Indian women in the 1985 Nairobi and 1995 Beijing UN Women's Conferences, where lesbianism had been more sympathetically discussed. The 1990s, however, was no sharp turning point; discretion and euphemism has continued to be common in women's same-sex relationships in India even after their decriminalization in 2018. In recognition of this complex environment, Women to Women changed its name to Stree Sangam (Confluence of Women), stressing an Indian rather than Western emphasis. Neither 'dyke' nor 'lesbian' could easily translate into this context.

Black feminists were another constituency who were recipients of (white) hostility and who expressed their own anger at the widespread racism of women's movements. Black, Asian and Latinx women faced constant battles to have their concerns taken seriously. Their feminist anger often had different targets from that of white women – rather than fighting for abortion rights, they wanted protection from medics and welfare workers who imposed unwanted abortion, sterilization and child removal. Women of colour sought protection from police violence, and justice in workplaces. The ambition of some feminists to speak for all women has in practice often proved arrogant and hurtful, and, as a result, anger has infused experiences and encounters between them.

Audre Lorde chose anger as her theme when she was invited to address the National Women's Studies Association in 1981. Her anger centred on the failure to recognize racism within the white women's movement, and on casual feminist talk of shared oppressions. Lorde challenged the audience in stark terms: 'What woman here is so enamoured of her own oppression that she cannot see her heelprint upon another woman's face?' Anger could be a destructive emotion, but Lorde wanted to reclaim it as a source of power. In her view, women of colour had learned 'to orchestrate those furies so that they do not tear us apart'. Anger was an emotion which women feared, but which could bring about change: 'focused with precision it can become a powerful source of energy serving progress and change . . . Anger is loaded with information and energy.'[15] This reclamation of anger proved difficult to contain without personal damage. Lorde reminded the audience that she spoke 'as a woman of Color who is not bent upon destruction, but upon survival'. She was frustrated that her white peers did not want to hear her anger. One woman had requested of Lorde: 'tell me how you feel but don't say it too harshly or I cannot hear you.' But Lorde remained confident that, as a productive process of clarification, anger could be distinguished from hatred, the emotion that characterized the 'death and destruction' of patriarchy, war and racism: 'anger between peers births change.'

Lorde's theorization of anger has gained renewed force in more recent decades, as a neoliberal injunction for all to feel happy has become more pervasive. Critics have talked of a late-twentieth-century ethic of 'drive-by' cheerfulness, capturing the shallow emotions of a world that is oriented to competitive consumption and deeply rooted forms of socialization in feminine compliance.[16] Shulamith Firestone wrote in her 1970 book *The Dialectic of Sex* that she had trained herself out of a phony smile, 'which is like a nervous tic on every teenage girl. And this meant that I smiled rarely, for in truth, when it came down to real smiling, I had less to smile about.' While other feminists dreamt of new worlds of gender equality or women's solidarities, Firestone's feminist dream was simple:

> My 'dream' action for the women's liberation movement: a smile boycott, at which declaration all women would instantly abandon their 'pleasing' smiles, henceforth smiling only when something pleased them.[17]

Today's embrace by women of their 'resting bitch face' resonates with Firestone's dream.

Recent work by Sara Ahmed and Barbara Ehrenreich has critically engaged with the way in which happiness has become a keystone aspiration of individuals and institutions in the context of global capitalism. This is an economic system where the happiness of the majority will always be sacrificed to the interests of the privileged, they argue. Ahmed's 'feminist killjoy' manifesto has instead offered 'feminist consciousness as a form of unhappiness'. She foregrounds embodied forms of emotion: 'Our bodies become our tools; rage becomes sickness. We vomit; we vomit out what we have been asked to take in.' For the feminist killjoy, the instinct of what must be rejected is a visceral feeling that recalled the 'gut feelings' of Sudsofloppen: 'Our guts become our feminist friends the more we are sickened.' Such feelings underpinned Ahmed's concept of 'the feminist snap' – the willingness 'to cause unhappiness, to support those who are causing unhappiness, to refuse reconciliation and healing if violence and harm are still embedded in the systems'.[18]

These are powerful statements of what feminist feelings might look and feel like. The articulacy of the feminist theorizing of emotion in the early twenty-first century should not blind us however to the long-standing nature of the political scrutiny of emotions, and their use to build and contest feminist activism. Spanish writer Concepción Arenal (1820–93), for example, described how women were held in 'deadly' contempt in nineteenth-century Spain. She had studied for a law degree at the University of Madrid in 1841, the first woman to enter Spanish higher education. To avoid opposition, she initially dressed as a man; throughout her life she was forced to use subterfuge to get her work published. Arenal was deeply committed to a rational mode in describing and attempting to raise women's status. Nonetheless, her account of women as 'sterilized and annihilated' by Spanish public opinion, which 'spits on her and tramples her underfoot', speaks to Arenal's 'feminist snap', her willingness to tell 'the truth, disagreeable though it be'.[19] Emotions inspired and drove her writing, gave force to her life projects and helped her combat the social contempt she encountered.

Love

While feminists have often stressed the critical power of anger, they have combined this with equally strong commitments to emotions of love and solidarity. A generation after Concepción Arenal, Anna Julia Cooper (1858–1964) was deeply committed to love as a feminist ethic, which grew out of her experience as an African American woman, daughter of an enslaved mother and the fourth African American woman to hold a doctorate, obtained from the prestigious Sorbonne university in Paris in 1924. Cooper argued that love, as a conventional emotion existing in heterosexual marriage, was a bond that limited women. Their education had been stifled and narrowed into an expectation that they would only use the alphabet to 'spell one verb, *amo*, to love'.[20] Marital love rendered women a plaything or a piece of property – a confinement that was particularly harshly experienced by African American women, whose poverty made a mockery of ideas of cherished womanhood and who experienced 'the most bitter, the most intense, the most unrelenting [prejudice] the world has ever seen'. Real love would be based on access to education; Cooper's life was dedicated to enhancing African American education to provide for 'the hungering of the soul for communion and love'.

This theme of love as a significant element of black feminist thinking persisted in the United States, with figures such as Alice Walker and groups such as the Combahee River Collective insisting on a politics which stems 'from a healthy love for ourselves, our sisters and our communities'.[21] Jamaican poet and feminist June Jordan (1936–2002) made 'where is the love?' the 'decisive question' of her political activism:

> I am a feminist, and what that means to me is much the same as the meaning of the fact that I am Black: it means that I must undertake to love myself and respect myself as though my very life depends upon self-love and self-respect. It means that I must everlastingly seek to cleanse myself of the hatred and the contempt that surrounds and permeates my identity, as a woman, and as a Black human being, in this particular world of ours.

Presented at a tense session of the National Black Writers Conference at Howard University in 1978, Jordan's principled black feminist love aimed to span women who differed from her as well as men; all could be embraced by a 'steady state deep caring and respect for every other human being'.[22]

How could such a love be generated and expressed? For many women it was the networks of organizing, both within nations and between nations, that actualized their emotions. The two Finnish delegates at the first conference of the International Council of Women (ICW), which met in Washington DC in 1888, were deeply invested in the feelings that could be generated by international feminist congresses. Alli Trygg-Helenius (1852–1926) talked of the 'golden cables of sympathy' that extended across the Atlantic. The 1888 conference, she told delegates, represented 'the great dream of my life', and she outlined her 'sincere belief in women's love, women's power, women's ability, women's energy which can never fail'.[23] Trygg-Helenius' own energies had gone into temperance work in Finland through the White Ribbon Association and the Young Women's Christian Association. Her collaborator, the writer and founder of the Finnish Women's Association, Alexandra Gripenberg (1857–1913), was more oriented to personal wellsprings of love that might flourish within the women's movement. After extensive travels in Britain and the United States, she wrote to an American friend in 1888 about the intense feelings amongst suffragists: 'Are you in love with Lucy Stone? I like her letters and speeches so much and her daughter whom I saw when in England, is delightful.' Treasurer of the ICW in the 1890s, Gripenberg travelled widely to support its work in other nations and was elected to the Finnish Parliament when women won the vote in 1906. Her conservative politics, however, distanced her from the more radical versions of feminist 'free love' that flourished amongst nineteenth-century literary and political radicals such as George Sand and Margaret Fuller. Sexual love outside of marriage or between women was, for someone like Gripenberg, a damaging passion. Conservative feminists who enjoyed 'activist emotions' of solidarity and personal friendship were constantly at pains to distance themselves from the dangers other emotions could pose.

For all their efforts, love was an emotion that could be infused with sexual desire between women. Audre Lorde, so insightful on anger, was also thoughtful on erotic feelings:

> The erotic is not a question only of what we do; it is a question of how acutely and fully we can feel in the doing. Once we know the extent to which we are capable of feeling that sense of satisfaction and completion, we can then observe which of our various life endeavors bring us closest to that fullness.

In a lecture given in 1978, Lorde attempted to distinguish the erotic from the pornographic, and to expand the erotic away from the bedroom and into a larger sense of life work. Work in a capitalist and patriarchal society, for Lorde, had become a duty, a source of oblivion, rather than the deep fulfilment that could come from 'that joy which we know ourselves to be capable of'.[24] Lorde used the strikingly tactile metaphor of margarine, recalling from her childhood the need to mix the yellow colouring into the 'soft pale mass' of the uncoloured fats. She visualized the erotic as a kernel which, like the margarine colouring, 'flows through and colors my life with a kind of energy that heightens and sensitizes and strengthens all my existence'.

Lorde's autobiography, *Zami: A New Spelling of My Name*, recounted her own lesbian desires, which after tentative experiments and setbacks, came to define her emotional world: 'The erotic is a resource within each of us that lies in a deeply female and spiritual plane, firmly rooted in the power of our unexpressed or unrecognized feeling.'[25] Andrea Dworkin, another radical feminist, was more specific about her feelings. She linked her sexuality to the recovery of a deep, embodied link to her mother:

> Being a lesbian means to me the memory of the mother, remembered in my own body, sought for, desired, found, and truly honoured. It means the memory of the womb, when we were one with our mothers, until birth when we were torn asunder. It means a return to that place inside, inside her, inside ourselves, to the tissues and the membranes, to the moisture and the blood.[26]

Motherhood

In Dworkin's visceral depiction of her connection to her mother's body, we get a glimpse of the centrality of motherhood as a site of feminist 'gut feeling'. Indeed, motherhood, actual or potential, has been at the heart of many historical versions of women's movements, ranging from the late-eighteenth-century American, French and Swiss republicans to the Communists and nationalists of postcolonial South and East Asia. It has not always been easy for feminists to embrace the demanding, emotionally intense and sometimes oppressive experiences of motherhood. It has been a site of class and race inequalities, as well as coercive interventions by medics and politicians. Attempts to socialize motherhood as part of a project of destroying the family were pursued in Maoist China, providing inspiration to Claudie Broyelle that China was pioneering a 'new concept of love'. Despite its emotional centrality, motherhood had inspired deep feelings of constraint and violence and was no easy rallying ground for activist women. Indeed, some have rejected any attempt to weave motherhood into feminism as essentialist and exclusionary, while for others it has formed the bedrock of feminist conviction. The feminist as a child-hating, maternity-shirking figure was a perennial anti-feminist cliché. Yet motherhood could provide an intense sense of shared embodiment for women, and a powerful claim for resources and citizenship.

In the late nineteenth century, Germany and Sweden saw the emergence of highly articulate forms of 'motherly feminism' in a context of deep demographic anxiety. Despite the absence of evidence, it was widely believed that there was an enormous gender imbalance in the population, such that large numbers of women would never be able to get married. This phenomenon, termed the *Frauenüberschuss* in Germany, gave rise to the concept of the 'women standing alone' (*alleinstehende Frauen*). In a social context in which being a wife and mother defined most women's legal existence, the single woman was unsettling and destabilizing. Her inability to rely on male support gave feminists the opportunity to assert women's rights to employment, to the vote and to an individualized existence.

'Women standing alone' was always a classed concept. Few tears were shed over the unmarried working-class woman, who was assumed to be safely absorbed into the labour market. But many anxious commentators feared that middle-class women who remained single and childless would destabilize their societies by becoming 'parasites'. Germany was not the only country where this idea of 'surplus' women was powerfully invoked. Britain, France and the United States also saw similar debates and fears that 'sexual anarchy' might ensue if marriage could no longer support and contain women. Of course, women existing outside of marriage was no new thing, and much of the late-nineteenth-century panic was only tenuously linked to the demographic reality. But these concerns created a historical moment that spanned continents, where motherhood became a powerful ideological point of anxiety and a resource for a particular formulation of feminism.

For Swedish feminist Ellen Key (1849–1926), it was women's maternal qualities that defined their social and political existence. Born into a politically active upper-class family, Key had worked as a teacher in Sweden, but became well known internationally for her writings on the 'woman question', the women's movement and childhood in the early twentieth century. Indeed, she was greeted with a degree of hyperbole in a number of countries as the 'new prophetess' of feminism. Confusingly, commentators have judged Key's later work anti-feminist due to her support for incentivizing women to motherhood. Nonetheless, she supported core feminist demands, such as women's rights to divorce and the vote, as well as an end to the status of illegitimacy for children born outside of marriage, and the abolition of women's legal incapacities. Key was increasingly drawn to socialism, and sought the separation of incomes within marriages, as well as the payment of women (by the state) for their work in raising children and (by husbands) for performing housework. All women should receive 'the same amount as a stranger in corresponding circumstances would receive in salary and cost of keep', Key declared in 1911.[27]

Ellen Key was widely influential throughout the world, with translations from Swedish into Japanese in 1913 and Chinese in 1923. The British sex radical and scientist Havelock Ellis introduced the English-language versions of her books in 1911, noting Key's particular prominence in Germany: 'It is in Germany that her fame has been made [where] the German women, awaking from a long period of quiescence, are inaugurating a new phase of the woman movement.' In Britain and America, the idea of surplus women had been used to argue for a range of policy interventions aimed at women, from colonial emigration to greater access to education and employment. Ellis feared that this would 'masculinize women' and 'ignored the claims of the race'.[28] Key, herself employed as a teacher, portrayed 'extreme' feminists as dogmatic and fanatical, all too ready to sacrifice harmony and racial progress to their logical end goal, 'the right of woman to individual, free development of her powers'. She offered a distinctive alternative, termed '*mutterschutz*'. This concept, which could be translated as 'protection of motherhood', took on a feminist cast through its insistence that *all* women's reproductive choices should be supported, to bear children or not according to their own choices. Even if unmarried, Key argued that mothers should receive material support without facing social stigma.

Supporters of this strand of feminism drew inspiration from Key's talk of women's spiritual and psychic power. She had argued that women's sweetness and tenderness, best expressed in motherhood, should be celebrated and offered as widely as possible to all women. She did allow that some women, lacking biological children, might be 'collective' or 'social' mothers They could take part in philanthropic or social policy initiatives that would still fulfil 'the great fundamental laws of nature' of motherhood. Key had herself remained childless and unmarried, but regarded teaching as a form of maternalism. This was a feminism that respected sexual 'difference': 'each sex pursues its course . . . and as an equal each helps the other in the different tasks'.[29]

In Germany, it was Helene Stöcker (1869–1943) who became the best-known proponent of *mutterschutz*. She took Key's emphasis on motherhood and turned it away from the more conservative direction that Key had taken, reminding us of the malleability and context-dependency of feminist ideologies. Stöcker helped found the organization Bund für Mutterschutz und Sexualreform (League for the Protection of Motherhood and Sexual Reform), editing its journals and advocating for the equality and state support of all children, legitimate or illegitimate. Stöcker also supported greater sex education and worked tirelessly for the peace movement. Her beliefs led her to support the freedoms of sexual minorities in Weimer Germany, and she lobbied the German Reichstag to prevent lesbianism being criminalized in the years after the First World War. Her league also sponsored homes for unwed mothers, and health clinics that provided contraception and, on occasion, abortion. Stöcker was insistent that motherhood should not rule out professional life, and in an essay titled 'The Sex Life of Teachers', she argued against the dismissal of women teachers on marriage. She was persecuted by the Nazis in the 1930s, and forced into exile, dying in New York City. As Ann Taylor Allen has argued, despite the conservative potential of maternalist feminism, it could be a powerful subversive force.[30]

Key and Stöcker were both, in different ways, iconoclastic radicals, dreaming of a very different society where the sexes had different kinds of rights and relationships. Nonetheless, the priority given to motherhood and the call for the protection of mothers by the state that was at the heart of Key's and Stöcker's feminism was not easy to translate across time and space. In Australia and Canada, for example, it was only white women who could look to the state for benign interventions. Mothers in Native American, Aboriginal Australian and First Nations communities found themselves subject to state violence and coercion that saw their children removed and raised in institutions. In the United States, the legacies of slavery and its removal of children were long-lasting, with African American and Native American women often viewed as workers rather than as mothers.[31] In West Africa, traditions of 'othermothering' saw a wide range of caregivers to children that decentred the care of birth mothers. Feminist approaches to motherhood that did not acknowledge these dynamics and injustices contributed to the sentiment amongst black and indigenous women that feminist ideas originating amongst white women were unable to speak to their needs.

In Latin America, there was a strong emphasis on child welfare and motherhood within the women's movement from the earliest years of the twentieth century. This region is important for its traditions of both conservative and radical Christianity, its indigenous feminisms, its civic activism and protest traditions, and the centrality of conflict and competition between North and South American feminisms. Latin American motherhood could be framed as a utopian and spiritual ideal. The dreams of a matriarchal society we encountered in Chapter 1 in Rokeya Sakhawat Hossain's *Sultana's Dream* and Charlotte Perkins Gilman's *Herland* were visible in a different form in indigenous Peru and Bolivia. In these settings, feminists could draw on the folk-memory of an Andean mother-goddess, Pachamama. This version of an indigenous matriarchy was a historically specific hybrid rather than a solely Andean tradition. Pachamama had become infused with beliefs about the Virgin Mary by Spanish colonial invaders, who also imposed taxation and inheritance systems premised on female dependency on male relatives. Nonetheless, ideas of a goddess-mother remained a powerful means of conveying an Incan cosmology of motherhood in balance with the environment.[32]

It was more common, however, for motherhood in early-twentieth-century Latin America to be framed in medicalized or nationalist terms. Feminist activists and social workers stressed the need for women's rights to be strengthened in order to better care for children. Physician Dr Julieta Lanteri Renshaw (1873–1932) had organized a series of feminist congresses in Argentina in the 1910s, and established the Liga para los Derechos de la Mujer y del Niño (League for Women and Children's Rights) in 1911. The emphasis on rights was echoed by the activism of Chilean feminist Marta Vergara (1898–1995), who was deeply involved in the Movimiento pro Emancipación de la Mujer Chilena (Movement for the Emancipation of Chilean Women) established in 1935, and in the Pan-American organizing that emerged in the 1920s and 30s for the maternity rights of women workers.[33] This emphasis on rights distinguished their approach from that of male professionals, who supported more authoritarian 'family welfare' approaches that had little feminist content and sometimes included draconian methods involving the removal of children from birth mothers.[34] But it was easy for the rights-based approach to get pushed aside by the urgent rhetoric of service to the nation. Bertha Lutz, a prominent Brazilian suffragist, framed women's emancipation in 1918 as a national duty that mothers had previously shirked:

> a woman ought not to live parasitically based on her sex, taking advantage of men's animal instincts, she [should] be useful, educate herself and her children . . . [Women] shall cease being one of the heavy links that chain our country to the past, and instead become valuable instruments in the progress of Brazil.[35]

Such rhetoric made it hard for Latin American maternalist feminists to develop a critique of unwilling motherhood. The entrenched position of the Catholic Church in the region, as well as the pro-natalist military governments that dominated the twentieth century, left abortion rights poorly developed across the twentieth century.[36] Illegal abortions were the largest cause of death amongst young women in Latin America in the late twentieth century. Even radical leftist regimes, with the exception of Cuba, have been reluctant to decriminalize abortion. Abortion was decriminalized in Chile in 2017 but remains illegal in all circumstances in Nicaragua and El Salvador.

Though reluctant to openly support abortion, mid-twentieth-century Latin American feminists were willing to argue for the expansion of sex education in similar terms to Helene Stöcker's *mutterschutz*. Maternal feminists of the mid twentieth century also offered support for poorer women to keep their children rather than give them up to institutional care, and gradually began to frame this in terms of 'child rights'. Where state 'endowment' of motherhood and provision of benefits had dominated earlier models, the 'rights of children' approach allowed for the evolution of more sensitive, less judgemental support for mothers. Motherhood could still be used for conservative mobilization, as witnessed in the 'empty pots and pans' marches by women against the leftist government of Chile's Salvador Allende in 1971. Yet the vigils and witnessing of the Argentinian Mothers of the Plaza de Mayo in the later 1970s made clear the potential of motherhood to take on wider significance. The love and care they owed their families made maternal feelings a powerful, militant force in contesting the abductions and violence Argentinians faced under military rule.[37]

Global Networks

Maternal feminism had been supported internationally through the Pan-American committees and congresses that linked activists in the United States to their Central and Latin American counterparts. In 1927, for example, the Havana Pan-American Child Congress saw the foregrounding of maternalist feminism under the influence of Katherine Lenroot (1891–1982) of the United States Children's Bureau, a federal agency dedicated to child welfare staffed almost exclusively by women. Lenroot provided Spanish translations of the pamphlets of the Children's Bureau and ensured that Latin American feminist social work was put into close dialogue with North American developments. As for earlier generations of women who worked transnationally, local leverage could be obtained through the 'golden cables of sympathy' that linked the struggles across national boundaries.

Nonetheless, it would be naïve to cast these transnational links as only supportive. They also elicited more negative emotions, entangled as they were with geopolitical tensions and ideological differences. There had long been tensions in relationships across the Americas, not helped by the widely voiced perception that the United States was a beacon of women's emancipation that would paternalistically extend a helping hand to its southern neighbours. Maria Estrela (1860–1946), the first female Brazilian medical doctor, had trained in the United States in the 1880s and termed it 'the country favoured by God to be the cradle of female emancipation'.[38] Such statements helped foster an uncomfortable sense of Latin American backwardness, as well as moments of significant resistance to the leadership of North American women and their attempts to set the feminist agenda.

This resistance to North American leadership came prominently into view during the first UN-sponsored World Conference on Women in July 1975, in Mexico City. This landmark conference was lobbied for by the Women's International Democratic Federation, and initially planned to be held in Communist-bloc East Berlin. Pressure from the United States saw it relocated to Mexico, but this did not put an end to the tensions that emerged over its organization and goals. The conference was divided into an elite conference, packed with the wives of presidents, such as Imelda Marcos of the Philippines (famed for her vast shoe collection). This was hardly a promising group to make plans for feminist change.

Fortunately, Mexico City also hosted a dynamic, grassroots 'Tribune', where non-governmental organizations (NGOs) and women's groups met. The Tribune was located a safe five kilometres from the main forum, yet its proceedings have been far more historically significant than those of the formal representatives of government power. Indeed, its dominance in the legacy of the Mexico City conference reflects a wider shift in feminist campaigning of the past fifty years, in which NGOs and supranational bodies such as the UN and the International Labour Organization have been very prominent.

Many 1975 Tribune participants were from the Americas, and the extremely diverse and challenging debates that it hosted were indicative of the lack of consensus of the women's movement in a political moment of Cold War tensions and postcolonial nationalism across this region. The Women's International Democratic Federation (WIDF), established in 1945 and representing activist women of left, Communist and anti-fascist ideologies, had sponsored a series of Latin American Women's Congresses (*Seminario Latinamericano de Mujeres*). The WIDF disassociated themselves from 'feminism', believing it 'bourgeois'. Nonetheless, their work on peace, childcare and equal pay galvanized demands for women's empowerment, and has recently been re-read as 'left feminism'.[39] Their third Latin American Congress, held in Lima in 1974, was dedicated to preparing position papers for Mexico City, working in close association with the Peruvian Communist Party. As historian Francesca Miller has argued, the Lima Congress was welcomed by the left-wing Peruvian military government in power as a means to demonstrate 'third world' nonalignment with the 'first

Figure 6.2
The 1975 Tribune in Mexico City, five kilometres from the official United Nations World Conference on Women

world' of the United States. Peruvian feminists did not however share the same goals and interests simply by living in a nation of the global South. The 1974 Congress revealed tensions between white Hispanic Peruvian women, often well educated, and poorer, indigenous Peruvian women, who prioritized land rights and material security rather than specific forms of gender oppression.[40]

These same tensions were dominant in the 1975 Mexico City Tribune, epitomized by the confrontation between Bolivian tin miner's wife Domitila Barrios de Chungara (1937–2012) and the actions of American feminist Betty Friedan. Friedan attended the conference with other members of the National Organization for Women, deliberately aiming to provide role models for women. During the conference, Friedan's 'Feminist Caucus' took on the new name of 'United Women of the Tribune' and, without any mandate, tried to influence the governmental conference on behalf of the Tribune.[41] Barrios de Chungara, a part-indigenous mother of seven, represented the Housewives' Committee of Siglo XX (a company-owned mining camp in Bolivia). She opposed Friedan's attempt to speak for other women, and to subsume their needs under a North American version of 'feminism'. Barrios de Chungara was hostile to demands for birth control, preferring to emphasize the value of a growing population in the struggle against transnational corporations and the dominance of the 'first world'. As an experienced union activist, she was determined to challenge the 'control over the microphone' that US women exerted at the Tribune, and to present feminism as a coalition with male *compañeros*. She perceived *gringa* (white) feminism as lesbian-dominated, a 'war against men'.

For her white feminism meant that 'if a man has ten mistresses, well, the woman should have ten lovers also. If a man spends all his money at the bar, partying, the women have to do the same thing.'[42] This was certainly a misrepresentation of feminist arguments, ignoring for example the emergence of sex-worker perspectives that were aligned with the anti-imperial, anti-racist politics of Barrios de Chungara herself.[43] Nonetheless, her interventions put some fundamental issues for poorer women – water, land rights, neo-colonialism and racial discrimination – centre stage in the UN World Plan of Action drawn up at the conference. Friedan allegedly termed this approach a 'war-like activity' that 'ignored women's problems'. Barrios de Chungara, 'moved by the anger I felt', denounced women like Friedan who 'show[ed] up all made up and combed like someone who has time to spend in an elegant beauty parlor and who can spend money on that'. Her own emotions were of shame and discomfort at finding herself separated from her tin mining community:

> Instead of feeling happy, I thought about how in the mine the people have to walk, how the women, even when they're pregnant, have to carry such heavy loads along such long roads . . . All that made me feel uncomfortable.[44]

Perhaps most startlingly for women's liberationists, the World Conference on Women voted against inserting 'sexism' into the list of obstacles women faced. Its Plan of Action talked of the dignity and worth of 'peoples' rather than 'women'. These decisions reflected the dominance of Soviet, East European, Latin American, African and Asian participants, often associated with the WIDF, whose anti-capitalist, anti-imperialist perspectives were pitted against forms of feminism associated with an agenda of privileged, 'first world' women's rights.[45]

Despite this hostility to some versions of feminism, the conference and the World Plan of Action led to a gradual reconciliation of left-wing and anti-colonial politics with feminisms, and a critical awareness that the anti-colonial left could not be trusted to safeguard women's access to resources and decision-making. Peru, for example, saw groups with a 'feminist intent' (*una intención feminista*) come together in 1978 spanning socialist, women's liberationist and indigenous perspectives.[46] The UN had responded to pressure from Communist-aligned members to include gender equality in its 1945 Charter, and in 1979 the General Assembly helped embolden such initiatives by adopting the Convention on the Elimination of All Forms of Discrimination Against Women (CEDAW). This treaty, which guarantees political, economic, social and legal rights for women, was widely ratified through the 1980s and helped kickstart the entrenchment of feminist claims in policy debates and legislation.[47]

The assertion of women's rights as part of, rather than opposed to larger struggles for land, security, human rights and justice within Latin American and Caribbean feminist groups was also spurred by a series of 'Feminist Encounters' (*Encuentros Feministas Latinoamericanas y del Caribe*) organized after 1981 which helped foster interactions between women's groups across the region.[48] Despite this open identification as 'feminist', the term still carried stigma. One participant at an early *Encuentro* noted the ongoing 'great prejudice there is against feminism' amongst indigenous women's groups, as a white, middle-class or 'imported' political movement.

K'iche' indigenous activist María Isabel Choxóm López, for example, described how widows in Guatemala had come together in solidarity groups that maintained an awkward relationship with ideas of feminism: 'We aren't in favour of a struggle between the sexes. Women and men have to come together to forge a new society, and within this new society, we each have to struggle for our place.' Nonetheless, it was clear to her that in Guatemala's long civil war,

> the most directly victimized are women and children. If you go to one of our demonstrations, you'll notice that most of us are women. And we're women who have discovered our capacity for struggle, our capacity for resistance. We've been left alone with four, five, six children, and we have to keep going. It gives me great hope.[49]

These contradictory emotions – hope, anger, love, shame – sum up something of the paradoxes of how feminisms developed within and through diverse historical moments and political discourses – of nationalism, internationalism, sexuality, race and motherhood. Hope underlay the utopian dreams of Chapter 1. Feminisms have also been fuelled by anger at the profound inequalities and violence faced by women, as well as compromised by their capacity to generate anger and bitterness between women. Feminists have often attempted to speak for all women, yet have been inattentive to the differences between them, prompting painful feelings of exclusion and disappointment. Feminisms have sometimes given women – and, on occasion, men – the opportunity to express and politically activate their feelings of love – towards other women, towards children, towards their nation. And perhaps most transformatively, they have given opportunities for the expression of self-love. As Audre Lorde perceptively put it,

> as we begin to recognize our deepest feelings, we begin to give up, of necessity, being satisfied with suffering and self-negation, and with the numbness which so often seems like their only alternative in our society. Our acts against oppression become integral with self, motivated and empowered from within.[50]

The emotions of historical actors are not always legible to us, particularly when reading them across several centuries or in regions of the world that have distinctive emotional cultures. We might imagine emotions, or even have the testimony of individuals but it is impossible to take for granted that the emotions they name as love, pride and so on, resemble ours. Emotions are shaped by the cultural context in which they are expressed. The anger of Kishida Toshiko is unlikely to feel and mean the same as that of Tanaka Mitsu or Shulamith Firestone. Some emotions will not leave traces in the historical record, and we can only speculate as to their existence. This is particularly the case where cultural and intellectual scripts constrained emotional expression. Writers such as Josefa Amar, who foregrounded women's reason as their claim to public life, were unlikely to openly voice their emotions, however intensely they may have been felt.

Other emotions simply can't be conveyed in a sufficiently fine-grained experiential form – to say that love was part of the feminist movement does little to capture its qualities and depth. And it would be naïve to ignore the fact that emotions might be performed to political ends, as the exchanges between Domitila Barrios de Chungara and Betty Friedan at the Mexico City conference suggest. The rhetorics adopted and emotions signalled were rooted in what historian Jocelyn Olcott terms 'cheap cabaret', performed for the conference or for a national audience in Cold War registers.[51] Similar scepticism emerged over the 'speaking bitterness' performances of Chinese women, as a more critical follow-up from Claudie Broyelle argued in 1980. She termed her 1973 work a 'day-dream', which 'presented a picture of China free of contradictions, or more precisely free of those contradictory emotions which even a short trip produces'.[52] Chinese women's formulaic assertions that 'we have happy lives' under Communism began to seem inauthentic when accounts of rapes, forced abortions and state conscription of labour during the Cultural Revolution emerged. 'Half of the sky has gone dark,' concluded one German visitor to China in 1982.[53]

While feminism was always a 'passionate politics', there were limits to the power of emotions to *change* the structures and everyday experiences that sparked feminist anger. Barbara Mehrhof, a radical feminist active in the New York group The Feminists in the early 1970s, argued in a polemic on rape that women's predominant emotion within a patriarchal society was terror. This was both a feeling imposed on women and also a tactic deployed by men.[54] She was dismissive of the 'emotions work' of consciousness-raising, arguing that it 'has the ability to organize great numbers of women, but to organize them for nothing'.[55] Instead, resonant with Ahmed's 'feminist snap', Mehrhof wanted collective action – women's own terror tactics – that would fight back against pervasive rape cultures. Mehrhof's dismissal of the talk and feelings of consciousness-raising as leading nowhere was an underestimation; exploring emotions made possible the 'feminist snap' and laid the basis for feminist action, the topic of the next chapter.

CHAPTER 7

Actions

Feminism has been explored in this book as an angry, creative, forceful claiming of women's rights, spaces and solidarity. But we've also seen versions of feminism that make a philosophical or utopian case for women's rights or empowerment without offering any kind of road map to achieve these goals. Some saw feminist reform as a passive historical process, assuming that change over time *inevitably* altered the status of women. The early Egyptian feminist writer Qasim Amin, for example, noted in his 1899 book, *The Liberation of Women* that change was already visible in terms of Egyptian gender norms:

> We have witnessed a decrease in the power of men . . . Is it not obvious that women in many families go out of the house to accomplish their business, that they work with men in their many concerns, that they seek recreation in a suitable environment where the air is pleasant, that they accompany their husbands on trips?

Amin (1863–1908) was clearly imagining elite families with the resources for leisure and travel. Despite his narrow range, his vision of the end of Egyptian patriarchy was vividly expressed. He described male power as 'a building bound for destruction and desolation, its foundations crumbled, its elements disintegrated, and its condition so deteriorated that each year a section of it collapses all by itself'. He did not think this crumbling was due to the resistance of women but 'a consequence of the increased intellectual development of men, and the moderation of their rulers'.

Educated in France, Qasim Amin was deeply invested in the possibilities of Egyptian nationalism and resistance to colonial rule. He saw women's position as a key area of national modernization, and this may have led him to be confident in the inevitability of change. The 'march of civilization', as despotism was replaced by enlightened self-rule, would, he thought, inevitably bring the collapse of the decaying house of male dominance. Veiling, for example, would disappear as 'the result of the societal changes which accompanied the change and progress of civilization'. He concluded his prescriptions for change:

> In order to improve the condition of the nation, it is imperative we improve the condition of women. If the reader proceeds to think about this major topic, with all its facets, he will be confronted by the truth, and its secrets will become clear to him.[1]

Many in the Egyptian women's movement were less sanguine about what simply thinking through the problem might achieve. Qasim Amin himself later acknowledged the limits of top-down change in his 1900 book, *The New Woman*. Responding to his critics, he acknowledged that 'In bringing about any kind of reform, it is not enough to identify the need for change, to order its implementation through governmental decrees, to lecture about it . . .' Instead, 'without women's involvement, it will be impossible to bring about any change in society.'[2] But even this revised position had little urgency – Amin envisaged change through women raising children to think differently, a 'natural, long-term course', rather than any activism on their own behalf.

His quietist advice was part of a broader confidence in the late nineteenth century that, without struggle, women's rights and equality were to be the characteristic of the twentieth century. Icons of the twentieth century showed it as having a female face, compared to the bearded male face of the nineteenth. In 1913, the National Council of Women of Canada confidently termed their periodical *Woman's Century: A Journal of Education and Progress for Canadian Women*. Similarly, *The Cosmopolitan*, a Jamaican journal edited by black feminist Una Marson, termed its era 'the age of women' in 1928. Yet women's experiences around the globe during the twentieth century were of painfully slow reform, withdrawal of rights when they experienced wars, coups and dictatorships, pervasive everyday violence, and the mockery or outlawing of feminist voices. Amin's collapsing house of patriarchy was only a dream, as distant as Rokeya Sakhawat Hossain's fantasized Ladyland.

In this chapter, I explore the strategies and experiences of those who wanted to actualize their feminist politics, rather than simply wait for it. We'll look at a broad repertoire of feminist actions, ranging from the publicity-seeking brilliance of suffrage campaigning, to intimate, personal refusals – to wash up, or to service men's emotional and sexual needs. Some actions have subverted other rituals, recasting them with feminist meaning. Turkish feminist Gul

Ozyegin notes that the apparently conventional and innocuous feminine act of giving out flowers on Mother's Day could be subversively reworked as a feminist protest in the context of Turkey's military dictatorship in the early 1980s. Indeed, it was only women who were able to protest openly:

> For us the military dictatorship granted activism denied other political groups. We were spared being arrested for gathering or demonstrations because of our sex, because we were women, because we were demonstrating on Mother's Day, carrying balloons and distributing flowers.[3]

Feminists have proved adept at exploiting acts of symbolic protest; most have rejected anything that could injure human life, though some have risked their own bodies. Feminism has been marked by its humanism, and its hopefulness for change. Radical feminist Andrea Dworkin produced some of the strongest denunciations of male domination, yet even she asked men in 1983:

> Have you ever wondered why we are not just in armed combat against you? It's not because there's a shortage of kitchen knives in this country. It is because we believe in your humanity, against all the evidence.[4]

From graffitiing sexist adverts that objectify women's bodies to physically mailing themselves as 'human letters' to the British Prime Minister in Downing Street in 1909, feminist activism has been creative and enormously diverse.

The Argument of the Stone

Some of the most notorious and iconic feminist actions emerged during campaigns for women's suffrage. They spanned refusals to cooperate with state efforts to conduct a census to cutting telegraph wires, stone throwing and arson. The Women's Social and Political Union (WSPU), founded in Manchester in 1903, was a highly innovative and creative political group which transformed the suffrage struggle in Britain into a media, courtroom and street spectacle. By actions such as persistently interrupting meetings, putting acid into post boxes, breaking shop windows, slashing art and, at their most extreme, planting bombs in unoccupied buildings, the WSPU members added urgency to the existing lobbying and mass petitioning that the British suffrage movement had deployed since the 1860s.

Members of the WSPU and the Irish Women's Franchise League pioneered techniques of stone throwing from 1908, smashing windows in shops, cars, government buildings and churches. Some undertook this 'argument of the stone' with humour; in 1909, a diminutive Manchester school teacher, Dora Marsden, wrapped a heavy iron ball in paper and labelled it 'bomb'. She then threw it through the window of a building where a Liberal politician was holding a meeting. Humour also marked the subversive efforts to invade and protest the masculine public sphere, such as the 1909 attempt by Daisy Solomon and Elspeth McClellan to mail themselves, using threepenny stamps, as 'human letters' to Prime Minister Asquith's residence on Downing Street. British postal regulations did not explicitly rule out humans as 'mailable

Figure 7.1
Daisy Solomon and Elspeth McClellan negotiate with police, a post boy and a Downing Street official in an attempt to get themselves mailed to the Prime Minister in February 1909

objects', and activists spotted that this oversight could get around the Prime Minister's refusal to accept their petitions and delegations. In some confusion, the post boy tasked to deliver them detailed on the official 'irregularity' form:

> I took the Ladies to Mr Asquith's house but the police would not let them go in. I went in but the butler would not sign the form because he did not have the letters to sign for, because the ladies themselves said they were the letters. And Mr Asquith refused to see them.

WSPU founder Emmeline Pankhurst (1858–1928) claimed the status of soldier, fighting 'a civil war waged by women' with 'revolutionary methods'. Breaking windows was 'the only means we consider open to voteless persons to bring about a political situation, which can only be solved by giving women the vote'. Lecturing to American audiences in attempts to raise funds and support, she aligned WSPU actions with the American War of Independence refusal to pay taxes without representation. Pankhurst noted that women 'broke the windows of shop-keepers where they spent most of their money when they bought their hats and their clothing'. As so often in feminist rhetoric of this period, class privileges were assumed rather than examined in her comment on hat shopping.[5]

The WSPU and other militant groups did not find it easy to root their political appeal in working-class communities. Nonetheless, it was not only middle-class women who took part in direct actions. Cissie Cahalan (1876–1948), a Dublin draper's assistant, for example, was heavily involved in the window-smashing Irish Women's Franchise League and also active in the Irish trade union movement. Emmeline Pankhurst's daughter Sylvia (1882–1960) worked closely in London's East End with working-class women such as Nellie Cressall (1882–1973), a mother of six who was later to become the first female mayor of London's borough of Poplar. For Cressall, her feminism was manifested through her demands for employment and childcare as much as the drama of marches and stone throwing.

The National Union of Women's Suffrage Societies was well established in the textile communities of the North-West. Female cotton weavers and winders saw their struggle as operating in alliance with working-class men. They were keen to establish universal suffrage in Britain rather than simple gender equality. The latter option, which kept property qualifications in place, disenfranchised the poor of both sexes; but when mobilized around 'adult suffrage', working-class activists were willing to speak at factory gates, join deputations, collect signatures and fundraise using familiar repertoires of campaigning techniques developed through the trade union and Chartist movements.

Suffragist stone throwing increased in coordination and scale as the campaign went on, with scores of women making simultaneous attacks on high-profile targets. Their actions led to prison sentences, and an escalation of tactics to include women chaining themselves to statues and railings outside Parliament and at the Prime Minister's residence, giving themselves time to make a speech while police struggled to remove them. In 1908, two members of the Women's Freedom League, Helen Fox and the Australian-born Muriel Matters, chained themselves to the ornate grille that separated women onlookers in the Ladies' Gallery from the male-only House of Commons. Freeing them required taking the grille down entirely, briefly dismantling the deeply resented symbol of women's political exclusion.

Over the course of the campaign the simple and accessible stone throwing was replaced by more complex and violent actions, such as arson and attacks on artworks, which could only be pursued by a small minority of dedicated activists. The bombing of London's iconic St Paul's Cathedral was foiled when a large device was found underneath the bishop's throne in 1913, but other bombs did explode in the homes of cabinet ministers, churches and public buildings across Ireland, Scotland, Wales and England. A famous painting of a nude, the Rokeby Venus, was slashed in London's National Gallery in 1914 by Mary Richardson (1883–1961), a Canadian WSPU member armed with a meat cleaver. The picture had recently been bought for the nation by a public appeal and featured the naked back and bottom of a woman whose face was hidden. Richardson's action was a protest at the arrest of the WSPU leader, Emmeline Pankhurst, the previous day. Pankhurst, Richardson argued, was more beautiful than the Venus depicted, but was suffering violence at the hands of the government. Later in life, however, she added that she disliked 'the way men visitors the gallery gaped' at a nude female body. The slashes in the picture were disturbingly akin to a violent assault, and resembled knife wounds. The press labelled Richardson a 'Ripper', referencing the famous late-nineteenth-century serial killer of London women.

WSPU militancy often incited violence or suffering onto the body of the protestor herself. The death of Emily Wilding

Davison (1872–1913), who threw herself under the hooves of the King's horse during the 1913 Derby while holding a 'Votes for Women' banner, has become an iconic example. Force-feeding in prison was another form of violence, imposed on suffrage protestors who adopted hunger strikes after their imprisonment for political actions. Suffrage militants commonly argued that women's protests were deliberately designed to avoid any damage to human life. Many believed that women's role as mothers meant that they intimately understood the value of human life and could never take lives. In reality, the actions taken sometimes did cause significant risks. Arson and bombing were hard to control, and there were some injuries as a result of acid attacks on the state-owned postal service. Violence was an important tactic, but could be unpredictable and problematic, losing mainstream public support for the women's cause and fuelling a spiral of ever more intense forms of government repression. Nonetheless, it was exported to other settings. Direct contact between the British and American movements saw the take-up of militant tactics in the United States, including window-breaking and hunger striking.

In China, however, it was contact with the anarchist movement that led early-twentieth-century suffragists to pursue tactics of militant interruption and confrontation. Chinese nationalists and radicals, paralleling Qasim Amin, had been calling for women to 'modernize', in order to achieve China's national development. Their goals included education, an end to foot-binding, and, for some, suffrage rights. These goals resonated with Enlightenment visions of modernity and natural rights. But it is also clear that Chinese traditions, such as the

Confucian idea of the 'learned wife' who could perform an important role in supporting her husband in politics or business, were also significant resources for Chinese women's suffragists.[6]

There was apparent support for feminist reforms within the Chinese Revolutionary Alliance led by Sun Yat-sen, which was attempting to bring down the Qing monarchy. When Qing rule collapsed in 1911, some provincial assemblies seemed set to enfranchise women. Reform was stymied by the new coalition between the Revolutionary Alliance and the Nationalist Party in 1912, which saw commitments to gender equality sidelined. Women activists from the Shenzhou Women's Suffrage Alliance reacted with rallies and petitions calling for equal rights. When the National Assembly in Nanjing responded by setting guards on Assembly meetings, women disregarded the 'audience seating' they were meant to use and sat amongst the deputies, pulling on their clothes and shouting over them to prevent proceedings. News reports emerged that, led by Tang Qunying (1871–1937), women protestors smashed windows with their hands, cutting themselves. Tang had been inspired by her involvement in militant anarchist circles while in exile in Japan from 1904.[7] She was reported in Chinese newspapers as confronting male politicians, such as Nationalist Party founder Song Jiaoren, who had betrayed women. On entering the Nationalist Party conference in August 1912, she

> walked to Song Jiaoren's seat [and] quickly raised her hands, scratched his forehead, twisted his beard, and boxed Song's ears with her delicate hands. The sound was so loud that everyone could hear the echo.[8]

Chinese women's suffrage continued to be strongly demanded by petitions and lobbying, particularly during the 'New Culture Movement' of the 1920s, when the provinces of Hunan, Guangdong, Sichuan and Zhejiang gave women equal citizenship rights. Both the Nationalist Party and the Chinese Communist Party supported women's equality in abstract terms, but their rivalry prevented the granting of women's suffrage until the 1936 National Constitution. Women's equal citizenship was cemented by their participation in the wartime People's Political Council and was confirmed by the Communist Party after it defeated the Nationalist Party in 1949.

British and Chinese women's use of force was designed to gain press interest, as well as compel their governments to respond. Their actions were reported globally, though largely repudiated by other activist women. The Brazilian suffrage-feminist Bertha Lutz (1894–1976), for example, introduced the first Brazilian women's suffrage association in 1918 as

> not an association of 'suffragettes' who would break windows along the street, but rather of Brazilians who understand that a woman ought not to live parasitically based on her sex, [but should be] useful, educate herself and her children and become capable of performing those political responsibilities which the future cannot fail to allot her.[9]

This caution and distancing from militancy was common across many feminist and women's movement groups worldwide. The bold and sometimes violent actions of militant suffragists offered others a simple means of gaining the political capital of moderation, with non-militant groups stressing

Figure 7.2
Julieta Lanteri voting in Buenos Aires in 1911, the first woman in Latin America to do so

that their requests were simple justice or pragmatism. This did not mean that they lacked creativity and radical intent. The case of feminist physician Dr Julieta Lanteri Renshaw demonstrates extreme persistence despite decades of setbacks. Lanteri was an Italian-born migrant to Argentina and is thought to be the first woman in Latin America to vote. She exploited the vagueness of Argentine law and persuaded the electoral authorities to let her vote in 1911 in the Buenos Aires city council elections. In that same year, it became a requirement to perform military service before voting, an amendment which definitively and deliberately excluded women. Undeterred, Lanteri ran for public office between 1918 and 1930, and unsuccessfully applied to undertake military service in 1929. In 1930, a fascist-leaning military coup saw the suspension of parties, elections and the constitution; Argentine women did not gain the national suffrage until 1947. Lanteri herself was killed in suspicious circumstances in a road accident in 1932, when a car driven by a far-right paramilitant ran her down on a Buenos Aires street. Her non-violent militancy had elicited murderous tactics in return.

Militancy and Violence Reworked

Suffrage actions of chalking and chaining remained an inspiration to later generations of activists. Australian protestors Merle Thornton and Rosalie Bognor, for example, chained themselves to a public bar in Brisbane in 1965, protesting the segregation of Australian pubs and hotels into mixed-sex and men-only spaces. Their efforts to lobby for change had been fruitless, so they resorted to a more militant protest. This tradition was extended by Zelda D'Aprano, who

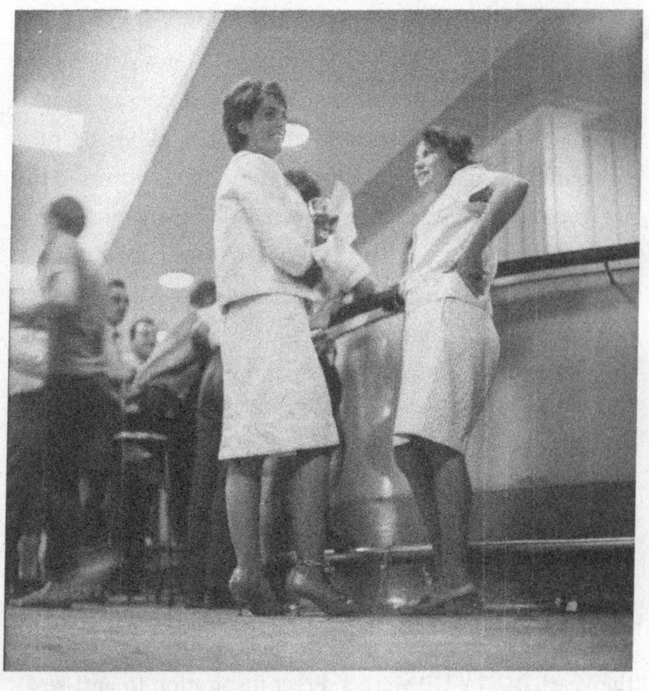

Figure 7.3
Rosalie Bognor and Merle Thornton protest women's exclusion from Australian public bars by chaining themselves to a bar rail, 1965

chained herself to the Melbourne Commonwealth Office in a protest over the gender pay gap in government employment. D'Aprano cited the British suffragettes as inspiration, but she had also been deeply involved in transnational anti-fascist organizing through the Italian-Australian movement Italia Libera.[10]

Australian activists continued to creatively contest sexism. The advertising graffiti collective BUGA-UP (Billboard Utilising Graffitists Against Unhealthy Promotions), active in the late 1970s and 80s, was a mixed-sex group of anonymous activists that targeted the sexism of the advertising industry. At risk of arrest and conviction, they targeted adverts that used women's bodies to sell (unrelated) products such as cars, jeans and electronic goods. The routine assumption of a male viewer was made clear by witty amendments – a Wrangler jeans advert that showed a man's crotch with the slogan 'For the Man who has Everything' was blazoned with 'Balls and Chained', plus the women's liberation symbol. A Tampax advert aimed at adolescent girls with the slogan 'Life would be much simpler if you didn't have to touch yourself internally' was awarded their 'Grand Bogey' prize of a golden spray can for 'the worst ad of the year'. BUGA-UP were a direct inspiration to anti-sexist men and feminist women in other countries, who also defaced and subverted adverts that demeaned women.

In the same time period, West Germany witnessed widespread debates about the uses of violence, rooted in the student and civil rights protest of 1968, the emergence of leftist terrorism in the 1970s, and an increasingly powerful women's movement. The 'speaking bitterness' techniques inspired by Maoist China had often also depicted violent retribution taken collectively by Chinese women against individual male abusers. Reports from China of women tying up and assaulting men were controversial amongst German feminists, as one recalled:

> At first, we were shocked by the reports of the beating of and spitting on the terrible, reactionary husbands. Our shock held a sense of guilt for the spontaneous desire to be able to use violence ourselves in the struggle . . .[11]

But the Maoist idea of '*fanshen*' – collective interventions that might include verbal and physical violence – became a powerful technique in German feminist circles in the late 1970s. Some feminist groups termed this 'counter-violence' – protests that might entail violence but were prompted by the systemic violence that patriarchal and capitalist structures inflicted on women. They rejected the association between feminism and the peace movement, and adopted a very different tone:

> We are sick of being reduced to these women's 'natural qualities,' that is, to impart peacefulness, the eternal mothers and social workers that make peace between irreconcilable contrasts; we are no 'peace women' because we cannot see peace occurring here or anywhere else on this world and because we cannot conjure up peace, but instead can only combat and destroy the causes of war.[12]

In a direct echo of earlier suffrage activists, West German students and feminists of the New Women's Movement (Neue Frauenbewegung) who supported violence were careful to reject violence directed against people. Instead, they opted for violence against property, such as the bombing of the Federal

Court of Justice in Karlsruhe in March 1975 to protest its unwillingness to grant abortion rights. The Rote Zora (Red Zora) group began to operate in 1977 and conducted a series of arson attacks in West Germany. The women involved were affiliated to a left-wing network called the Revolutionary Cells, though they had found interacting with leftist men frustrating. Whatever their politics, Red Zora women discovered, men found it hard to change their everyday treatment of women as sexual partners. Red Zora became an independent guerrilla group from 1984, relishing the chance to express themselves politically in ways not normally open to women:

> Personally, we found it tremendously liberating to break with the feminine peaceableness that was imposed on us and to take a conscious decision for violent means in our politics.[13]

Red Zora's early attacks had been largely on sex shops but they went on to adopt a global perspective in the 1980s, leading to the bombing of the Philippines consulate to protest its complicity with sex tourism. The high-profile events of the UN 'decade for women' (1976–86), and the global conferences that had taken place in Mexico City, Copenhagen and Nairobi, had raised the profile of women's lives and experiences of discrimination in the global South.

Red Zora's most sustained action was prompted by a letter to the German women's movement from workers at a clothing factory in South Korea, who worked for the German fashion firm Adler. Facing poor working conditions, the women workers had asked for 'sisterly help'. After more conventional protests to the company had failed, Red Zora carried out a string of bombings at Adler shops. They used slow-burning devices that were designed to set off sprinkler systems and destroy the stock, avoiding any threat to human life. The resulting economic costs were an important part of the ultimately successful campaign to force change on Adler's South Korean factory floor.

Strikes

The activists of Red Zora might have imagined that South Koreans were exploited 'third world' sisters who needed the intervention of the more liberated women of Germany. 'Third worldism' could be an important platform for the black, Latinx and Asian women's movements, as Kumari Jayawardena's 1986 book, *Feminism and Nationalism in the Third World*, suggested. But wielded by white women activists, it could also serve to clump together women of the poorer countries of the global South and present them as victims. This both obscured issues of race amongst women of the global North and encouraged a kind of worthy paternalism towards 'third world women'. But the South Korean appeal for help came from a country with well-established traditions of female worker protest. Women had been brought into the industrial workforce by South Korean leader Park Chung Hee, aiming to boost export industries after his seizure of power by military coup in 1961. Facing deeply exploitative working conditions, women workers organized through the South Korean trade unions, aided by the election of female union leaders Chu Kilcha and Yi Yŏngsuk in the 1970s. Male workers were not always supportive of such leadership. The election of Yi Yŏngsuk, for example, led to male workers in one factory locking female co-workers in their dormitory, so that the election could be re-run without women's votes. Female workers, incensed, broke out of the dormitory and staged a sit-in on the factory floor. When riot police broke into their factory, women took off their work clothes, believing semi-nakedness would deter and embarrass the police. Many were beaten and arrested. Despite this setback, the larger picture is one of militant female workers, such as those at YH Trading who not only contested their own conditions but in 1979 led to a political revolution that brought down the autocratic rule of President Park Chung Hee.[14]

Strikes proved a powerful weapon for women workers, often undertaken through the labour movement. Direct action via boycotts, sit-ins and strikes had been the bread and butter of what Dorothy Cobble has termed 'the other women's movement' – that of the labour activists such as Domitila Barrios de Chungara, Maida Springer Kemp and Pauline Newman for whom strikes were a routine tactic.[15] Some of these actions were taken in support of workplace organizing by male workers. The wives of miners were important and highly visible figures in strikes such as that undertaken against the Empire Zinc Company in 1950–52 in New Mexico. The Mexican-American miners were banned from picketing their workplace, but their place was taken by the Ladies Auxiliary, made up of miners' wives. Similar actions were taken by miners' wives in the British miners' strike of 1984–5, which saw women occupy pits, picket and fundraise across the country. Male workers could be deeply ambivalent about such actions, and their wives sometimes found unexpected opportunities for greater social confidence, employment and redistribution of housework. But the overall commitment was to shared struggles across both sexes for social justice and community survival.

Strikes, however, could also be redeployed in more intimate contexts. Nelly Roussel (1878–1922), a French mother of three, was passionately opposed to women's unwilling reproduction of 'cannon fodder' for military and economic purposes. She supported birth control for all women, a right not gained in France until the Pill was legalized in 1967. Writing in the early twentieth century, Roussel declared that 'Feminism should proclaim above all else, "liberty for motherhood," the first, the most sacred, and nevertheless . . . the least discussed and least respected of liberties.'[16] In 1904, she proposed a birth strike, in protest at the state's pro-natalist policies. Roussel's radical claims were combined with strategic uses of dedications in her books, photographs and sculptures, which presented her as primarily a mother. Despite spending long periods away from her children, she was widely celebrated as a devoted mother, and perhaps as a result, she escaped the police harassment and arrest that other birth-control activists faced in France.[17] Roussel also demanded women's rights to sexual pleasure, and to pain relief during childbirth. But despite her charisma and her high profile in the media, she had few resources to organize a collective response, and the idea of a birth strike remained just an oratorical claim rather than a realistic tactic.

Some activists, however, found a strike perfectly realizable, even if it encompassed the entire public sphere. On 24 October 1975, Icelandic feminists took the unusual step of designating the day a national 'day off' for women, in recognition of their hard work in homes and workplaces, and their low pay compared to men. An extraordinarily high number, estimated to be 90 per cent, of Icelandic women took up this 'strike' invitation. Their refusal to teach, print newspapers, service airlines and gut fish led to an almost total shutdown of Icelandic schools, industry and commerce. If fathers wanted to work, they had to take their children with them. The following year, the Icelandic parliament passed equal rights legislation, and five years later the first woman was elected Iceland's president. The protest has been repeated every ten years and was recently the inspiration for Polish activists who successfully protested against the withdrawal of Poland's already very limited abortion rights in 2016.

The Icelandic protest had in turn been inspired by the much smaller strike called by American women on 26 August 1970, the fiftieth anniversary of American women's enfranchisement in 1920. The action had been proposed by Betty Friedan, the president of the National Organization for Women (NOW), and called on women to take whatever action made sense in their lives. One organizer fantasized:

> Women who work in offices are going to over-ink their machines . . . Secretaries are going to put all their letters into the wrong envelopes. Waitresses will put salt into sugar bowls. Wives are going to feed their husbands Swanson's Frozen Mexican Dinners and watch their old men get Montezuma's Revenge. Some wives aren't going to feed their husbands anything.[18]

She proposed a motto for the day: 'Don't Iron While the Strike is Hot!'

In Washington DC, the range of groups coordinating the event reveals the complex coalition of interests that made up the 'women's movement' at that historical moment. NOW members joined women from the National Welfare Rights Organization, the Young Socialist Alliance, the DC Women's Liberation Movement (DCWLM), Federally Employed Women and the Alliance of Union Women. Their commitments ranged widely, from stopping the Vietnam War to ending sexism in the union movement, addressing black and working-class women's poverty and ending patriarchy. Some sought a constitutional amendment, the Equal Rights Amendment (ERA). Others, such as the DCWLM, rejected the ERA as a white, middle-class, reformist goal that would do little to change the status quo. This resonated with the Washington DC members of the National Welfare Rights Organization (NWRO), largely low-income African American women. Their primary concern was poverty, and they lobbied and struck for better housing, cheaper transport and better health care. These 'welfare activists' were also sceptical about paid work as a form of liberation. Having experienced low-paid employment under poor conditions, as well as the compulsion to work – without reference to the needs of children – built into the welfare system, activists such as Etta Horn were always careful to distinguish their activism from women's liberation calls for access to employment. Horn, a former domestic worker, a mother of seven and an active church member, was involved in protests over police racism and a boycott of department stores that refused to offer credit to welfare recipients. The NWRO did not term its actions feminist, but as historian Anne Valk has argued, they developed an analysis of motherhood as uniquely exploited and unpaid under systemic forms of 'male supremacy'. The disproportionate numbers of women amongst welfare recipients and their talk of 'male supremacy' gave this work a strong affinity with feminist campaigning.[19]

The strike in 1970 inspired varied tactics across the United States. The Federally Employed Women were prohibited by law from striking and called for members to 'fight with wits – not bricks'. The Chicago Women's Liberation Union paid an impromptu visit to a meatpacking workplace where a woman had been sacked for bringing her child to work, and persuaded managers to reinstate her. In Washington, NOW placed a consumer boycott at the heart of their action. In protest at sexist advertising, they specified *Cosmopolitan* magazine, a brand of cigarettes, a dishwashing liquid and a 'feminine hygiene' spray as targets. The DCWLM marched to the local women's prison and announced that 'male supremacy incarcerated all women.' They threw rocks at the prison windows, shouted to the women inside, and later attempted to raise bail money to free them. Nonetheless, their engagement with imprisoned women was fairly superficial and efforts to sponsor bail or create further links to women in the criminal justice system were sparse. Coalition building could seem costly; the DCWLM concluded that working with NOW represented 'energy wasted in working with groups with different priorities'. Other US women's groups disliked the involvement of men in the strike. The Chicago Women's Liberation Union reflected that, in its rallies, 'the men seemed to dominate much of the crowd and had an inordinate impact. Once again an event was not fully ours and we were a show for the men.'[20]

Pickets

Another tactic deployed from the labour movement was the picket, traditionally used to enforce workplace strikes but, like the strike, capable of being reworked to sites of women's subordination. In 1971, for example, a group of around forty protestors picketed a 'Hot Pants Contest' at a tavern in Seattle, arguing that it objectified women; in the same year, a group of Irish women were frustrated that the Seanad (Parliament) would not give time for a bill on women's access to contraception. They used prams to picket the parliament building, Leinster House, and changed the lyrics of the civil rights anthem 'We Shall Not Be Moved' to sing 'We shall not conceive.' Some women broke into the building by climbing through a window into the men's toilets, which they then occupied. Their frustration at the parliamentary impasse on contraception led to a foundational moment in the Irish Women's Liberation Movement on 22 May 1971. A group of women invited television crews to follow them as they travelled to Belfast to break the ban on contraception in the Republic of Ireland. They bought condoms and spermicide jelly, but their plans to buy the contraceptive pill were foiled. Though it had been legal in Great Britain since 1962, the Pill could only be issued on prescription. Instead, they bought hundreds of packets of aspirin, which they suspected customs officials would not be able to distinguish from contraceptives. On their arrival by train back in Dublin, the protestors declared their actions to customs officials, waved the condoms and swallowed some of the aspirins. Surrounded by supporters chanting 'let them through', officials did not dare arrest them. Their actions of civil disobedience gained extensive publicity; but change was still slow. Despite a ruling in 1973 by the Irish Supreme Court that contraception was a 'marital right', the government were still unwilling to make provision, citing the opposition of the Catholic Church. Legislation in 1980 eventually gave limited access to contraception but only to married couples. A slow process of amendments over the subsequent fifteen years gradually expanded who could access birth control. Abortion in the Irish Republic was decriminalized in a historic referendum in 2018, followed belatedly by Northern Ireland in 2019.

Japanese and Korean women used pickets to protest the commercial sex trade, focusing particularly on its 'tourism' dimension. Japan and its former colonial territory, Korea, had a long-standing system of 'red light' or 'pleasure districts'. Brothels could be legally licensed, and systems of indentured labour sometimes governed the lives of sex workers. Korean women termed '*kisaeng*', for example, had an established role as tolerated providers of sexual entertainment for elite men. After larger numbers of Japanese settlers came to Korea in the later nineteenth century, prostitution thrived in Korean ports. When Japan declared Korea its protectorate from 1905, the authorities introduced a more formal system of regulated sex tourism. This system helped pave the way to the sexual enslavement of many Korean and Chinese women in 'comfort stations' during Japan's military conflicts between 1937 and 1945. Forced to provide sex for Japanese troops, 'comfort women' were coerced into brothels; around three-quarters died or were killed during their incarceration. Japan's defeat and the establishment of the two Koreas as independent nations from 1948 did not prevent the subsequent establishment of routine sex-tourism from Japan to South Korea. Corporate sponsorship and men-only package tours grew rapidly in the 1970s. Indeed, the Second World War 'comfort women' went unrecognized as a major atrocity until the late twentieth century. Organized by the Korean Council for the Women Drafted for Military Sexual Slavery by Japan, weekly demonstrations by women at the Japanese Embassy in Seoul from 1992 to 1994 finally forced a process of apologies and compensation.[21]

Like many men from the United States and Europe, sex tourists from Japan travelled to South Korea as well as the Philippines in the 1970s. The South Korean government actively supported sex tourism as a means of bringing foreign revenue into the country and cooperated with Japanese companies to profit from women's sexual labour. The rise of a more assertive women's movement began to challenge this system. Koreans picketed Seoul's Gimpo Airport to protest the arrival of Japanese men, and, in 1974, Japanese women picketed men's departure from Tokyo's Haneda Airport.[22] Protestors were particularly incensed by the organized nature of Japanese sex-tourism packages. Japanese firms supplied meals and hotels and so monopolized the profits, leaving Korean sex workers very poorly paid.

When greater regulation was eventually brought to this sector and threatened its profitability, many women from South Korea and other destinations were brought to Japan to work in bars and massage parlours, often without access to their passports or funds to leave exploitative employment. As a result, protests at airports were supplemented by Japanese women setting up shelters to house migrant women fleeing sexual and labour exploitation.

The growth of 'sex shops' in the later twentieth century, selling pornography and sex toys, and the growth of sexually explicit content more generally in the media, were a prompt to picketing for many women's liberation groups. In 1981, the San Francisco Women Against Violence in Pornography and Media newsletter offered its readers a 'how-to guide', titled 'Organizing an Anti-Porn Picket', envisaged as a tactic that might be used at cinemas, television studios and sex shops. They stressed the need to involve the media, to use creative slogans, and to use chanting and music to emphasize active resistance. The civil rights songs 'We Shall Overcome,' 'Fight Back' and 'We Shall Not Be Moved' were listed as suitable.

In London, women on a 'Reclaim the Night' march in 1978 picketed then invaded a sex shop and plastered pornographic magazines with protest stickers; sixteen women were arrested. They had explicitly referenced the window-smashing suffragettes as inspiration.[23] Other tactics of graffitiing and fire-bombing sex shops were to follow. 'Reclaim the Night' was the slogan under which marches through urban spaces to protest male violence against women became known in the 1970s. The first such march recorded in feminist media took place in Brussels in March 1976, and quickly spread to Rome, Berlin, and then to a synchronized series of marches across West Germany on 30 April 1977. The marches were prompted by the rapes and harassment routinely suffered by women on city streets, particularly in red light areas. They featured women holding flaming torches and using musical instruments and improvised percussion to invade hostile spaces by sound and light. They were held in Leeds, London and seven other British cities later in 1977, with the actions in Leeds being particularly oriented to the 'Yorkshire Ripper' murders of women committed by Peter Sutcliffe between 1975 and 1980. The Yorkshire police had told women in Leeds to stay at home at night for safety, and this prompted an angry feminist response: why should women confine themselves in response to male violence? Feminists proposed instead that men should be subject to a curfew. The Leeds Revolutionary Feminist group fly-posted fake police posters that addressed 'all men in West Yorkshire', asking that

> out of consideration for the safety of women, please ensure you are indoors by 8pm each evening, so that women can go about their business without the fear you may provoke.

'Reclaim the Night' marches are still common today, and their defiant reclaiming of space was echoed in the global 'SlutWalk' movement that originated in 2011 in protest at advice from police in Toronto that women should avoid dressing like 'sluts' to evade sexual assault. Both formats were controversial in relation to sex workers, who resented the noisy disruption of their working environments and for whom the appropriation of 'slut' was not always welcome. It was possible to find common ground in the struggle against male violence, but this was not always sensitively done. Sex workers were regarded as victims or colluders by many in the women's liberation movement, and judgemental models of 'rescue' that had been prevalent in the nineteenth century were still visible in the late twentieth. This was a source of enormous tension within the women's movement, which was slow to listen to the perspectives of women and non-binary individuals who found themselves selling sex. Any attempt to 'reclaim' space or offensive categories such as 'slut' ran the risk of creating new boundaries of access and belonging.

Bodies and Nakedness

Inspired by protests at the 1968 Miss America contest in Atlantic City, 'bra burner' has become a shorthand name for a feminist. Yet despite its historical notoriety, no bras were burned on this occasion. Though feminists in the 1970s did encourage women to go braless, bra-burning was an image deployed mostly by anti-feminists, indicating the dangerous, subversive nature of women's bodies when uncontrolled by clothing, by men and by the state. Despite this stereotyping, breasts and women's bodies more generally have been prominent sites of feminist protest.

In 2008, a group of Ukrainian feminists calling themselves FEMEN (ФЕМЕН) decided to campaign against the sex trafficking of women in Europe and former Soviet-bloc countries such as Ukraine and Moldova. Their previous efforts to gain publicity had attracted little attention. But by removing their tops and blazoning slogans on their bare torsos, they managed to generate global press coverage. Spontaneous and provocative, they aimed to subvert the media's obsession with women's breasts and reconnect feminism with popular audiences. A protest at the attempts to restrict abortion rights in Ukraine saw activists' chests painted with the slogan 'My body is my business'. FEMEN subversively claimed reproductive autonomy *and* acknowledged, tongue in cheek, the entrepreneurial uses women make of their bodies. For the individuals involved, FEMEN protests have considerable costs; FEMEN activists were forced to leave

Ukraine in 2013 and claimed asylum in France after receiving death threats.

FEMEN's activists regarded their feminism as different from the feminism they considered either 'historical' or 'American', which focused on equal rights. Instead, they used terms such as 'ultra feminism' or 'neo-feminist' to capture their sense of feminine distinctiveness. One member, Anna Hutsol, commented:

> feminism should stop being marginal. It has to be popular. It must be cool and fun. That's why I'm FEMEN. I want feminism to be popular and light, ever so light.[24]

This stance draws on well-established traditions of seeing feminism as a distorting import of American, colonial or Western origin. This is interwoven with another well-worn narrative of rejection of the goals of past generations of feminists, rebranding it as 'new'.

Like South Korea in the 1970s, post-Soviet Ukraine in the 1990s and 2000s had become a sex-tourism destination. FEMEN's topless protests highlighted the sexual exploitation of women this involved. Was this a brilliant publicity stunt, or a capitulation to the male gaze? Certainly, portraits of their breasts were sometimes recirculated for men's titillation in the media. Their bodies were frequently slim, young and conformed to patriarchal beauty standards. FEMEN's members aimed to subvert men's exploitation of women's bodies, but they did not showcase any fat, ageing or non-normative bodies.

Subsequent FEMEN protests were criticized for adopting an anti-religious stance which became notorious for its focus on Islam. In 2013, FEMEN organized a 'topless jihad' in five European cities, to support Muslim women who via social media, had also adopted the technique of topless or nude protests. Despite claims for its 'newness', critics termed FEMEN Islamophobic or neo-colonial, dangerously echoing past efforts by Euro-Americans to 'save brown women from brown men', as postcolonial scholar Gayatri Spivak famously argued.[25]

The topless or nude protest was not however a FEMEN invention and has a much longer history, as the actions of South Korean workers in the 1970s and Nigerian market traders in the 1920s suggest. The problematic Islamophobic and racialized aspects of FEMEN's use of women's bodies in protest obscures the ways in which African and African American women – free and enslaved – have also displayed their bodies as acts of protest. Such protests took on a particular meaning in the United States, where African American women have been historically treated as sexually available. Black women's bodies, whether labouring or eroticized, have been put on display, ridiculed and exploited. To take to the platform or pulpit, as black orators such as Frances Harper, Ida B. Wells and Maria Stewart did in the nineteenth and early twentieth centuries, was to court visibility in a way that was particularly costly for black women. Former slave and abolitionist Sojourner Truth famously chose to display her breasts to a white audience in Indiana in 1858 when they claimed she was not a woman. She reminded her audience that her breasts had suckled white babies, and that slavery had separated her from her own children. Finally, she invited audience members also to suckle. This brilliant, subversive gesture shamed her audience, and epitomizes Truth's refusal to be silenced by sceptics. However, the political uses of black women's bodies have not been easy to negotiate, and protests that involve nakedness are always undertaken in environments where race, faith and class will shape the meanings of women's bodies.[26]

Despite the global diversity of feminism, threads of common inspiration, borrowing and shared techniques are visible within the means by which feminists have contested exclusion, claimed their spaces and made their voices heard. The catalysts have been disruptive moments of economic and demographic change, war or regime change. Activists have drawn on their experiences of political organizing within other campaigns – for democracy or the abolition of slavery, for civil rights or religious change, seeking national liberation or better pay. All too often, these other struggles have been disappointing for women, who have found themselves marginalized and not taken seriously. They have turned in frustration to feminist actions, though many have maintained prior commitments to the causes of labour, nation or faith. They have sometimes been able to meld different causes; as we have seen, anarchist disruption and trade union collective actions were particularly amenable to feminist adaptation.

The meaning of an action is variable, according to its setting and its personal significance. 'Militancy', if it means anything in this enormously diverse terrain, is best understood as relating not to the degree of force used but to the personal costs of commitment and courage entailed. Baring a breast or offering a flower can be imbued with militancy in the appropriate context. Most feminist activism has been designed to celebrate life; yet the deaths of dogged, unstoppable campaigners such as Julieta Lanteri, Funmilayo Ransome-Kuti and others at the hands of paramilitaries, police and soldiers shows how it has been deeply risky for those involved.

CHAPTER 8

Songs

What is it like to hear feminism?[1] Historical distance and the intangible nature of sound mean that there are limits to the aural archive. But by reading historical documents against the grain, it is possible to 'hear feminism' even at the distance of several centuries. The traces of its rich soundtrack of oratory, songs, chants and keening gives us a final entry point into understanding the useable past of feminisms. In 1982, a set of lyrics was penned by protestor and lesbian revolutionary Gillian Booth, with the help of other women at Greenham Common. It asked in stark terms:

Which side are you on
which side are you on
are you on the other side from me
which side are you on?

Are you on the side that don't like life
are you on the side of racial strife
are you on the side that beats your wife
which side are you on?

Are you on the side who loves to hunt
are you on the side of the National Front

are you on the side who calls me cunt
which side are you on?

Linking the powerful, emotive issues of racism, domestic violence, foxhunting and fascism, this feminist song was very much of its historical moment and British location. 'Which Side Are You On?' has a longer history, however, which makes visible a complex musical and political heritage. It was originally written by American trade unionist Florence Reece (1900–1986) in 1931, inspired by her experiences of her striking male relatives – coal miners in Harlan County, Kentucky. Reece's husband, Sam, was a union organizer. They had suffered raids on their home, witnessed by their seven children. Far from the women-only activism of Greenham Common, Reece sought solidarity with men, and took a male persona in her lyrics:

My daddy was a miner,
And I'm a miner's son,
He'll be with you fellow workers
Until this battle's won.

The chorus of 'Which Side Are You On?' addressed men, calling for their affiliation to the union:

Which side are you on boys?
Which side are you on?

Reece appealed to the ideals of solidarity and endurance associated with 'being a man':

Oh workers can you stand it?
Oh tell me how you can?

Will you be a lousy scab
Or will you be a man?

Like many working-class women seeking social justice through collective action, Florence Reece stressed the shared interests of male and female workers. Her song was used across a range of labour struggles, became a civil rights song in the 1960s, and was reused for other miners' strikes around the world. It gives us a sense of the connections and rich musical heritage of feminist, labour and anti-fascist movements as they shared and rewrote songs across struggles and national borders.

Feminist campaigners have long recognized the power of song to foster solidarity and subvert the status quo. From Ethel Smyth's suffrage anthem 'The March of the Women' (1910), to Russian punks Pussy Riot's 'Kill the Sexist' a century later, songs and music have been vehicles for feminist dissent. Songs have sometimes been simple chants such as *Un Violador en tu Camino* (*A Rapist in your Path*), a chant and dance written by Chilean feminist collective Las Tesis in 2019 and performed globally. Other feminist songs have brought with them the infrastructure of bands, recording studios and distribution networks. In most histories, however, feminist movements have typically been presented through texts and speeches, and it can be hard to think beyond this frame, to 'hear' feminism as a creative practice. Women's exclusion from many sorts of cultural production has been a profound ingredient of their oppression. The arts are vehicles for cultural power and voice, and women's marginalization in the past two centuries from composing and performing music, writing and directing films, plays, radio and television, making artworks and publishing books, has left their lives, truths and visions muted. It has also left them poorer, lacking access to professional roles in music and the arts.

Nonetheless, there *are* traces of how women have made culture, explored here through music. The archives of feminist activism have tantalizing glimpses of the music that accompanied women and men in their struggles. The Swedish writer Ellen Key, for example, described how, in the early twentieth century,

> At a Scandinavian meeting on the woman's question, a cantata was sung which proclaimed that the human race under the supremacy of man had stumbled in darkness and crime. But the race was now to be newly born from the soul of woman, the sunrise would scatter the darkness of night, and the advent of the Messiah was certain.[2]

Key's feminism was a visionary religious affair. Music captured its creative impetus and ability to tap into deep spiritual and emotional sources of mobilization. Unfortunately, however, we still know nothing about what the cantata sounded like.

'Hearing feminism' does not only have to capture musical performance; the feminist archive can also convey other kinds of sound qualities. A crucial moment in Iranian feminist history, for example, was captured by the American feminist Kate Millett, who tape-recorded her thoughts throughout her thirteen-day visit to the country during the 1979 Iranian revolution. Accidentally, she also recorded in the background the animated conversations and shouted slogans of Iranian activist women, who supported the insurrection against the

American-backed dictator Reza Shah Pahlavi, and wanted to ensure women's rights were part of the new Islamic Republic. They encountered increasing opposition from the revolutionary leader Ayatollah Khomeini, but the tapes that allow their activism to be heard reveal the other possible directions the revolution might have taken. Islamic and secular feminists envisaged a 'free society' and a 'free life'. As scholar Negar Mottahedeh has argued, Kate Millett did not always understand their priorities, but her presence there created a feminist soundscape of extraordinary intensity.[3]

Listening to earlier feminisms, prior to the easy availability of recording equipment, can be harder. Descriptions in words sometimes are all we have. The celebrated French orator for birth control Nelly Roussel (1878–1922), for example, was noted for her musical voice of 'pure crystal whose pathetic vibrations filled huge rooms'.[4] Roussel was famed for her ability to use her voice to connect emotionally with her audiences, despite the controversial nature of her topic. But it was more typical that women activists found it hard to get their voices heard. Anna Julia Cooper, for example, was born into slavery in 1858, and went on to live a life of extraordinary achievement and transnational mobility. She studied at Oberlin College and the Sorbonne in Paris and was an active speaker in the black civil rights and women's movements. Her book, *A Voice from the South*, published in 1892, was structured musically. The first part was called *Soprano Obligato* and discussed womanhood. The second part, *Tutti Ad Libitum*, reflected on race in American culture; Cooper referred to the voice of the Negro as 'one muffled strain' or 'a jarring cadenza' in the American South. But she was

Figure 8.1
Anna Julia Cooper, the fourth African American woman to receive a doctorate, and a lifelong campaigner for civil rights and education

even more aware of the absence of black women's voices, described as striking a 'mute and voiceless note'.[5] Cooper invited her readers to think in musical terms about who could speak, and to note the silences.

Suffrage Music

The creative protests associated with the suffrage campaigners are well known for their use of drama, colour and costume. Their music has been less closely examined, perhaps because its uses were often ephemeral and unlikely to be captured in archives. From adapted Chartist songs of the nineteenth century to specially commissioned compositions of the twentieth, songs were inspirational within the movement and published in its numerous songbooks. It is unsurprising that the British suffrage movement was oriented to music, given the environment of the radical choirs, brass bands and orchestras of the time. Movements such as the Clarion socialists and the temperance campaigners used music very widely to galvanize their followers. Edward Carpenter's socialist hymn 'England Arise' was sung at meetings and fairs, though the socialist movement also produced anti-feminist ditties, such as the reworked children's nursery rhyme published in the *Manchester Monthly Herald* in April 1898:

> Rock-a-bye, baby, for father is near,
> Mother is biking, she never is here!
> Out in the park she's scorching all day
> Or at some meeting is talking away!
> She's the king-pin at the women's rights show,
> Teaching poor husbands the way they should go!

It was composer Ethel Smyth (1858–1944) who produced music for the set-piece galas and marches of the WSPU. Despite her father's opposition, Smyth had been determined to study music, and she composed a wide variety of works, including an opera, *Der Wald*, which was staged at the Metropolitan Opera in New York in 1903. Until the 2016 season, it remained the only female-composed opera performed in that venue.

Ethel Smyth had joined the WSPU in 1910 and was jailed in Holloway Prison for two months in 1912 after breaking windows. She was memorably glimpsed conducting WSPU prisoners from her prison window, using a toothbrush, as other prisoners sang in the courtyard below. They were singing Smyth's most famous contribution to the women's movement, 'The March of the Women'. Composed as a rousing, stirring march, it was later given words by writer Cicely Hamilton. *Votes for Women* described it as 'the fiery spirit of revolution united with religious solemnity . . . It is at once a hymn and a call to battle.' Smyth described a 1911 performance in the Albert Hall, a prestigious central London setting where suffragette oratory and fund-raising was staged: 'A Suffragette choir had been sternly drilled . . . We had the organ, and I think a cornet to blast forth the tune.'

Smyth's public status as a celebrated composer was just as useful to the WSPU as her musical contributions, and they placed her centre stage in the spectacle of women's achievements that accompanied their claims to citizenship. Smyth recalled, 'it was wonderful processing up the centre aisle of the Albert Hall in Mus. Doc. robes at Mrs Pankhurst's side,

Figure 8.2
Composer Ethel Smyth speaking at a WSPU meeting, the London Pavilion, 1912

and being presented with a beautiful baton, encircled by a golden collar.'[6]

Smyth's promising career began to be curtailed by encroaching deafness in 1913, but even before this, she had often been pigeon-holed as a 'lady composer'. A review of *Der Wald* in the British *Daily Mail* noted patronizingly, 'The charm and quaintness of it will appeal more than its attempt to mirror intense human emotion and to this extent it is feminine, according to all tradition.' This kind of rhetoric was not new. 'Ladies' orchestras' made up of white women had begun touring in Europe and America in the 1870s, but despite their high musical standards they tended to be attractive to audiences as a visual curiosity rather than as musical performers. One review in the *New York Times* of the Viennese Ladies' Orchestra in 1874 patronizingly described 'the Viennese ladies, with their uniformity of pretty costumes and (may it be added) their uniformity of pretty faces.'[7] Female performers struggled to be treated as professionals. They had relatively little access to concert halls, and instead played in vaudeville and theatre orchestras, as well as parks, fairs and parties.

For women orchestral players, paid work was always precarious. After the First World War, for example, the Hallé Orchestra in Manchester had sacked all the women musicians they had used during the war. This was not only to make way for returning servicemen, who were widely believed to have the first claim on any employment. The musical directors also argued that women could not be accommodated on tours, and that their presence challenged the 'unity of style' of the orchestra. Smyth, a campaigning member of the

Society of Women Musicians, recognized that this kind of prejudice did not simply prevent women earning their living but also made careers in composition virtually impossible since orchestral playing was an essential training. She was scathing about the world of classical music:

> Bullying and cowardice, meanness and jealousy, are not pretty qualities, and I wonder if men have a notion with what contempt women view these attempts to prevent them from earning their livelihood . . . [8]

Music was, for Smyth, as much about women's access to employment as it was a vehicle for protest and solidarity.

Gospel, Blues and Racial Exclusion

In addition to segregation of gender, racial segregation was widely practised in American musical venues. Black female musicians were even less likely than their white counterparts to gain employment. Racial segregation also limited access to music for audiences of African and Asian Americans. This issue became a flashpoint for the performance of feminist music. In 1925, the International Council of Women (ICW), an international network founded in 1888, met in Washington DC. Their programme included an 'All-American Musical Festival', intended to showcase national culture to the international audience. The ICW, however, had always tried to avoid radicalism and controversy. The festival's organizers caved in to local demands for racially segregated seating in the Memorial Continental Hall. Incensed, the prominent African American orator Hallie Quinn Brown called for a boycott by performers. Brown (*c.* 1845–1949), a musician and a member of the National Association of Colored Women, had represented the United States at the 1899 ICW in London. Born to formerly enslaved parents, she was prominent in teaching, suffrage and anti-lynching activism as well as on the international lecture-circuit where she performed songs from the African American spiritual tradition. Brown angrily denounced the ICW's lack of principle: 'this is a gathering of women of the world here and color finds no place in it.' After her appeal, two hundred musicians boycotted the ICW festival.

Hallie Quinn Brown drew her musical inspiration from gospel, a realm to which African American women had easy access. Performing and listening to music in Christian settings of churches, missionary meetings and revival camps was a means of religious inspiration and sometimes authority and power for women who could rarely progress up the hierarchies of their churches. Hymn singing was not often done under the name of feminism. Yet it was nonetheless a source of power, as witnessed in the life of Amanda Berry Smith (1837–1915), born into slavery in Maryland, but still able to live a life of transnational influence through speaking and missionary tours in Britain, India and Liberia. Smith was known for her strong singing voice, which became central to her ministry within the African Methodist Episcopal Church. Decades of labour as a domestic servant and laundress gave way to Smith's association with Methodist missions and the Women's Christian Temperance Union, eventually bringing her to Liberia in 1882 for an eight-year mission. Smith's autobiography describes her singing on trains and carts, on tree stumps, in tents and churches. In Britain, she was patronizingly advertised to audiences as a gospel singer and 'converted slave girl'. Summing up her faith, Smith's autobiography cited a hymn:

> The peace of Christ keeps fresh my heart,
> A fountain ever springing;
> All things are mine since I am His,
> How can I keep from singing?[9]

Smith's ministry was oriented to the love of Jesus and trust in God and did not overtly take up feminist issues. Nonetheless, historian Patricia Schechter notes her refusal to be excluded on account of her sex from any gathering, and her scepticism about descriptions of Liberia as a place where men could 'be men'. Smith never sought ordination, though she coyly noted the astonishment of a large Methodist conference at her singing, 'especially as the question of ordination of women never was mooted in the Conference. But how they have advanced since then.' She was wary of men's propensity to seek wives who would advance their careers and labour in their homes. Widowed twice, and burying four out of her five children before they reached adulthood, Smith was well aware of the costs of marriage and motherhood and deliberately preserved her personal autonomy in her spiritual and temperance work.

Smith's musical horizons were narrow – she relied on a limited repertoire of well-known gospel hymns and was not impressed by the musical traditions of countries she visited. On a visit to Burma in 1881, she noted,

> I heard a great sound of music, such as they have there; I can't describe it; it couldn't be described by music that we

> hear here; tin-pans and tambourines, and something like the noise that a stove pipe, or something of that kind would make. Oh, it was a jingle.

Despite these prejudices, her singing created intimate, sympathetic bonds with congregations across the world. It gave her power within her church, facilitated her transnational mobility and allowed her to self-identify as a woman who 'generally carried out what I undertook'.[10]

The Music Industry and 'Women's Culture'

Amanda Berry Smith's famed singing voice was not recorded and we must try to hear it through her letters and contemporary descriptions. She died in 1915, at a moment when poor-quality recordings on wax or celluloid cylinders were being displaced by the new system of discs made of shellac or vinyl. This allowed for the rapid development of mass-produced gramophones and, with them, record companies and celebrity artists. As music became increasingly commercialized and marketed, the music industry's tendency to appropriate women's creative energies, to control their artistic choices and to sexually objectify their presentation to audiences became an area of feminist concern. In the booming world of popular music after the Second World War, women musicians were routinely paid less than men, and were judged by their appearance. As musicologist Jacqueline Warwick has argued, the American 'girl groups' of this period were 'grotesquely twisted' in terms of posture, weight, dance moves and sexuality. She focuses on the commercially successful all-female group The Crystals, whose producer Phil Spector insisted, against their preferences, that they record in 1963 the song 'He Hit Me (And It Felt Like A Kiss)'. It included disturbing lyrics that implied that women might welcome intimate-partner violence because men's jealousy proved the depth of their love.

The band 'absolutely hated' the song, which, unlike their usual upbeat doo-wop sound, was dirge-like. Wide condemnation of its lyrics forced its eventual withdrawal from circulation, though the song remained on their 1963 album, *He's A Rebel*.[11] This incident reflects the wider culture of the American-dominated music industry, where mostly male executives and powerful companies profited from songs that glorified heterosexual romance and patriarchal authority. In 1976, the American feminist journal *Quest* ran a feature on music that noted

> In its lust for profits, [the music industry] manipulates us to feel we should buy whatever it markets. Instead of recording music that is as varied as the individuals or cultures who create it, commercial music offers us a limited selection of items that have been programmed to sell.

The authors were optimistic about the prospect of women making 'meaningful statements about women's feelings through and around music' and encouraged politically active women to support feminist and lesbian performers so that 'most importantly, we can listen to what we hear'.[12]

Women's liberationists offered training workshops for women, so that they could join or replace the predominantly male sound engineers. They founded their own record labels, such as the commercially successful collective Olivia Records, established in Washington DC in 1973 and active for twenty years in producing predominantly lesbian-identified music. They may have appreciated the irony that their first single, 'Lady', performed by collective member Meg Christian, was written by the same songwriting team (Carole King and Gerry Goffin) that had authored 'He Hit Me (And It Felt Like A Kiss)'. Olivia's later output, however, sponsored the creative autonomy of lesbian and feminist musicians, and inspired the creation of numerous further labels, bands and festivals. Music, often produced on shoestring budgets, became key to efforts to create alternative women's (or wimmins'/womyns') culture across the United States. Numerous feminist choirs flourished in the 1970s, including the Anna Crusis Women's Choir, the Bread and Roses Feminist Singers and the Philadelphia Feminist Choir.

The black women's movement in the United States was central to this exploration of 'women's culture' in dance, song and art. The Combahee River Collective sponsored a tour titled 'The Varied Voices of Black Women' in 1978, to celebrate black lesbian identity and explore the race and class dimensions of 'women's music'.[13] African American performers such as blues singer Elizabeth Cotten (1893–1987), folk-pop artist Tracy Chapman and the all-women band Sweet Honey in the Rock were reflective of the diversity and power of women of colour in the US political music scene. Created by Bernice Johnson Reagon, an African American singer and historian, Sweet Honey in the Rock first performed in 1973. Their audiences were racially diverse, and unlike many in the 'women's culture' movement, the band were always committed to playing for mixed-sex audiences. Reagon had been active in the civil rights movement and was briefly jailed in

1961, an experience that she had navigated through song. Along with her fellow prisoners, she formed the Freedom Singers, affiliating to the Student Nonviolent Coordinating Committee and adapting the Southern black musical tradition to the politics of the 1960s. By the 1970s, Reagon turned to campaigns to end violence against women, and wrote a song titled 'Joan Little' in honour of the African American woman who escaped from prison in 1974 after murdering a prison warder who tried to rape her. Sweet Honey in the Rock premiered this song in 1976 and played at benefits to support Little's legal costs. Joan Little was eventually acquitted of murder, and became an iconic figure of resistance.

Sweet Honey in the Rock participated in the booming women's music scene of clubs, festivals and recording labels. Their tour of West Coast United States was sponsored by the lesbian record label Olivia Records in 1977, and the band became a powerful player within the lesbian cultural networks of California, as well as internationally. Donna Pieters of the Lewisham Black Women's Group organized their tour of Britain in 1983 and described them as

> the soundtrack to the Women's Movement . . . For women in the Black Women's Movement, Sweet Honey embodied everything that represented them; you'd go to everyone's house and it was 'Oh Sweet Honey!' At a Sweet Honey concert you see everyone you know.[14]

Music helped make possible the communities of women's and feminist activism.

Sweet Honey in the Rock identified as 'Black women singers' rather than as feminist, and remained wary of the largely white, middle-class nature of the 'women's culture' movement. Elizabeth Cotten's life is particularly revealing of the ways in which music could be a site of generous exchange and emotional bonding, but also of appropriation and racial exclusion. Cotten came from a poor African American musical family in North Carolina. She had begun working as a domestic worker at the age of thirteen and was later employed as a maid to the Seeger family of well-known folk singers. Via the Seegers, Cotten gained opportunities to record and later tour; her songs became part of the folk revival of the 1960s and helped link the African American blues tradition to left-wing and labour politics. Peggy Seeger went on to write powerful feminist songs such as 'I'm Gonna Be An Engineer' (1972) and 'Carry Greenham Home' (1999). Cotten was an important link for the Seegers to African American music traditions, but their interactions were begun through the unequal relationship of domestic employment that, as Frances Beal pointed out, had done so much to shape and trouble the relationships between white and black women.

Feminist record labels and music distributors in Europe, such as Denmark's Face the Music and Sweden's Lilith Öronfröyd, were inspired by and imported American feminist artists, but were keen to develop women's music scenes in their own countries. In Britain, too, there was a strong emphasis on creative empowerment amongst bands and labels connected to the women's liberation movement. Stroppy Cow, a London-based label, encouraged 'women to make their own kind of music in their own time and space without the counterproductive pressures of commercialism'. Activists tried to demystify who counted as a 'musician' by skill-sharing. They founded bands whose titles reflect their subversiveness – The Harpies, Proper Little Madams, Ova, Friggin' Little Bits. The all-women band Rainbow Trout could reportedly clear men out of venues by the aggressive lyrics of 'Kerb Crawler':

> later with the boys, you'll laugh and joke
> you're a bunch of pigs who like to poke . . .
> They see a woman walking down the street
> . . . just another piece of meat
> to a kerb crawler.[15]

Musicians also explored songs of the past, forging links back to earlier generations through folk songs that captured female experiences. Women's liberation music was allied to similar creative subversion in theatre and film, and feminist songs were often part of wider performances of feminist agit-prop, disco, stand-up and satire which flourished in 1970s public spaces, bars, coffee shops, universities, picket lines, squats and rallies.

While some feminist music makers challenged the 'star-system' of the music industry, emphasizing grassroots empowerment as a political tactic, others became frustrated by their lack of access to mainstream music channels. Feminist and women's bookshops sold their records, but Rainbow Trout's Carole Nelson noted, 'Radio's still not playing women's music. Any of us wanting to get a look in are in for a really tough time.' The collective Drastic on Plastic, based in Perth, Australia, aimed to contest this exclusion from the airwaves. Their name celebrated plastic, not only as the vinyl of records but also 'in the sense of formative, procreative and flexible'. In 1983, they founded a weekly half-hour show, later extended to two hours, that saw presenter Lorraine Clifford play music made by women, such as punk band The Slits.[16]

If radio was hard to crack, feminist performance found its stride in the alternative settings of women's music festivals, such as the Taranaki Women's Music Festival in New Zealand. Often low-budget, these festivals created intense experiences of community and space away from the commonplace sexual harassment of mixed-sex gigs and festivals. It frustrated one festival-goer, however, that Taranaki's organizers hired male sound engineers. She requested a less sophisticated sound desk in future if that would allow women to be employed. Only in a women-only environment would lesbians 'be able to take off their tops and be openly affectionate', she complained. Tensions over who could attend were reproduced in the vaster setting of Michigan Womyn's Music Festival (1976–2015). Michigan attracted audiences of 10,000 largely white, lesbian women, and enforced a strict women-only policy. This was interpreted as 'women-born women', thus refusing transwomen entry. Despite the potential for destabilizing binary forms of gender associated with the growing prominence of queer politics, the women's liberation movement was divided on whether individuals could transition across or align with multiple genders.

The creation of 'women's culture' in the 1970s and 80s had sometimes been presented as rooted in a biologically or genetically given version of femininity, leading to beleaguered efforts to police the boundaries of 'female'. Olivia Records, for example, saw controversy over its employment of a transwoman, Sandy Stone. The idea of 'men' choosing to become 'women' has been seen as an invasion of sisterhood, and an attempt by those already in receipt of the 'patriarchal dividend' to also experience the emotional solidarities shared by women. Mary Daly, Robin Morgan, Gloria Steinem and Janice Raymond were high-profile proponents in the United States of a position that now terms itself 'gender critical' feminism. Morgan, the high-profile feminist author of *No More Miss America!* (1968) and *Sisterhood Is Powerful* (1970), and later an editor of the American feminist magazine *Ms.*, was incensed at the West Coast Lesbian Conference in 1973 when a transsexual woman, Beth Elliott, was invited to sing:

> I will not call a male 'she'; thirty-two years of suffering in this androcentric society, and of surviving, have earned me the title 'woman'; one walk down the street by a male transvestite, five minutes of his being hassled (which *he* may enjoy), and then he dares, he *dares* to think he understands our pain? No, in our mothers' names and in our own, we must not call him sister.[17]

Elliott had also faced vicious attacks, as well as ejection from the San Francisco chapter of the lesbian group the Daughters of Bilitis. Morgan's position was shared by many radical and revolutionary feminists, such as the British Sheila Jeffreys and Australian Germaine Greer. The violence of the rhetoric is clear from Janice Raymond's *The Transsexual Empire* (1979). Raymond, a former nun and research student of Mary Daly's, argued that 'All transsexuals rape women's bodies by reducing the female form to an artefact, appropriating this body for themselves.' Female to male transitions were also greeted with hostility; Stephen Whittle was active in women's liberation and lesbian circles in Manchester before his transition. He faced prejudice and exclusion during the process of transition, particularly when seeking to maintain his participation in feminist circles. There was, however, also a questioning of gender binaries within the movement, as we saw in Kate Millett's idea of 'bisex'. As scholar D-M Withers has recently argued, we must be careful not to casually dismiss feminism's past as monolithically hostile to trans people. Withers argues that the women's liberation movement 'contributed substantially to the *trans*formation of sex by making gender legible as a social practice.'[18]

Sandy Stone of Olivia Records answered Raymond in 1987 with 'The *Empire* Strikes Back: A Posttranssexual Manifesto'. She argued that transsexuals should give up the practice of passing and should instead reclaim unorthodox embodiment, named by philosopher Donna Haraway as 'promises of monsters' that we might today read as queer.[19] As for singer Beth Elliott when a vote was taken at the West Coast Lesbian Conference in 1973, a majority of the audience wanted to hear her sing. She performed, but then left the conference and withdrew from radical feminist circles.

The Menacing Hum of Women's Liberation

Peggy Seeger's 'Carry Greenham Home' was a late-comer to an already rich music landscape in the women's peace movement. The Greenham Common Peace Camp was a women-only protest against the hosting of American nuclear missiles at RAF Greenham Common, a NATO 'stand-by base' in Berkshire, England. It was one of the most enduring protests in the history of the women's movement, lasting for nineteen years. The protests had been launched by a march in 1981 undertaken by thirty-six women and four men, starting in Wales. Called 'Women for Life on Earth', the marchers had been inspired by the example of an earlier peace march from Copenhagen to Paris. They walked the 120 miles to Greenham but found very little press interest in their actions until, echoing Edwardian suffrage tactics, they chained themselves to the perimeter fence of the base. The peace camp attracted more than 30,000 women who gathered to 'embrace the base' by forming a human chain around the nine-mile perimeter in December 1982. As one participant described it,

> hand in hand in hand, for nine miles we formed a living chain to lock in the horrors of war, to stand between them and our world and to say: we will meet your violence with a loving embrace, for it is the surest way to defuse it. How strong I felt when I joined my voice to the waves of voices shouting 'Freedom' and when the echoes from so far away drifted across the base.[20]

Men visited the camp, though some areas were declared women-only. They provided support such as childcare, but it was women who set up and inhabited the permanent camps. The different gates giving entry to the base took on their own distinctive characters and were named after the colours of the rainbow. Violet Gate protestors identified as religious and adopted songs that focused on 'mother earth'; Orange Gate was safe for children, and strongly associated with music; Green Gate was militantly women-only; Yellow Gate had a strong anti-racist focus. In this demanding environment, lacking running water, electricity and telephone connections, creative actions such as singing, dancing and weaving became powerful everyday projects. Songs were frequently adapted from other formats. Well-known songs with simple, repetitive lyrics, sometimes termed 'zipper songs' for their ability to be swiftly amended in new contexts, were effective in providing immediate protest resources. The Greenham Common protestors, for example, amended the nursery rhyme 'Frère Jacques' to the simple lyrics,

> We are women,
> we are strong,
> we say no,
> to the bomb.

Forty-four women famously invaded the base on 1 January 1983 and danced for an hour on top of a silo while singing to the accompaniment of saxophones and violins, before their eventual arrest. Regular efforts to cut the fence followed, with one action later that year managing to cut down four miles of fence before police could intervene. Protestors also followed army personnel on exercises on Salisbury Plain, holding hands and singing to make military training impossible.[21]

The Greenham Common Peace Camp was influential, and similar camps were set up at other bases. Katrina, a protestor at Waddington nuclear base in Lincolnshire, described her feelings at being part it:

> the camp is blossoming, a women's culture is growing. It's brightly coloured, confident and new. We spin webs across the gates, sing out with new songs, learn to juggle and blockade the main gates for two weeks . . . The atmosphere

> is excitable, like shedding a dowdy skin and emerging vividly painted. The sense of our power is intoxicating.[22]

The cost was high; regular evictions by bailiffs destroyed tents and campfires at Greenham, sometimes on a daily basis, until a donation from musician and artist Yoko Ono meant that an area of land next to the base was purchased and could remain free of police harassment. The experience of a woman-run, democratic and anti-hierarchical space was often hard to manage, with conflicts over tactics, accountability and inclusivity common. 'Women' was a category that did not easily capture the different interests within the camp. Yet for all that, it was deeply empowering to experiment with 'women's culture', lesbian sexuality and women's space on the doorstep of a militarized, deeply masculine, Cold War missile site.

Recordings from the camp reveal the songs being performed at the gates and fence of the US airbase, prompting angry attempts from police and base personnel to silence the protestors. Some songs used harmony, and many were accompanied by improvised percussion. Lines from Greenham songs such as 'You Can't Kill the Spirit' became slogans, graffitied across the world and turned into stickers. Songs did not only focus on peace and the nuclear threat; 'Reclaim the Night' was a well-known Greenham song that referenced the marches against male violence taking place across the world in the late 1970s. The *Chant Down Greenham* songbook included songs about witches, referencing the eco-feminism of Mary Daly with lines such as 'weave your power with the wind, we will change and we will spin'. This emphasis saw some borrowing of Native American and Aboriginal Australian iconography of spiders and serpents. 'You Can't Kill the Spirit' was a song originally written by Chicana activist Naomi Littlebear Morena to contest landgrabs of Native American territory. This borrowing was potentially enriching and reflects the magpie-like assembly of 'feminist mosaics' from multiple sources. But it could also be a clumsy claiming of a musical heritage, with little appreciation of how such appropriation could be a form of white privilege.

In keeping with this interest in historic and spiritual sources of 'womanly' power, women at Greenham adopted the use of 'keening' – a mourning lament with roots in Celtic cultures but also dating back to Ancient Greece and Rome. It expressed the protestors' devastating sense of loss at the prospect of nuclear war, and was a way of making their protest both political and emotional. The originating walk by Women for Life on Earth had been accompanied by keening. Though one marcher, Jayne, had never heard of this practice, she recalled:

> it was like a healing, to wail out my distress and frustration at what the base represented . . . As the sounds came deep from inside me there was a buzzing in my ears and I thought I was going to pass out – but instead the tears just flowed. Merisa [a fellow marcher] was also crying and we put our arms around each other. For me it was like the completion of the whole experience of the march and chaining action. In fact, it was the completion of my whole life up to that point.[23]

A protest at the Westminster Houses of Parliament by Greenham women in 1982 was described as a 'keening action', using sound to get across the physical barriers to entry. Wearing

Figure 8.3
A protestor from the 'keening' protest in Parliament Square, January 1982

black and holding each other, the women filled Westminster Square with the eerie noise of wordless grief. One protestor commented: 'Had we just gone there and stood outside with a banner we could easily have been ignored, but by using sound we could actually penetrate the building.'[24] Keening and humming was also a useful way to make a feminist presence felt within hostile spaces; a group of Greenham Common protestors attended the Annual General Meeting of the Rio Tinto Zinc mining company in 1984 to protest the company's violence against communities in Australia, Panama and Namibia. When the all-male, all-white board members were perceived to be lying, feminists hummed or keened to disrupt the meeting. Chants that named individual board members, followed by 'Blood on your hands: warmongers!' led to the ejection of three women. However, the resulting vigorous protests meant that the meeting could not continue until these women were re-admitted. Recognizing the importance of sound to this action, the protestors taped the entire meeting and made the recording available to other campaigners, deliberately fostering the borrowing of sound-invasion tactics.

Keening was not only an expression of collective mourning but, as scholar Margaret Laware suggests, also evoked women's role as 'bridges between the living and the dead and as mediators between different realms' of past, present and future. The marking of anniversaries of the bombings of Hiroshima and Nagasaki by keening represented this sense of history, women's mourning, and the loss of future through war. Commemorating nuclear actions around the world was part of a global orientation that led Greenham Common protestors to speak internationally and to join other sites of protest. In 1983, Greenham women travelled to Comiso, Sicily, prompted by rumours of it becoming a NATO missile installation. They encountered brutal police actions against them, and when scores of protestors were arrested, they surrounded the provincial prison, Carcere Ragusa, to carry out a 'shouting action' of songs and other encouragement. The prisoners were not allowed to shout back, but regulations did not forbid singing. They used song to give updates on their situation, including how the police had broken the arm of one woman.

As it had for jailed suffragist Ethel Smyth, singing also pervaded the prison experiences of peace protestors in Britain. Women jailed in Holloway Prison for their peace activism in the 1980s were asked to assemble Alien Space Invader toys as part of the 'voluntary' labour prisoners could undertake. One prisoner, Sarah Green, recalled:

> Women were expected to fit guns on to the machines and put them in boxes . . . We sat at our table humming and I informed the man in charge that we did not intend to take part in the work because these were war toys . . . We started singing, 'Take the toys away from the boys'. The man was extremely disturbed and shouted to the women guards, 'Get them out of here!' Most of the women were very amused by this. We were not asked to work again.[25]

Tactics of humming, singing, chanting and keening proved powerful in contesting arrests and prison, in laying claim to a sonic space, and in mourning the loss of future that nuclear missiles represented. As suggested by a line in one of the popular protest camp songs, Holly Near's 'We Are a Gentle Angry People', there was a deep feeling that protestors were 'singing, singing for our lives'.[26]

Riot Grrrl

In the 1990s, an alternative music scene developed alongside a new generation of feminist activists. Rather than the autonomy and 'women's culture' emphasis of women's liberation music, riot grrrl emerged as a music and a movement that bridged women's, avant-garde and popular culture, though still sharing the early women's movement ambition to make rather than consume culture. Drawing on punk and alternative rock, riot grrrl generated a critical account of girlhood rooted in feelings and everyday experiences.

Sometimes it is simply the choice of instrument that makes a feminist statement – women and girls choosing the trombone or tuba today may still face gendered resistance. My own musical experiences as a player of an instrument strongly coded 'male' – the Irish uilleann pipes – reflect this, with astonishment expressed to me in Irish traditional music sessions at encountering a 'girl piper' in the 1990s. This was far from the distorted electric guitars of riot grrrl, but I shared something of their power in my deliberate choice of an unlikely or shocking instrument. Reclaiming 'girl' from its diminutive associations, riot grrrl lyrics and poems described girlhood as a site of power and friendship, but also of harassment, rape and self-harm. Bodies were centre stage in this exploration of the experiences of young women. Enjoyment of the fluidity of gender and sexuality suggests the queer potential of this movement which embraced non-binary gender, passing, bisexuality, pansexuality, asexuality and other formulations of desire. But riot grrrl also raised concerns about body image, eating and the immense pressures of growing up female in the late twentieth century that have remained urgently troubling for today's young women.[27]

Riot grrrl operated at the interface of DIY zines, poetry and bands, subversively crossing cultural genres and trying to break down the boundaries between performer and 'fans' – the latter often a culturally demeaning, female-dominated category. Riot grrrl music used shouting and screaming, just as the zines used capitals, scrawl and made-up words. The band Bikini Kill, founded in Olympia, Washington, in 1990, gave out colour-in zines and lyric sheets at gigs, and its audiences produced zines that were a mash-up of scrapbook, diary, photomontage and manifesto. Riot grrrl saw a proliferation of 'text-objects': handwritten, cut and pasted, typed on old-tech typewriters and reproduced on new-tech photocopiers. Despite their DIY status and tiny circulation, zines sometimes prompted heavy-handed state responses: the Canadian government, for example, banned the riot grrrl zine *Thorn* for its expressions of rage and violence.

Zines could form a new 'material' version of the talk that had previously underpinned consciousness-raising, by including highly personal, confessional material about issues such as sexual assault, self-esteem and friendships. They also self-consciously recirculated and reworked historical material, such as avant-garde artist Mina Loy's 1914 'Feminist Manifesto', which had insisted that women 'leave off looking to men to find out what you are not – seek within yourselves to find out what you are'. Loy's modernist, eugenic commitments were not an easy fit into later mosaics of feminist self-expression, but her iconoclasm, and her belief that 'women must destroy in themselves the desire to be loved', were reworked for later generations. In this spirit, even the 1963 song 'He Hit Me (And It Felt Like A Kiss)' could be reused after the punk, alternative-rock and riot grrrl movements had suggested new ways to confront the sexist violence of everyday life and the music industry. Courtney Love, lead singer of Hole, performed the song in 1995 in a sneering, angry mode. She changed the words to remove talk of a kiss and sang instead 'when he hit me, he made me his'.[28]

It was significant that riot grrrl originated on the West Coast of the United States, a location that had also hosted an earlier dynamic women's liberation music scene. But this location was quickly transcended as music tapes and zines circulated throughout Asia, Europe and Latin America. Riot grrrl scenes developed in Brazil, Russia and Indonesia, though the concerns and formats adopted were transformed as the music travelled. Russia's Pussy Riot, established in 2011 by the feminist collective Voina (War), became globally prominent and influential after their 2012 performance of a 'Punk Prayer' in Moscow's Orthodox Christian Cathedral of Christ the Saviour. Their filmed performance, released on social media, led to international notoriety and the arrest and conviction of three band members. Though some dismissed them as Western-influenced pranksters, Pussy Riot's support for LGBT rights and their anti-authoritarian stance provoked beatings, arrests and imprisonment. Indonesian riot grrrl bands such as Virgin Oi! cited Pussy Riot as inspiration for their songs which expressed resistance to rape and patriarchal family authority. But the versions of 'liberation' generated within the global North have not always been helpful to those negotiating a complex postcolonial landscape. Indonesian riot grrrls, for example, have resisted American and Russian depictions of Islam as a stand-in for women's oppression. Sporting their own 'look' of black headscarves and black jeans, they have sought their own locally generated forms of empowerment that are sensitive to their Islamic heritage.[29]

International Women's Day and State Feminism

Indonesia's regional authorities in Aceh, a province that had suffered a long rebellion against the government, were deeply concerned by the rise of punk amongst its young men and women in the early twenty-first century. In a notorious action, the police arrested sixty-four people at a punk gig in 2011. Detainees of both sexes were held without charge for a week, forced to shave their heads, pray and take communal 'cleansing' baths. Though punk and riot grrrl were tolerated in other Indonesian provinces, in post-conflict Aceh, sharia law was interpreted as forbidding them.

Indonesia had its own alternative for a feminist song. Kartini, who was introduced in Chapter 1 as taking inspiration from the work of Pandita Ramabai, went on to become widely heralded by Indonesia's nationalists as well as by the Communist-feminist mass movement Gerwani in the 1950s and early 60s.[30] This was taken to a height during the secular, military Suharto regime (1968–98), which designated Kartini a 'national heroine'. Reflecting this mythic status, Kartini has been celebrated in Indonesia on 'Kartini Day' on 21 April.

Memorials to Kartini were accompanied by 'her' song, 'Ibu Kita Kartini' (Our Mother Kartini), written in 1931 by nationalist W. R. Supratman, who also composed the Indonesian national anthem. The regular beat and predictable harmonies make this melody instantly recognizable as one penned for decorous, choreographed public occasions. Its lyrics claimed Kartini as an Indonesian princess and 'the nation's warrior'. Her status as a maternal, aristocratic national heroine, depicted on bank notes and in state-sponsored ceremonies, was an element of President Suharto's 'New Order' project of establishing himself as 'Father-President' and centralizing power through Javanese dominance over the archipelago.[31] Yet Kartini's rebellious non-conformity was also claimed by Suharto's opponents, including Indonesian feminists who used Kartini Day in 1998 to protest his policies, assert women's rights and reclaim a space for Islamic feminism.

Kartini's song is a reminder of the power of music to celebrate the status quo and support the legitimacy of political regimes. The celebrations around another 'designated day' can reveal something of the processes by which subversive music can become orthodox. International Women's Day was launched in 1909 as a socialist-inspired occasion for celebration and protest. It was initially organized by the Socialist Party of America in New York on 23 February, then marked in Copenhagen in 1910 at a meeting of the socialist Second International. Sponsored by Clara Zetkin, its observance spread rapidly to Vienna as well as other cities in Germany, Switzerland and Denmark in 1911, to the Netherlands and Sweden in 1912 and, after the support of Alexandra Kollontai, to Russia in 1913. The early events saw demands for the vote, and for equal employment rights; during the First World War some protestors combined this with calls for peace. We know from historical descriptions that women marched under banners on these occasions, but often only fleeting records remain that convey International Women's Day as a multi-sensory and auditory experience. In Beijing, following Third Communist International (Comintern) instructions, the occasion was marked from 1924. Protestors sang the Communist anthem, the Internationale. Its lyrics spoke for workers and peasants and included the unfortunate line 'The earth belongs only to men'. Nonetheless, the Internationale was sung widely by women socialists in support of their vision of emancipation.

In China, after the breakdown of the alliance between the Nationalist Party and the Chinese Communist Party, both sides attempted to use International Women's Day to assert their party line. The Nationalist Party became increasingly anxious to impose its own influence. By 1934, as Louise Edwards has documented, International Women's Day was celebrated in Nationalist-controlled terrain by party songs which stressed the immediate context – the need to boycott Japanese goods, for example – rather than world revolution and women workers' emancipation. The Chinese Communist Party, meanwhile, was hosting its own International Women's Day celebrations in its area of control, the Jiangxi Soviet, established by Mao Zedong in 1931. It commissioned its own songs, one of which ran:

'Commemorate March 8'
We want to enthusiastically shout:

> Long live the Communist Party!
> Long live the liberation of the Working Women! . . .
> Destroy the imperialist Nationalist Party!
> Raise the red flag over the entire territory of China,
> To enable working women of China to achieve a thorough liberation.

Another song included the line: 'Women of the Soviet have already achieved liberation . . . The Nationalist Party are running dogs of the imperialists.' There was little distinctive feminist influence in either setting, with International Women's Day becoming exploited by competing parties to demonstrate their authority over Chinese women. Where in earlier years it had been a transnational assertion of the revolutionary empowerment of women workers, it became a predictably choreographed set-piece of party propaganda.[32] Songs could change their meaning; 'feminist' music could celebrate rather than unseat orthodoxy.

The American feminist journal *Quest* had argued in 1976:

> A song, because of its emotional power, can evoke a level of energy in an audience unparalleled by any article or speech, simply because music speaks to our spirits as well as to our intellects. Feminist musicians have only begun to tap this potential power.

The authors were wrong, however, about the recent invention of feminist music; this chapter has shown a much longer and more varied history. Music helped women suffragists, socialists, liberationists and lesbians create communities, satirize opponents, fundraise, and invade spaces where they were not welcome. For riot grrrls, music was anarchic protest, and gave voice to their complex feelings. For African American musicians, gospel songs, jazz and blues gave them a powerful repertoire that fed into their activism and empowerment. Beyoncé's embrace of feminism in her 2013 tour sits perfectly comfortably within this tradition. The historical record, however, also shows African American women as frequently exploited through contracts with record labels and segregated performance spaces.

Trying to recapture what the women's movement 'sounded like' is difficult at a historical distance. Nonetheless, refusing to see feminism only as a textual affair is important. It was Rita Mae Brown who, in 1974, challenged her peers to pay more attention to multi-sensory elements of feminism:

> The Women's Movement, due to its largely white, middle-class composition, leans heavily on words at the expense of other forms of communication. As a child raised in a poor white community, I was taught 'Don't listen to what people say, watch what they do.' After watching women change as a result of feminism, I'd like to . . . encourage the reader to become more aware of the non-verbal as one area of that change.[33]

My own mosaic metaphor brings to mind how we might see the patterns of feminisms, and imaginatively feel and touch its creations. But in attempting to hear feminism's soundscape, we might turn instead to historian Nancy Hewitt's idea of feminist radio waves. Hewitt suggests that rather than seeing successive 'ocean waves' of feminism, we might imagine competing, simultaneous broadcasts, some loud and clear, others disrupted by static. This helps capture the global multiplicity and inequality of voice that was poorly captured by tired talk of first, second and third wave feminism. Radio broadcasts are not neutral but can be creative, innovative and even vitriolic. The 'radio waves' metaphor is suggestive of the disagreements between feminisms. But it reminds us that we can literally or imaginatively hear feminisms, through their shouts, keening, music and song.[34]

Songs and music are not easy political or protest tools. They intensify sentiments and offer complex, elusive or double meanings. Their messages are often interpreted according to the listener's needs.[35] A song, therefore, is not simply a heart-warming icon of solidarity, but does different cultural and political work when performed in different contexts. Recognizing the historical origins and travels of a song such as 'Which Side Are You On?' or the Internationale can help us understand the breadth and complexity of the different strands of modern feminism, its reuse strategies, its cultural entrepreneurship, and its awkward moments of ideological or racial appropriation. Listening to feminism gives us a better sense of its eclectic, dynamic, angry and joyful inventiveness.

CONCLUSION
Global Feminisms

In 1911, Hiratsuka Raichō published a famous opening editorial in *Seitō* magazine:

> In the beginning, Woman was truly the sun. She was a genuine person. Now, Woman is the moon. She is a sickly, pale moon, living through others, shining by the light of others.[1]

We encountered Hiratsuka in her study, divided between Western and Japanese furnishings; her *Seitō* editorial also speaks to this interweaving of influences. Hiratsuka and her contemporaries in Japan drew on Western texts by Ibsen, Ellen Key and John Stuart Mill to challenge Confucian ideas of female obedience to male relatives. However, they also found inspiration in local or culturally specific sources, such as Hiratsuka's solar imagery. The sun was of religious significance as a Shinto goddess as well as symbolic of Japan's imperial rulers. It was no accident that this was the image chosen to open Japan's most significant feminist publication of the early twentieth century.[2] The cultivation of Japanese symbolism did not, however, prevent *Seitō* from being banned by the state when its demands and ideas became too bold.

Seitō provides a powerful example of the global and local

influences that have shaped activists seeking women's rights, emancipation or gender justice. When I undertook this project of a global history of feminisms, I did so to counter the hard-to-shake European and North American dominance of many existing accounts, and to reflect the new historical writing that has begun to show a much more diverse landscape. I anticipated stories of plural, divergent feminisms, and many have indeed emerged in these chapters.

But I did not expect the degree to which I would also encounter borrowing, cross-border influence and sharings. Global influences, far from being exceptional, are widely present in the networks, the intellectual traditions and the practices of the majority of feminist campaigns and lives.

This book has traced the evolution of global feminist themes that span a remarkable range of concerns: women's rights to property, education and citizenship; pacifism, anti-fascism, the welfare and protection of mothers and children; social justice, labour rights and human rights; sexual autonomy, cultural expression and reproductive rights. A linear account of change over time does not easily capture global patterns of feminist mobilization on these issues. The Euro-American periodization of feminism around two 'waves' of the 1890s–1920s ('suffrage') and the 1970s–80s ('women's liberation') directs our attention away from important movements such as international feminist-pacifism in the 1920s and 30s, and the 'left feminism' of the Communist and labour movements from the 1940s to 60s. Moreover, there are circles in the mosaic of feminisms that defy linearity. Feminist politics were often traversed by other distinctive or local campaigns and concerns. The varying pace of campaigns for demands such as the vote meant that these issues could be resolved in the nineteenth century in New Zealand but still be at play in the twenty-first century in Kuwait and Saudi Arabia. Rights won did not always stay won, and often needed defending or regaining after setbacks. There were repeated motifs in the patterns that emerged: national self-determination, peace activism and socialism, for example, have been persistently threaded into feminisms over the past two and a half centuries. The mosaic thus saw overlapping patterns, as well as new shards and tiles.

Feminists imagined the world, though often imperfectly, as the setting for their struggles. Anne Knight, Quaker and traveller during the revolutions of 1848, for example, published a polemic in the French feminist journal *La Voix des Femmes* citing women's exercise of political power amongst 'African tribes', Native American Huron peoples, Anglo-Saxons and Gauls.[3] These were vaguely imagined entities, juxtaposing so-called 'primitives' to older 'civilizations' and suggestive of Knight's commitment to the civilizational hierarchies of her time. But the list gives us a glimpse of her expansive vision of the globe, spanned by what she termed a shared 'struggle for liberty'.

Knight's global imagination was problematic for its racial hierarchies, but its global reach was echoed by later developments such as the 'new woman', and political groups such as anti-colonial women's movements. All were premised on an imagined global terrain, but also characterized by what came to be a stronger sense of how the imagined world might be undermined by the realities of exclusion and marginality. Knight had the privilege of transnational mobility, travelling to revolutionary Paris. This privilege was shared by students such as Anna Julia Cooper, well-off activists such as Funmilayo Ransome-Kuti and literary figures such as Mina Loy. Other figures we've encountered did not travel, or did so through necessity rather than choice. The exile of Tang Qunying in Japan, the search for work and flight from unwilling marriage of Ernestine Rose and the flight from persecution of Meena Keshwar Kamal remind us that global mobilities have not always been a privilege.

In addition to physical mobilities, the borrowing and shared insights of feminists around the world have been facilitated by the modernizing communications infrastructure of the past two and a half centuries. The speeding up and expansion of postal services in the nineteenth century, followed by the telegraph, telephone, printing, photography, tape-recorders and radio, all made for a world of connections and networks. Kathy Davis has argued that the travels and reprints of *Our Bodies, Ourselves*, for example, created a 'global feminist imagined community' which gained its strength because it did not impose common interests or goals. This text allowed for a shared politics of knowledge based on reprinting, adapting and translating.[4] These are practices that continue in twenty-first-century digital media and remain in dialogue with older genres and technologies.

My focus on the imagined and tangible 'global' in this book would have been barely possible twenty years ago. Recent historical research has hugely expanded understanding of the transnational and international networks that fostered links between nations and activist groups. This has thrown extensive new light on the operations of bodies such as the Women's Christian Temperance Union, the International Woman Suffrage Alliance, the International Council of Women and the Women's International Democratic Federation. Pan-Asian, Pan-Arab, Pan-American and Pan-African politics have also emerged as important sources of inspiration and leadership roles for activists largely located in the global South. These networks and political projects fostered friendships, provided resources for congresses and travel, and battled for their respective ideological or religious positions.[5] The archive sources that recount their work tend to over-celebrate the victories and solidarities they fostered. They are sometimes strategically silent about the differences that emerged between women. The alliances and international networks produced were often fragile. Historians have noted the assumed leadership of Euro-American women, and the marginalization of those who spoke non-European languages or had non-Christian faith backgrounds, in organizations such as the International Council of Women. The Peruvian National Council of Women withdrew in frustration from the International Council in 1937, arguing that it 'lacks a truly international spirit, since it is obviously dominated by British-Nordic-Slav majority . . .'[6] Other networks were infiltrated by surveillance and intelligence agencies, or were deeply compromised by war, propaganda or doctrinaire politics. Nonetheless, understanding how international organizations operated and evolved has helped bring into view new historical actors and to rethink the 'when' of feminisms.

Internationalism is not the only framework, however; global histories also focus on the idea of 'connected' or 'entangled' histories. These concepts are helpful for capturing the wider dynamics of global interactions, often under conditions of inequality. They displace the macro perspective of world history approached through nations and international relations. Anne Knight's Quakerism or Pandita Ramabai's complex negotiation between Christianity and Hinduism, for example, are forms of connection and entanglement that exceed the categories of the national or international. There are many peoples and organizations that fall between the cracks of nationhood. I've told the stories of transient individuals such as Amanda Berry Smith, of borderlands, refugees and diasporas, and of relationships between regions, ethnic groups or religious affiliations that don't straightforwardly relate to any nation state. Moreover, the local remains an important dimension in understanding the resonances of actions such as observing International Women's Day or protesting male violence. Keeping in view the local, international, transnational and regional gives us exciting new ways of framing feminist history. I've focused on feminist practices and how they might be seen, heard and touched, through anthems and protest songs, shoes and veils, stones and bolt-cutters. The creation of physical space has been a recurrent theme, helping to anchor these histories in physical, material locations and to understand better what it meant to have rights and access to space. This helps us to document how the 'feminist mosaic' of campaigns, people and ideas was cemented and stabilized or, on occasion, dissolved and remade. This approach helps unpick the orthodox canon of feminist foremothers and reveals pieces of the mosaic that were previously obscured.

Inclusion and Exclusion

A focus on how feminism was enacted, dreamt and lived through uses and practices allows us to better hear the voices of figures at the grassroots, of the young, the poor, the illiterate, and to put them into dialogue with the amplified voices of the privileged. By no means are all the figures discussed in this book feminists – many would not have heard of this word, and some would angrily repudiate it. But they can nonetheless be placed within a critical feminist history, one that helps us understand feminisms' tensions and possibilities across a broad canvas. I've also focused on the participation of men, who have sometimes been allies or even active creators and participants in the striking, picketing, singing, theorizing and dreaming surveyed in this book. I do not overlook the infuriating character of many attempts to work with men, who often proved flaky, over-sexed, emotionally needy or selfish. But to ignore men's and women's cooperation would be a deliberate historical effacement, as well as a loss of hope for future change.

We see occasional moments in these histories of individuals such as Elsie Clews Parsons who were playfully ready to cross-dress or identify as both male and female. The widely read work of Judith Butler provided theoretical underpinning for the idea of gender as a performance that could support more than two positions. Her 1990 book *Gender Trouble* argued that individuals were not easily divided into male and female. Gender is no inner essence, Butler declared, but is remade by repeated performances in forms specific to time and place. Gender could be understood as a plastic process rather than a state of being. Building on Butler's work, the term 'transgender' became adopted to indicate non-binary gender fluidity in the 1990s. Jack Halberstam's *Female Masculinity* (1998) made more visible the existence of transgender men and helped cement the connections between feminist and queer theory.

The question of 'trans' remains extremely controversial in contemporary feminisms, a lightning rod for the reassertion of essentialist forms of identity politics. Trans-feminist Raewyn Connell has suggested that feminisms should be alert to the problems that transgender individuals face, some of which are shared with 'born female' women – poverty, labour-market exclusion, abuse, and legal, medical and civic limbo. This helps roots feminisms in a concept of embodied, gendered practices and material contexts, replacing divisive talk of gender as performance or as bio-genetic.[7] This is an area where, despite today's hard-fought battles between proponents of 'gender critical' and 'trans-friendly' feminisms, we are likely to see new histories being written that reveal a deeper history of gender non-conformity, from which activists will have much to learn.

The stories I've told in this book have returned again and again to the injuries and inequities of poverty, class, caste and social status within the history of feminisms. For women living lives of structural material disadvantage due to informal or uncertain employment, poor access to education, or stigmatizing or hard manual labour, feminism could seem, at best, irrelevant to their concerns. Rights to higher education or access to the professions, for example, have seemed abstract or redundant to those living economically precarious lives. Nonetheless, there have been coalitions and collaborations between groups stressing social justice or workers' rights and those identifying as feminist. Moreover, working-class women have always been part of feminist campaigns for the vote, for peace and for reproductive rights. As Chapter 7 showed, workers' organizations have been a rich source of inspiration for feminist tactics of strikes, pickets and boycotts.

Racial prejudice has also been profoundly significant in shaping global feminisms. There is an important story to tell about the white privilege that allowed Shulamith Firestone to wave aside racism as simply 'sexism extended', and German feminist Karin Schrader-Klebert to argue that 'women are the Negroes of all nations'.[8] The hierarchies of race have often excluded individuals of black, Asian and Latinx descent from the spaces, institutions and visions of the future created by white feminists. This has led to calls to dismantle 'white peoples' organizations' and create new feminisms 'with diversity at their core and people of color as their leaders'.[9] This story of racial privilege can be paired with an alternative story of the innovation and leadership that women of colour have exercised, despite opposition. Their organizations and campaigns have influenced how democracy, human rights and sexual autonomy are understood. Women of colour have not played a reactive role to white racism, but have shaped feminism through their agency and analysis, sometimes by following, as Benita Roth suggests, 'separate roads'.[10] Sensitivity to racial inequalities have placed them at the forefront of developing the intersectional approaches that have deeply influenced this book, as well as at the cutting edge of other kinds of theorizing and activism.

A commitment to diversity underpins this book, yet there are limits to the extent of historical recovery. The writing of history is always dependent on the survival of sources – of letters, pamphlets, magazines, photographs, outfits, badges, and all the ephemera that might help us see feminisms past. But mosaic pieces may be lost, destroyed or buried, and their survival is not just a matter of chance – it depends on access to power and resources. The records of feminist protest and ideas are not well archived for the poor, working-class, migrant or ethnic-minority activists who sought change. That means that all feminist histories will be partial affairs, skewed towards those who wanted to or were able to claim the mantle of feminism and who could make their voices heard. The more marginalized, or those who were wary of being termed a 'feminist', are obscured. Nonetheless, a self-consciously global, critical history can attend to and preserve what has survived, and point to the missing mosaic tiles.

The Useable Past

What sort of relationship to the past should those involved in today's campaigns sustain? The past can offer inspiration for ideas and methods. Chalking pavements, hunger striking, parody and satire, passionate friendships, producing zines and writing books – these all remain an active part of today's feminist politics. A rich relationship to the past can infuse contemporary activism and ideas with a sense of history and possibility. There are significant continuities in the feminist landscape – women's bodies continue to be subject to scrutiny, violence and control; activists continue to feel love and anger, to use writing and song as tools for change, and to create and appropriate their own 'things' and spaces.

However, the emphasis on repeated patterns and continuities risks downplaying historical distance. Feminist concerns, or attempts to address the 'woman question', were sometimes rooted in very different contexts to today's campaigns. Mary Wollstonecraft's 'wild wish' to see women educated and even politically active, for example, was rooted in her compelling religious faith in a Supreme Being. The distinctive eighteenth-century intellectual and religious debates that produced her faith are unlikely to be echoed today. In recognition of this distance, historian Judith Allen warns that we should avoid being too familiar with our historical subjects by referring to them by their first names. She also insists that we should not condemn feminist forebears for failing to hold 'our' values.[11]

The past can be a significant resource for feminists without validating or reproducing its limitations and violence. Feminists of other eras were sometimes complicit in racial injustice, class prejudice, anti-Semitism, gung-ho imperialism, or simple neglect of issues that now seem compelling. The troubling past, however, should not only provoke renunciation or disillusion. It can be approached for comparison, imaginative reconstruction and historically informed criticism. We should be suspicious of attempts to flatten and simplify the landscape of feminisms, or to ignore its irredeemable ideological differences. Understanding this makes feminist history more useable today. It shouldn't surprise us that women want different things. But feminisms stand or fall according to the uses made of diversity.

A recognition that feminists have not agreed on a single programme in the past can help reduce the toxicity of today's disputes. It is normal, and productive, for any social movement to have many goals and strategies and to mean different things to different people. My account pluralizes feminisms in order to expand the possible and inspire new feminist dreams. My selections of feminist iconic moments, objects and places are of course influenced by my own experiences, the books I've read, music I've played, places I've lived in and the privileges I've had. Others will have very different demands of the past, and their own dreams, songs and actions to put forward. This useable history offers inspiration and talking points; not all will agree with my choices, and this dissent is welcomed. There is no definitive selection, and feminism remains an evolving, politically relevant politics.

What Next?

In 1971, the American feminist Betty Friedan wondered, 'In the year 2000 will some harassed, guilty daughter of my daughter's generation have to start all over again?'[12] She would have been astounded that, in the 2020s, feminism remains such an urgent, pressing concern. Hundreds of thousands of women have marched, sung and danced in Chilean, Turkish, Mexican, Brazilian and Spanish cities in recent years to protest violence against women and the inadequate response of police and the courts; Swiss women have struck against unequal pay and cultures of sexism, vividly making their point by ringing cathedral bells and singing in train stations, 'If it's women's will, everything will stand still.'

Eco-feminists have shown how women, as the majority of the world's poor, are bearing the brunt of climate change. Climate justice has emerged as a major feminist issue, fought for by activists such as Honduran Berta Cáceres (1971–2016), born the very year that Friedan queried the feminist future.

Cáceres was assassinated in 2016 by individuals linked to the Honduran military and to a dam-building company which she had opposed. Women's rights activists continue to face violent and deadly state-led and corporate harassment, with activists recently jailed in Saudi Arabia, Russia, Uganda and elsewhere. Feminists have been viciously targeted as part of the rise of populist and racist politics. Brazilian president Jair Bolsonaro has demanded that all references to feminism be removed from school textbooks. Leaked documents in 2019 revealed that the Apple Corporation scripted its digital assistant Siri to never use the word 'feminism', even if directly asked about it. Reproductive rights and justice are sharply threatened: in Nicaragua, El Salvador and the US state of Alabama, abortion is banned in virtually all circumstances, leaving poor and young women particularly vulnerable to arrest and unwanted pregnancies. The cost to women and to the planet is incalculable; the global feminist challenge could not be clearer.

Friedan's question implied that feminism was a wearying campaign, an attempt to reach an 'end state' of gender equality. Dreams however must evolve, and to 'do feminism' isn't an end state but a journey. A global history reveals the depth, breadth and diversity of the longing and determination to achieve gender justice. The global perspective helps us sustain a more tentative sense of how coalitions between women, or between the sexes, might both form and fail; shared interests must always be provisional and cannot be taken for granted. Friedan feared that twenty-first-century campaigners might have to 'start over'. But the richness of the global feminist past suggests otherwise.

Acknowledgements

This book has only been made possible through a collaborative process of putting heads together. I am particularly indebted to the following generous friends and scholars who have suggested readings, provided inspiration and read my work: Chloe Kattar, Maria DiCenzo, Kristina Schulz, Anna Bull, Isidora Grubacki, Francisca de Haan, Deborah Cohen, Mary Chapman, D-M Withers, Heidi Kurvinen, Khurram Jowiya, Zoe Strimpel, Rosa Campbell, Mikiko Eto, Zoe Thomas, Natalie Thomlinson, Florence Sutcliffe-Braithwaite and Maud Bracke.

The Emmets – Lucy Bland, Laura Carter, Niamh Gallagher, Julia Laite, Helen McCarthy, Deborah Thom – have been a close support, and read chapters in early versions with their usual subtlety and thoughtfulness. Margaretta Jolly and Polly Russell, crucial figures in the expanding history of feminisms in recent years, have been friends and mentors to this work – I'm lucky to have them. Judith Allen inspired the chapter on song by breaking out into a feminist number in a London pub, as well as offering her marvellous historical insight. My thanks also go to Graham Copekoga for his photography. The Murray Edwards fellowship has given me a warm academic home and I especially thank Rachel Leow for her assistance. Chika Tonooka,

Manuel Arroyo-Kalin, Julie Barrau, Silke Zimmer-Merkle and Joelle Patient have helped me with questions of translation, and Ben Griffin has been a friend and collaborator on many shared projects – my grateful thanks to all. My graduate students have brought me into contact with histories and ideas I would not otherwise have encountered, and I am enriched by my work with them. I'm especially grateful to Holly Nielsen, whose feminist cross-stitch masterpiece inspired the chapter on feminist objects. Casiana Ionita, who twisted my arm in the first place to write this book, has supported me with her enthusiasm and nose for a good sentence. Ben Sinyor and Jane Birdsell have helped enormously with the final stages.

My family have also read much of this book, and I'd like to thank them for this and so much more. They have sustained me, distracted me, and made my writing possible. To my inspirational nieces, I can't resist quoting feminist poet Dollie Radford:

To you my nieces, who must face
Our right and wrong, and take your place
As future leaders.

And I, meanwhile, shall still pursue
All that is weird and wild and new,
In song and ballet,

In lecture, drama, verse and prose,
With every cult that comes and goes
Your aunt will dally.*

* 'From Our Emancipated Aunt in Town', Dollie Radford, *Songs and Other Verses* (London: Philadelphia: John Lane, 1895).

In a nod to the spatial turn, I'd like to dedicate this book, written in Cambridge, UK, and Kerry, Ireland, to a specific space that has long been important to me – South Front Two of the Cambridge University Library. A treasure trove of histories of feminisms, its unmistakeable smell and feel has accompanied this book, and indeed my life as a historian, for over twenty years. It's a privilege to have access to such a space, and I'm deeply grateful to the University Library staff who look after it, as well as to the scholars, translators and publishers who have filled its shelves. This book could not have been written without them.

Notes

INTRODUCTION

1. *Western Echo* (3 January 1886), cited in Audrey Gadzekpo, 'The Hidden History of Women in Ghanaian Print Culture', in Oyèrónkẹ́ Oyěwùmí, *African Gender Studies: A Reader* (Palgrave Macmillan, 2005), 282.
2. Chela Sandoval, *Methodology of the Oppressed* (University of Minnesota Press, 2000).
3. Adele Murdolo, 'Safe Homes for Immigrant and Refugee Women: Narrating Alternative Histories of the Women's Refuge Movement in Australia', *Frontiers: A Journal of Women Studies* 35:3 (2014), 146.
4. https://www.ipsos.com/sites/default/files/2017-03/global-advisor-feminism-charts-2017.pdf.
5. *Emporia Daily Gazette*, Kansas, USA (27 November 1897), vol. 7.
6. *The Times* (18 June 1906), 6.
7. For a video introducing some of the concepts of feminism, see https://www.youtube.com/watch?v=H_GBrIntUq8.
8. Mina Roces, 'Is the Suffragist an American Colonial Construct? Defining "the Filipino Woman" in Colonial Philippines', in Louise P. Edwards and Mina Roces (eds.), *Women's Suffrage in Asia: Gender, Nationalism and Democracy* (Routledge, 2005), 29.
9. Asunción Lavrín, *Women, Feminism, and Social Change in Argentina, Chile, and Uruguay, 1890–1940* (University of Nebraska Press, 1995), 26–36.
10. Mary Louise Roberts, *Disruptive Acts* (University of Chicago Press, 2002), 39.
11. Johanna Gehmacher, 'In/Visible Transfers: Translation as a Crucial Practice in Transnational Women's Movements around 1900', *German Historical Institute London Bulletin* 41:2 (2019), 3–44.
12. Natalia Novikova, 'Early Historical Accounts of the Russian Women's Movement: A Political Dialogue or a Dispute?', *Women's History Review* 20:4 (2011), 509–19.

13. Frances Watkins Harper, 'We Are All Bound Up Together': speech at the 11th National Woman's Rights Convention in New York, May 1866.
14. June Edith Hahner, *Emancipating the Female Sex: The Struggle for Women's Rights in Brazil, 1850–1940* (Duke University Press, 1990), 26–30, 209–10.
15. Bonnie S. Anderson, *Joyous Greetings: The First International Women's Movement, 1830–1860* (Oxford University Press, 2001).
16. Francisca de Haan, 'Writing Inter-Transnational History: The Case of Women's Movements and Feminisms', in Barbara Haider-Wilson, William D. Godsey and Wolfgang Mueller (eds.), *Internationale Geschichte in Theorie und Praxis/International History in Theory and Practice* (Verlag der Österreichischen Akademie der Wissenschaften, 2017), 501–36.
17. Kathy Davis, *The Making of Our Bodies, Ourselves: How Feminism Travels across Borders* (Duke University Press, 2008).
18. Nancy Hewitt's metaphor of radio waves has brilliantly signalled this idea of feminist voices of varying volumes: Nancy A. Hewitt (ed.), *No Permanent Waves: Recasting Histories of U.S. Feminism* (Rutgers University Press, 2010).
19. Kathryn Gleadle, 'The Imagined Communities of Women's History: Current Debates and Emerging Themes, a Rhizomatic Approach', *Women's History Review* 22:4 (2013), 524–40.
20. Kathryn Gleadle and Zoë Thomas, 'Global Feminisms, *c.* 1870–1930: Vocabularies and Concepts – A Comparative Approach', *Women's History Review* 27:7 (2018), 1209–24.
21. Kimberly Springer, *Living for the Revolution: Black Feminist Organizations, 1968–1980* (Duke University Press, 2005).
22. bell hooks, *Talking Back: Thinking Feminist, Thinking Black* (Sheba Feminist, 1989).
23. Mrinalini Sinha, 'Mapping the Imperial Social Formation: A Modest Proposal for Feminist History', *Signs* 25:4 (2000), 1077–82
24. 'Use' is critically explored by Sara Ahmed, *What's the Use? On the Uses of Use* (Duke University Press, 2019).
25. Kathleen A. Laughlin *et al.*, 'Is It Time to Jump Ship? Historians Rethink the Waves Metaphor', *Feminist Formations* 22:1 (2010), 97.

CHAPTER 1: DREAMS

1. Charles Fourier, 'Marriage and the Family System', quoted in Charles Fourier, Jonathan Beecher and Richard Bienvenu (ed. and trans.),

The Utopian Vision of Charles Fourier: Selected Texts on Work, Love, and Passionate Attraction (Beacon Press, 1971), 177.

2. Cited in Shirin Akhtar, 'East Bengal Women's Education, Literature and Journalism', in Francisca de Haan *et al.* (eds.), *Women's Activism: Global Perspectives from the 1890s to the Present* (Routledge, 2013), 110.
3. Bharati Ray, *Early Feminists of Colonial India* (Oxford University Press, 2012).
4. Barnita Bagchi, 'Ladylands and Sacrificial Holes', in Barnita Bagchi (ed.), *The Politics of the (Im)Possible: Utopia and Dystopia Reconsidered* (Sage, 2012).
5. Judith A. Allen, *The Feminism of Charlotte Perkins Gilman: Sexualities, Histories, Progressivism* (University of Chicago Press, 2009), 354.
6. Linda Edmondson, 'Feminism and Equality in an Authoritarian State: The Politics of Women's Liberation in Late Imperial Russia', in Sylvia Paletschek and Bianka Pietrow-Ennker (eds.), *Women's Emancipation Movements in the Nineteenth Century: A European Perspective* (Stanford University Press, 2004), 221–39.
7. Alexandra Kollontai, *Working Woman and Mother*, republished in *Selected Writings of Alexandra Kollontai*, trans. Alix Holt (Allison & Busby, 1978), 134.
8. Ibid., 135.
9. Alexandra Kollontai, *A Great Love*, trans. Cathy Porter (London: Virago, 1981), 76.
10. Kollontai, *Selected Writings*, 134.
11. Padma Anagol, *The Emergence of Feminism in India, 1850–1920* (Ashgate, 2005); Meera Kosambi, 'Multiple Contestations: Pandita Ramabai's Educational and Missionary Activities in Late Nineteenth-Century India and Abroad', *Women's History Review* 7:2 (1998), 193–208.
12. Ramabai Sarasvati, *The High-Caste Hindu Woman*, (G. Bell & Sons, 1888), 64.
13. Ibid., 202. See also Uma Chakravarti, *Rewriting History: The Life and Times of Pandita Ramabai* (Zubaan, 2013).
14. Sarasvati, *High-Caste Hindu Woman*, 56–57.
15. Kartini, quoted in Kumari Jayawardena, *Feminism and Nationalism in the Third World* (Kali for Women, 1986), 137.
16. Jo Ellen Jacobs and Paula Harms Payne (eds.), *The Complete Works of Harriet Taylor Mill* (Indiana University Press, 1998).
17. Linda M. G. Zerilli, *Signifying Woman: Culture and Chaos in Rousseau, Burke, and Mill* (Cornell University Press, 1994), 96.
18. J. S. Mill to Harriet Taylor Mill, 17 February 1857, quoted ibid., 95.

19. Mary Trigg, *Feminism as Life's Work: Four Modern American Women through Two World Wars* (Rutgers University Press, 2014), 124.
20. 'Hunger (for Audre Lorde)', in Adrienne Rich, *The Dream of a Common Language: Poems 1974–1977* (W. W. Norton and Co., 1993), 13.
21. 'An Open Letter to Mary Daly', in Audre Lorde, *Sister Outsider: Essays and Speeches* (Crossing, 2007).
22. Pratibha Parmar, 'Other Kinds of Dreams', *Feminist Review* 31 (1989), 55–65.
23. Iris Marion Young, 'The Complexities of Coalition', *Dissent Magazine* (Winter 1997).
24. Audre Lorde, *Zami: A New Spelling of My Name* (Penguin Classics, 2018), 223, 197.

CHAPTER 2: IDEAS

1. Ifi Amadiume, *Male Daughters, Female Husbands: Gender and Sex in an African Society* (Zed Books, 2015).
2. Josefa Amar y Borbón, *In Defence of Women*, trans. Joanna M. Barker (Modern Humanities Research Association, 2018), 100.
3. Mary Nash, 'The Rise of the Women's Movement in Nineteenth-Century Spain', in Sylvia Paletschek and Bianka Pietrow-Ennker (eds.), *Women's Emancipation Movements in the Nineteenth Century: A European Perspective* (Stanford University Press and Eurospan, 2004), 243–62; Juan Pro, 'Thinking of a Utopian Future: Fourierism in Nineteenth-Century Spain', *Utopian Studies* 26:2 (2015), 329–48.
4. Christine Arkinstall, 'A Feminist Press Gains Ground in Spain, 1822–66', in Silvia Bermúdez and Roberta Johnson (eds.), *A New History of Iberian Feminisms* (University of Toronto Press, 2018), 123.
5. This British publication has been attributed to Lady Mary Wortley Montagu (1689–1762), and to Lady Sophia Fermor (1724–45). On the translation of this text, see Charlotte Hammond Matthews, *Gender, Race and Patriotism in the Works of Nísia Floresta* (Cambridge University Press, 2013).
6. Despite the Brazilian declaration as an independent republic in 1889, there was no national women's suffrage until 1932, when the decision by the 'frontier' state of Rio Grande do Norte to enfranchise women in 1927 was taken up the federal government. Suffrage was lost again when a series of dictatorships ('Estado Novo', 1937–45, and military rule, 1964–85) took over.

7. Lewis Henry Morgan, *Ancient Society* (University of Arizona Press, 1985), 54, 505.
8. Friedrich Engels, *The Origin of the Family, Private Property, and the State* (Penguin Classics, 2010), 27.
9. Olive Schreiner, *Women and Labour* (Virago Press 1978), 97–8.
10. August Bebel. *Woman and Socialism*, trans. Meta L Stern (Socialist Literature Co., 1910), 6–7.
11. Marilyn J. Boxer, 'Rethinking the Socialist Construction and International Career of the Concept "Bourgeois Feminism"', *American Historical Review* 112:1 (2007), 131–58.
12. August Bebel, *Woman in the Past, Present and Future* (Zwan, 1988), 264.
13. Elizabeth Cady Stanton, 'Address', in Ellen Carol DuBois and Richard Cándida Smith, *Elizabeth Cady Stanton, Feminist as Thinker: A Reader in Documents and Essays*, (New York University Press, 2007), 96–7.
14. Eleanor F. Rathbone, *The Disinherited Family: A Plea for the Family* (Edward Arnold, 1924), 215, 269.
15. Susan Pedersen, *Eleanor Rathbone and the Politics of Conscience* (Yale University Press, 2004), 246–56.
16. Antoinette Burton, *Burdens of History: British Feminists, Indian Women, and Imperial Culture, 1865–1915* (University of North Carolina Press, 1994).
17. Charlotte Perkins Gilman, *The Man-Made World, Or, Our Androcentric Culture* (Charlton Company, 1914), 15.
18. Ibid., p. 16.
19. Charlotte Perkins Gilman, *Women and Economics* (Courier Corporation, 2012), 120.
20. Schreiner to Karl Pearson, 10 September 1886, University College London special collections, Karl Pearson, 840/4/3/61–64.
21. Louise P. Edwards, *Gender, Politics, and Democracy: Women's Suffrage in China* (Stanford University Press, 2008).
22. Schreiner to Mrs John X. Merriman, [undated] 1912, National Library of South Africa, Special Collections, Cape Town: MSC 15/1912:211.
23. Ling Qichao, 'On Women's Education' (1897), in Lydia He Liu *et al.*, *The Birth of Chinese Feminism: Essential Texts in Transnational Theory* (Columbia University Press, 2013), 203.
24. Jin Tianhe, 'The Women's Bell' (1903), reprinted ibid.
25. Ibid., 11.
26. Tani E. Barlow, *The Question of Women in Chinese Feminism* (Duke University Press, 2004), 49–59, 274.

27. He-Yin Zhen, 'The Feminist Manifesto' (1907), in Liu *et al.*, *Birth of Chinese Feminism*, 184.
28. Barlow, *The Question of Women*, 105–6.
29. He-Yin Zhen, 'The Feminist Manifesto' (1907), in Liu *et al.*, *Birth of Chinese Feminism*, 182–3.
30. Kate Millett, Preface to Japanese edition of *Sexual Politics*, quoted in Laurel Fredrickson, 'Trap: Kate Millett, Japan, Fluxus and Feminism', *Women & Performance: A Journal of Feminist Theory* 19:3 (2009), 337–67.
31. Shulamith Firestone and Anne Koedt (eds.), *Notes from the Second Year: Women's Liberation: Major Writings of the Radical Feminists* (New York Radical Feminists, 1970).
32. Ibid.
33. Mary Daly, 'The Spiritual Dimension of Women's Liberation', in Anne Koedt, Ellen Levine and Anita Rapone (eds.), *Radical Feminism* (Quadrangle Books, 1973).
34. Mary Daly, *Gyn/Ecology: The Metaethics of Radical Feminism* (Beacon Press, 1978), 28.
35. Ibid., 32.
36. Aileen Moreton-Robinson, *Talkin' Up to the White Woman: Aboriginal Women and Feminism* (University of Queensland Press, 2000), 24.
37. Women in Publishing Industry Group in Britain, 'Non-Sexist Code of Practice for Book Publishing', 1982.
38. Hélène Cixous, 'The Laugh of the Medusa', *Signs* 1:4 (1976), 876.
39. Assia Djebar, *Ces Voix qui m'assiègent*, cited in Jane Hiddleston, 'Feminism and the Question of "Woman" in Assia Djebar's *Vaste est la prison*', *Research in African Literatures* 35:4 (2004), 92–3.
40. Robin Thompson, 'Mary Daly's Gyn/Ecology', *The Amazon* (August–September 1980), 9–11.
41. Pavla Miller, *Patriarchy* (Routledge, 2017); Seungsook Moon, 'Carving Out Space: Civil Society and the Women's Movement in South Korea', *Journal of Asian Studies* 61:2 (May 2002), 473.
42. Barbara Burris, 'Fourth World Manifesto', in Anne Koedt (ed.), *Notes from the Third Year: Women's Liberation* (New York Radical Feminists, 1972), 342.
43. Frances M. Beal, 'Double Jeopardy: To Be Black and Female', *Meridians* 8:2 (2008), 169.
44. Claudia Jones, 'An End to the Neglect of the Problems of Negro Women' (1949), in *Claudia Jones: Beyond Containment: Autobiographical Reflections, Essays and Poems* (Ayebia Clarke, 2011), 80; Denise Lynn, 'Socialist Feminism and Triple Oppression: Claudia Jones and African American Women in American Communism', *Journal for the Study of Radicalism* 8:2 (2014), 1–20.

45. Beal, 'Double Jeopardy', 175.
46. Deborah K. King, 'Multiple Jeopardy, Multiple Consciousness: The Context of a Black Feminist Ideology', *Signs* 14:1 (1988), 47.
47. Kimberlé Crenshaw, 'Mapping the Margins: Intersectionality, Identity Politics, and Violence against Women of Color', *Stanford Law Review* 43:6 (1991), 1241–99.
48. 'Feminism, a Transformational Politics', in bell hooks, *Talking Back: Thinking Feminist, Thinking Black* (Sheba Feminist Press, 1989), 419–21.
49. Philippe De Wolf, 'Male Feminism: Men's Participation in Women's Emancipation Movements and Debates. Case Studies from Belgium and France (1967–1984)', *European Review of History* 22:1 (2015), 77–100.
50. R. W. Connell, 'The Politics of Changing Men', *Australian Humanities Review* (December 1996).

CHAPTER 3: SPACES

1. Margaret Mary Finnegan, *Selling Suffrage: Consumer Culture and Votes for Women*, Popular Cultures, Everyday Lives (Columbia University Press, 1999), 49.
2. Maud Bracke, *Women and the Reinvention of the Political: Feminism in Italy, 1968–1983* (Routledge, 2014).
3. Roger Fulford, *Votes for Women: The Story of a Struggle* (Faber and Faber, 1957), 103.
4. Virginia Woolf, *A Room of One's Own* (Penguin, 2004); Margaret Llewelyn Davies, *Life as We Have Known It, by Cooperative Working Women* (Virago, 1977).
5. Dina Lowy, *The Japanese 'New Woman': Images of Gender and Modernity* (Rutgers University Press, 2007), 11.
6. 'The Good Fairy', *Quest* 1 (1974), 61.
7. Mrs (Anna) Jameson, *The Communion of Labour: A Second Lecture on the Social Employments of Women* (Longman, Brown, Green, Longmans, & Roberts, 1856).
8. H. Martineau, 'Female Industry', *Edinburgh Review* 109 (1859), 336.
9. Mya May Hla Oung,'The Women of Burma', *Buddhism: An Illustrated Quarterly Review* (September 1903), 62, 81.
10. Ellen Jordan and Anne Bridger, '"An Unexpected Recruit to Feminism": Jessie Boucherett's "Feminist Life" and the Importance of Being Wealthy', *Women's History Review* 15:3 (2006), 385–412.

11. Ethel Snowden, *The Feminist Movement* (Collins, 1913), 216–17.
12. Rosemary Feurer, 'The Meaning of "Sisterhood": The British Women's Movement and Protective Labor Legislation, 1870–1900', *Victorian Studies* 31:2 (1988), 233–60.
13. Dorothy Sue Cobble, 'More than Sex Equality: Feminism after Suffrage', in Dorothy Sue Cobble, Linda Gordon and Astrid Henry, *Feminism Unfinished: A Short, Surprising History of American Women's Movements* (Liveright Publishing Corporation, 2014).
14. Patricia Ann Schechter, *Exploring the Decolonial Imaginary: Four Transnational Lives* (Palgrave Macmillan, 2012).
15. Maria Odila Leite da Silva Dias, *Power and Everyday Life: The Lives of Working Women in Nineteenth-Century Brazil* (Polity Press, 1995), 32–3.
16. See Toyin Falola and Adam Paddock, *The Women's War of 1929: A History of Anti-Colonial Resistance in Eastern Nigeria* (Carolina Academic Press, 2011).
17. 1929 Commission of Inquiry, cited in Caroline Ifeka-Moller, 'Female Militancy and Colonial Revolt', in Shirley Ardener, *Perceiving Women* (Wiley, 1975), 129.
18. Cheryl Johnson-Odim, *For Women and the Nation: Funmilayo Ransome-Kuti of Nigeria* (University of Illinois Press, 1997).
19. Ayesha Imam, The Dynamics of WINning: An Analysis of Women in Nigeria (WIN)', in M. Jacqui Alexander and Chandra Talpade Mohanty (eds.), *Feminist Genealogies, Colonial Legacies, Democratic Futures* (Routledge, 1997), 282.
20. Ibid., 286.
21. Bene E. Madunagu, 'The Nigerian Feminist Movement: Lessons from "Women in Nigeria", WIN', *Review of African Political Economy*, 35:118 (December 2008), 666–72.
22. A. Finn Enke, *Finding the Movement: Sexuality, Contested Space, and Feminist Activism* (Duke University Press, 2008).
23. Alexandra Ketchum, '"The Place We've Always Wanted to Go But Never Could Find": Finding Woman Space in Feminist Restaurants and Cafés in Ontario, 1974–1982', *Feminist Studies* 44:1 (2018), 126–52.
24. Joshua Clark Davis, *From Head Shops to Whole Foods: The Rise and Fall of Activist Entrepreneurs* (Columbia University Press, 2017).
25. Ibid., 156–7.
26. Alice Echols, *Daring to Be Bad: Radical Feminism in America, 1967–1975* (University of Minnesota Press, 1989), 280.
27. Ann Phoenix, 'Re-Narrating Feminist Stories', in Mary Evans and Kathy Davis (eds.), *Transatlantic Conversations: Feminism as Travelling Theory* (Routledge, 2016).

28. 'Feminist Forum', *Women's Studies International Forum* 11:6 (1 January 1988), 14.
29. Kristen Hogan, *The Feminist Bookstore Movement: Lesbian Antiracism and Feminist Accountability* (Duke University Press, 2016).
30. Elizabeth Cady Stanton, Introduction to *The Woman's Bible* (1898; reprinted by Polygon, 1985).
31. Betty Livingston Adams, *Black Women's Christian Activism: Seeking Social Justice in a Northern Suburb* (New York University Press, 2016).
32. Ibid., 28–8.
33. Ibid., 31.
34. Ibid., 37.
35. Ibid., 78.
36. Johnson to Wilson, 5 August 1919, quoted ibid., 84.
37. Ibid., 113, 150.
38. Sheila Shaver, 'Gender, Class and the Welfare State: The Case of Income Security in Australia', *Feminist Review* 32 (1989), 90–110.
39. Rosa Campbell, 'A Global History of Australian Women's Liberation 1968–1990' (forthcoming PhD dissertation, University of Cambridge); Tikka Jan Wilson, 'Feminism and Institutionalized Racism: Inclusion and Exclusion at an Australian Feminist Refuge', *Feminist Review* 52 (1996), 1–26.
40. Adele Murdolo, 'Safe Homes for Immigrant and Refugee Women: Narrating Alternative Histories of the Women's Refuge Movement in Australia', *Frontiers: A Journal of Women Studies* 35:3 (2014), 135.
41. Ibid., 138.

CHAPTER 4: OBJECTS

1. George Thompson (1834), cited in Gail Malmgreen, 'Anne Knight and the Radical Subculture', *Quaker History* 71:2 (1982), 105.
2. Ibid., 106.
3. Bonnie S. Anderson, *Joyous Greetings: The First International Women's Movement, 1830–1860* (Oxford University Press, 2001), 22.
4. Samuel Allen (1841), cited in Malmgreen, 'Anne Knight and the Radical Subculture', 106.
5. Cited in Margaret L. Laware, 'Circling the Missiles and Staining Them Red: Feminist Rhetorical Invention and Strategies of Resistance at the Women's Peace Camp at Greenham Common,' *NWSA Journal* 16:3 (2004), 18–41.

6. 'Pint Size', *Spare Rib* 96 (July 1980), 11.
7. Silver Moon, 'Boltcutters', in Alison Bartlett and Margaret Henderson (eds.), *Things That Liberate: An Australian Feminist Wunderkammer* (Cambridge Scholars, 2013), 61.
8. Alison Bartlett and Margaret Henderson, 'What Is a Feminist Object? Feminist Material Culture and the Making of the Activist Object', *Journal of Australian Studies* 40:2 (2016), 170.
9. Pankhurst, cited in Laura E. Nym Mayhall, 'The Rhetorics of Slavery and Citizenship: Suffragist Discourse and Canonical Texts in Britain, 1880–1914', *Gender & History* 13:3 (2001), 481.
10. Elizabeth Crawford, *The Women's Suffrage Movement: A Reference Guide, 1866–1928* (Psychology Press, 2001), 550.
11. Ibid., 137.
12. *Votes for Women* (1908), cited in Krista Lysack, *Come Buy, Come Buy: Shopping and the Culture of Consumption in Victorian Women's Writing* (Ohio University Press, 2008).
13. Elizabeth Crawford, 'Our Readers Are Careful Buyers: Creating Goods for the Suffrage Market', in Miranda Garrett and Zoë Thomas (eds.), *Suffrage and the Arts: Visual Culture, Politics and Enterprise* (Bloomsbury Visual Arts, 2019).
14. Jessica Ellen Sewell, *Women and the Everyday City: Public Space in San Francisco, 1890–1915*, Architecture, Landscape, and American Culture Series (University of Minnesota Press, 2011), 140–42.
15. Margaret Mary Finnegan, *Selling Suffrage: Consumer Culture and Votes for Women*, Everyday Lives (Columbia University Press, 1999), 122–4.
16. Crawford, *Women's Suffrage Movement*, 537.
17. Ibid, 149; Kenneth Florey, *Women's Suffrage Memorabilia: An Illustrated Historical Study* (McFarland & Company, Inc., 2013), 107.
18. Finnegan, *Selling Suffrage*, 126–28.
19. Ornella Moscucci, *The Science of Woman: Gynaecology and Gender in England, 1800–1929*, (Cambridge University Press, 1990). Andrea Dworkin, *Autobiography*, Contemporary Authors Autobiography Series 22 (Gale, 1995), 14.
20. Adrienne Sallay, 'Pocket Mirror', in Bartlett and Henderson, *Things That Liberate*, 138.
21. Donna J. Haraway, 'The Virtual Speculum in the New World Order', *Feminist Review* 55 (1997), 45.
22. Kathy Davis, *The Making of Our Bodies, Ourselves: How Feminism Travels across Borders* (Duke University Press, 2008).

23. Ester Shapiro, cited ibid., 180–81.
24. Susan Magarey, 'Tampon', in Bartlett and Henderson, *Things That Liberate*, 188–90.
25. Theresa Munford, 'China: Rough Brown Paper for Periods', *Spare Rib* 100 (November 1980), 15.
26. 'How to . . .', *Lesbian Connection* (March/April 1986), 13–14.
27. Susanne Gannon, 'Sea Sponges', Bartlett and Henderson, *Things That Liberate*, 165.
28. Amanda Sebestyen, 'Blood Money', *Spare Rib* 65 (December 1977), 8.
29. 'A Sponge?' *Bread and Roses* 1:2 (1978), 2.
30. Jean Taylor, 'Gestetner', in Bartlett and Henderson, *Things That Liberate*, 95.
31. Jennifer S. Duncan, 'French Feminism's Struggle to Become Global', in Francisca de Haan *et al.* (eds.), *Women's Activism: Global Perspectives from the 1890s to the Present* (Routledge, 2013), 183–97.
32. Jennifer Leigh Disney, *Women's Activism and Feminist Agency in Mozambique and Nicaragua* (Temple University Press, 2009).
33. Ifi Amadiume, *Male Daughters, Female Husbands: Gender and Sex in an African Society* (Zed Books, 2015); Oyèrónkẹ́ Oyěwùmí, *The Invention of Women: Making an African Sense of Western Gender Discourses* (University of Minnesota Press, 1997).
34. Penny A. Weiss and Megan Brueske (eds.), *Feminist Manifestos: A Global Documentary Reader* (NYU Press, 2018).
35. Susan Magarey, *Dangerous Ideas: Women's Liberation – Women's Studies – Around the world* (University of Adelaide Press, 2014), 33.
36. Bartlett and Henderson, 'What Is a Feminist Object?', 169.
37. Urvashi Butalia and Ritu Menon, *Making a Difference: Feminist Publishing in the South*, (Bellagio Publishing Network, 1995), 19–20.
38. *Feminist Bookstore News* (September–October 1986), 27. On Virago, see Catherine Riley, *The Virago Story: Assessing the Impact of a Feminist Publishing Phenomenon* (Berghahn Books, 2018).
39. Simone Murray, 'The Cuala Press: Women, Publishing, and the Conflicted Genealogies of "Feminist Publishing"', *Women's Studies International Forum* 27:5 (2004), 489–506.
40. Butalia and Menon, *Making a Difference*, 23–4.
41. Joan Marie Johnson, *Funding Feminism: Monied Women, Philanthropy, and the Women's Movement, 1870–1967*, (University of North Carolina Press, 2017), 223.
42. Deni Fuller 'The Women's Symbol', in Bartlett and Henderson, *Things That Liberate*, 215–16.

CHAPTER 5: LOOKS

1. Elsie Clews Parsons, *The Journal of a Feminist*, Subversive Women 5 (Thoemmes Press, 1994), 86.
2. Samuel Edwards, *George Sand: A Biography of the First Modern, Liberated Woman* (McKay, 1972).
3. Chandra Talpade Mohanty, 'Under Western Eyes: Feminist Scholarship and Colonial Discourses', *Boundary* 12:3 (1984), 333–58.
4. Mina Roces, 'Is the Suffragist an American Colonial Construct? Defining "the Filipino Woman" in Colonial Philippines', in Louise P. Edwards and Mina Roces (eds.), *Women's Suffrage in Asia: Gender, Nationalism and Democracy* (London: Routledge, 2005), 24–58.
5. Marshall Foletta, 'Angelina Grimké: Asceticism, Millenarianism, and Reform', *New England Quarterly* 80:2 (2007), 179–217.
6. Bonnie S. Anderson, *Joyous Greetings: The First International Women's Movement, 1830–1860* (Oxford University Press, 2001), 59.
7. Barbara Hamill Sato, *The New Japanese Woman: Modernity, Media, and Women in Interwar Japan* (Duke University Press, 2003); Dina Lowy, *The Japanese 'New Woman': Images of Gender and Modernity* (Rutgers University Press, 2007).
8. Dorothy Ko, 'Jazzing into Modernity: High Heels, Platforms, and Lotus Shoes', in Valerie Steele and John S. Major (eds.), *China Chic: East Meets West* (Yale University Press, 1999). See also Joan Judge, 'Sinology, Feminist History, and Everydayness in the Early Republican Periodical Press', *Signs* 40:3 (2015), 563–87.
9. *Votes for Women* (30 July 1908), 348, quoted in Wendy Parkins, 'The Epidemic of Purple, White and Green: Fashion and the Suffragette Movement in Britain 1908–14', in Wendy Parkins (eds.) *Fashioning the Body Politic* (Berg Publishers, 2002), 102.
10. Gul Ozyegin, 'My Father, an Agent of State Feminism and Other Unrelatable Conversations' in Kathy Davis and Mary Evans (eds.), *Transatlantic Conversations: Feminism as Travelling Theory* (Ashgate, 2011), 37.
11. Marie-Thérèse McGivern interviewed by Rachel Cohen on 9 February 2012, *Sisterhood and After: The Women's Liberation Oral History Project, 2010–2013* (British Library Sound & Moving Image © The British Library and The University of Sussex). Henceforth, *Sisterhood and After*.
12. Cited in Delia Davin, 'Of Dogma, Dicta and Washing Machines: Women in the Peoples Republic of China', in Sonia Kruks, Rayna Rapp and Marilyn

B. Young (eds.), *Promissory Notes: Women in the Transition to Socialism* (Monthly Review Press, 1989), 357.

13. Sarah Franklin, 'A Feminist Transatlantic Education' in Davis and Evans, *Transatlantic Conversations*.
14. Sue Katz, 'Working Class Dykes: Class Conflict in the Lesbian/Feminist Movements in the 1970s', *The Sixties* 10:2 (2017), 281–9.
15. Alison Bartlett, 'Bras', in Alison Bartlett and Margaret Henderson (eds.), *Things That Liberate: An Australian Feminist Wunderkammer* (Cambridge Scholars, 2013), 75.
16. Margaret L. Laware, 'Circling the Missiles and Staining Them Red: Feminist Rhetorical Invention and Strategies of Resistance at the Women's Peace Camp at Greenham Common', *NWSA Journal* 16:3 (2004), 30–31.
17. Valerie Wise interviewed by Freya Johnson Ross in September 2011, *Sisterhood and After*.
18. Sara Dowse, 'Blouse', in Bartlett and Henderson, *Things That Liberate*.
19. Alice Echols, *Daring to Be Bad: Radical Feminism in America, 1967–1975* (University of Minnesota Press, 1989), 92–95.
20. For an activist's account of the Albert Hall protest in London, see https://www.bl.uk/collection-items/jo-robinson-miss-world-contest.
21. Sandie Wyles interviewed by Rachel Cohen in July 2011, *Sisterhood and After*.
22. Constance Lytton, *Prisons and Prisoners: Some Personal Experiences* (Cambridge University Press, 2011), 239.
23. Lekkie Hopkins, 'Overalls', in Bartlett and Henderson, *Things That Liberate*.
24. Nett Hart, 'But Can She Type? Meet Me Up Front', *Feminist Bookstore News*, 15:5 (1993), 65
25. Katz, 'Working Class Dykes', 284–5. See also Echols, *Daring to be Bad*, 225, on similar dynamics in a Washington lesbian collective.
26. Sojourner Truth, quoted in Margaret Mary Finnegan, *Selling Suffrage: Consumer Culture and Votes for Women* (Columbia University Press, 1999), 22.
27. Hart, 'But Can She Type?'
28. Elizabeth Cady Stanton, 'Address', in DuBois and Smith, *Elizabeth Cady Stanton, Feminist as Thinker*, 96–7
29. Virginia Woolf, *A Room of One's Own; Three Guineas* (Vintage, 1996), 127–8.
30. Ibid.
31. Pete Six [Goodridge] interviewed by Lucy Delap on 29 September 2012, *Unbecoming Men Collection* (British Library Sound & Moving Image, British Library). Henceforth, *Unbecoming Men Collection*.

32. Aidan White, 'Laying Down Machismo and Taking Up Knitting,' *Guardian* (16 July 1985), 8.
33. John Colvin, 'Dressing for Myself', *Man* 23 (Spring 1986), 12.
34. John Colvin interviewed by Lucy Delap on 7 April 2013, *Unbecoming Men Collection*.
35. Flora Tristan, *Flora Tristan, Utopian Feminist: Her Travel Diaries and Personal Crusade* (Indiana University Press, 1993), 29, 31–2.
36. Leila Ahmed, *Women and Gender in Islam: Historical Roots of a Modern Debate* (Yale University Press, 1992), 150.
37. *Daily Alta California* (14 June 1851).
38. Margot Badran, *Feminists, Islam, and Nation: Gender and the Making of Modern Egypt* (Princeton University Press, 1995); Marie Sandell, *The Rise of Women's Transnational Activism: Identity and Sisterhood between the World Wars* (I. B. Tauris, 2015), 76.
39. Ahmed, *Women and Gender in Islam*, 197–202; Saba Mahmood, *Politics of Piety: The Islamic Revival and the Feminist Subject* (Princeton University Press, 2005).
40. Laura Bier, *Revolutionary Womanhood: Feminisms, Modernity, and the State in Nasser's Egypt* (Stanford University Press, 2011).
41. Rachel Rinaldo, *Mobilizing Piety: Islam and Feminism in Indonesia* (Oxford University Press, 2013).
42. Carla Jones, 'Fashion and Faith in Urban Indonesia', *Fashion Theory* 11:2/3 (2007), 211–32.
43. Ayesha Khan, *The Women's Movement in Pakistan: Activism, Islam and Democracy* (I. B. Tauris, 2018), 94–5.
44. Anne E. Brodsky, *With All Our Strength: The Revolutionary Association of the Women of Afghanistan* (Routledge, 2003).
45. Amina Wadud, *Qur'an and Woman: Rereading the Sacred Text from a Woman's Perspective* (Oxford University Press, 1999).
46. Ziba Mir-Hosseini, *Islam and Gender: The Religious Debate in Contemporary Iran* (I. B. Tauris, 2000); Haleh Afshar, *Islam and Feminisms: An Iranian Case-Study* (Macmillan Press, 1998).
47. bell hooks, *Black Looks: Race and Representation* (South End Press, 1992), 7.
48. *New York Times* (14 October 1917), 35.
49. Anthony, cited in Amy Kesselman, 'The "Freedom Suit": Feminism and Dress Reform in the United States, 1848–1875', *Gender and Society* 5:4 (1991), 500.

CHAPTER 6: FEELINGS

1. Chude Pamela Allen, 'Free Space', in Anne Koedt (ed.), *Notes from the Third Year: Women's Liberation* (New York Radical Feminists, 1972).
2. Claudie Broyelle, *Women's Liberation in China* (Harvester Press, 1977); Quinn Slobodian, 'Guerrilla Mothers and Distant Doubles: West German Feminists Look at China and Vietnam, 1968–1982', *Studies in Contemporary History/Zeithistorische Forschungen* 12 (2015).
3. Alice Echols, *Daring to Be Bad: Radical Feminism in America, 1967–1975* (University of Minnesota Press, 1989), 147.
4. Sudsofloppen, 'The Sudsofloppen Paper', appendix to Chude Pamela Allen, *Free Space: A Perspective on the Small Group in Women's Liberation* (Times Change Press, 1969), 45 (emphasis added).
5. Mitsu, quoted in Setsu Shigematsu, *Scream from the Shadows: The Women's Liberation Movement in Japan* (University of Minnesota Press, 2012), 110, 25.
6. Ibid.
7. Betty Friedan, 'A Dialogue with Simone De Beauvoir', in *'It Changed My Life': Writings on the Women's Movement* (Harvard University Press, 1998), 160.
8. Republished in Koedt, *Notes from the Third Year.*
9. Rita Mae Brown, 'Women Who Love Men Hate Them', *The Furies* (Fall 1972), 14–15.
10. 'CLIT statement 2', *off our backs* (1 July 1974), 13.
11. Adrienne Rich, 'Compulsory Heterosexuality and Lesbian Existence', *Signs* 5:4 (1980), 631–60; Jeska Rees, '"Taking Your Politics Seriously": Lesbian History and the Women's Liberation Movement in England', in Sonja Tiernan and Mary McAuliffe (eds.), *Sapphists and Sexologists* (Cambridge Scholars Publishing, 2009).
12. 'editorials, challenges, clit', *off our backs* (1 July 1974), 1.
13. Cited in Rees, 'Taking your Politics Seriously', 89.
14. Naisargi N. Dave, 'To Render Real the Imagined: An Ethnographic History of Lesbian Community in India', *Signs* 35:3 (2010), 595–619.
15. Audre Lorde, 'The Uses of Anger', in *Sister Outsider: Essays and Speeches* (Crossing, 2007), 124–33.
16. Christina Kotchemidova, 'From Good Cheer to "Drive-By Smiling": A Social History of Cheerfulness', *Journal of Social History* 39:1 (2005), 5–37.
17. Shulamith Firestone, *The Dialectic of Sex: The Case for Feminist Revolution* (The Women's Press, 1979).

18. Barbara Ehrenreich, *Smile or Die: How Positive Thinking Fooled America and the World* (London: Granta, 2009); Sara Ahmed, *The Promise of Happiness* (Duke University Press, 2010), 53.
19. Concepción Arenal, 'Spain', in Theodore Stanton (ed.), *The Woman Question in Europe: A Series of Original Essays* (S. Low, Marston, Searle, and Rivington, 1884).
20. Anna Julia Cooper, *The Voice of Anna Julia Cooper: Including A Voice from the South and Other Important Essays, Papers, and Letters* (Rowman & Littlefield, 1998), 72. See also Vivian M. May, 'Anna Julia Cooper's Black Feminist Love-Politics', *Hypatia* 32:1 (2017), 35–53.
21. Jennifer C. Nash, 'Practicing Love: Black Feminism, Love-Politics, and Post-Intersectionality', *Meridians* 11:2 (2011), 1–24.
22. June Jordan, *Some of Us Did Not Die: New and Selected Essays* (Basic Books, 2003).
23. Margaret H. McFadden, *Golden Cables of Sympathy: The Transatlantic Sources of Nineteenth-Century Feminism* (University Press of Kentucky, 1999), 177.
24. Lorde, 'The Uses of the Erotic: The Erotic as Power', in *Sister Outsider*, 54–7.
25. Ibid., 53; Audre Lorde, *Zami: A New Spelling of My Name* (Penguin Classics, 2018).
26. Andrea Dworkin, 'What is Lesbian Pride?' *Second Wave* (Fall 1975), 9.
27. Ellen Key, *Love and Marriage*, trans. Arthur G. Chater (G. P. Putnam, 1911), 382.
28. Havelock Ellis, Introduction to ibid., xiii, and Ellen Key, *The Woman Movement* (G. P. Putnam, 1912), xii.
29. Ibid., 44, 57, 223, 215.
30. Ann Allen, 'Maternalism in German Feminist Movements', *Journal of Women's History* 5:2 (1993), 99.
31. Eileen Boris, 'The Power of Motherhood: Black and White Activist Women Redefine the "Political"', *Yale Journal of Law and Feminism* 2:1 (1989), 25–49.
32. Miriam Tola, 'Between Pachamama and Mother Earth: Gender, Political Ontology and the Rights of Nature in Contemporary Bolivia', *Feminist Review* 118 (2018), 25–40.
33. Katherine M. Marino, 'Marta Vergara, Popular-Front Pan-American Feminism and the Transnational Struggle for Working Women's Rights in the 1930s', *Gender & History* 26:3 (2014), 642–60.
34. Donna J. Guy, 'The Politics of Pan-American Cooperation: Maternalist Feminism and the Child Rights Movement, 1913–1960', *Gender & History* 10:3 (1998), 449–69.

35. Bertha Lutz in *Revista Da Semana* (23 December 1918), cited in June Edith Hahner, *Emancipating the Female Sex: The Struggle for Women's Rights in Brazil, 1850–1940* (Duke University Press, 1990), 222.
36. Francesca Miller, *Latin American Women and the Search for Social Justice* (University Press of New England, 1991).
37. Jadwiga E. Pieper Mooney, 'Militant Motherhood Re-Visited: Women's Participation and Political Power in Argentina and Chile', *History Compass* 5:3 (2007), 975–94.
38. Maria Estrela in *A Mulher*, cited in Hahner, *Emancipating the Female Sex*, 59.
39. Francisca de Haan, 'Continuing Cold War Paradigms in Western Historiography of Transnational Women's Organisations: The Case of the Women's International Democratic Federation (WIDF)', *Women's History Review* 19:4 (2010), 547–73.
40. Miller, *Latin American Women*, 197.
41. Jocelyn Olcott, *International Women's Year: The Greatest Consciousness-Raising Event in History* (Oxford University Press, 2017).
42. Domitila Barrios de Chungara, *Let Me Speak! Testimony of Domitila, a Woman of the Bolivian Mines* (Monthly Review Press, 1978), 199.
43. Jocelyn Olcott, 'Cold War Conflicts and Cheap Cabaret: Sexual Politics at the 1975 United Nations International Women's Year Conference', *Gender & History* 22:3 (2010), 733–54.
44. Barrios de Chungara, *Let We Speak!* 202, 205.
45. Katharine McGregor, 'Opposing Colonialism: The Women's International Democratic Federation and Decolonisation Struggles in Vietnam and Algeria 1945–1965', *Women's History Review* 25:6 (2016), 925–44; Francisca de Haan, 'Eugénie Cotton, Pak Chong-Ae, and Claudia Jones: Rethinking Transnational Feminism and International Politics', *Journal of Women's History* 25:4 (2013), 174–89.
46. Miller, *Latin American Women*, 198–203.
47. Celia Donert, 'Women's Rights in Cold War Europe: Disentangling Feminist Histories', *Past & Present* 218:8 (2013), 180–202; Susanne Zwingel, *Translating International Women's Rights: The CEDAW Convention in Context* (Palgrave Macmillan, 2016).
48. Edna Acosta-Belén and Christine E. Bose, 'U.S. Latina and Latin American Feminisms: Hemispheric Encounters', *Signs* 25:4 (2000), 1113–19.
49. Emilie Smith-Ayala, *The Granddaughters of Ixmucané: Guatemalan Women Speak* (Women's Press, 1991), 123–4.
50. Lorde, 'The Uses of the Erotic', 58.
51. Olcott, 'Cold War Conflicts'.

52. Claudie Broyelle, *China: A Second Look*, trans. Sarah Matthews (Harvester Press, 1980), 7. See also Marilyn B. Young, 'Chicken Little in China: Women after the Cultural Revolution', in Sonia Kruks, Rayna Rapp and Marilyn B. Young (eds.), *Promissory Notes: Women in the Transition to Socialism* (Monthly Review Press, 1989).
53. Slobodian, 'Guerrilla Mothers and Distant Doubles', 24.
54. Barbara Mehrhof and Pamela Kearon, 'Rape: An Act of Terror', in Anne Koedt, Ellen Levine and Anita Rapone (eds.), *Radical Feminism* (Quadrangle Books, 1973).
55. Mehrhof, cited in Echols, *Daring to Be Bad*, 148.

CHAPTER 7: ACTIONS

1. Qasim Amin in Sharon M. Harris and Linda K. Hughes (eds.), *A Feminist Reader: Feminist Thought from Sappho to Satrapi*, vol. II (Cambridge University Press, 2013), 507, 510.
2. Ibid., 511.
3. Gul Ozyegin, 'My Father, an Agent of State Feminism and Other Unrelatable Conversations', in Mary Evans and Kathy Davis (eds.), *Transatlantic Conversations: Feminism as Travelling Theory* (Routledge, 2016), 37.
4. Andrea Dworkin, *Last Days at Hot Slit: The Radical Feminism of Andrea Dworkin* (MIT Press, 2019), 208.
5. A. Palmer, 'Report on Why No Signature Was Obtained', The Postal Museum, POST 30/1655a. Emmeline Pankhurst, 'When Civil War Is Waged by Women', cited in Miriam Schneir (ed.), *Feminism: The Essential Historical Writings* (Random House, 1972), 301.
6. Susan Mann, *Precious Records: Women in China's Long Eighteenth Century* (Stanford University Press, 1997).
7. Louise P. Edwards, 'Chinese Women's Campaigns for Suffrage', in Edwards and Mina Roces (eds.), *Women's Suffrage in Asia: Gender, Nationalism and Democracy* (Routledge, 2005), 60–62.
8. *Shenzhou Daily* (27 August 1912), cited in Yuxin Ma, *Women Journalists and Feminism in China, 1898–1937* (Cambria Press, 2010).
9. Lutz, cited in June Edith Hahner, *Emancipating the Female Sex: The Struggle for Women's Rights in Brazil, 1850–1940* (Duke University Press, 1990), 224.
10. I'm grateful to Rosa Campbell for elucidating this connection.

11. Anon., Afterword to *Kinhua* (1969), cited in Quinn Slobodian, 'Guerrilla Mothers and Distant Doubles: West German Feminists Look at China and Vietnam, 1968–1982', *Studies in Contemporary History/Zeithistorische Forschungen* 12 (2015), 14.
12. *Frauen gegen imperialistischen Krieg*, cited in Patricia Melzer, '"'Women of Peace' We Are Not": Feminist Militants in the West German *Autonomen* and the Women's Movement', *German Studies Review* 40:2 (2017), 313–32.
13. Red Zora, quoted in Katharina Karcher, 'How (Not) to "Hollaback": Towards a Transnational Debate on the "Red Zora" and Militant Tactics in the Feminist Struggle against Gender-Based Violence', *Feminist Media Studies* 16:1 (2015), 1–16.
14. Barbara Molony, *Gender in Modern East Asia: An Integrated History* (Westview Press, 2016), 434–5.
15. Dorothy Sue Cobble, *The Other Women's Movement: Workplace Justice and Social Rights in Modern America* (Princeton University Press, 2004).
16. Karen Offen, *European Feminisms, 1700–1950: A Political History* (Stanford University Press, 1999), 241.
17. Elinor Accampo, *Private Life, Public Image: Motherhood and Militancy in the Self-Construction of Nelly Roussel, 1900–1922* (University of California Press, 2000), 240–41.
18. Miss Ruby Tuesday, *East Village Other* (18 August 1970), 7.
19. Anne M. Valk, *Radical Sisters: Second-Wave Feminism and Black Liberation in Washington, D.C.* (University of Illinois Press, 2008).
20. *Chicago Women's Liberation Union News* (1 September 1970), 2.
21. Seung-kyung Kim and Na-Young Lee, 'Shared History and the Responsibility for Justice: The Korean Council for the Women Drafted for Military Sexual Slavery by Japan', in Barbara Molony and Jennifer Nelson (eds.), *Women's Activism and 'Second Wave' Feminism* (Bloomsbury Academic, 2017).
22. Okpyo Moon, 'Japanese Tourists in Korea', in Sylvie Guichard-Anguis and Okpyo Moon (eds.), *Japanese Tourism and Travel Culture* (Routledge, 2011).
23. Jeska Rees, 'A Look Back at Anger: The Women's Liberation Movement in 1978', *Women's History Review* 19:3 (2010), 337–56.
24. Maria Mayerchyk and Olga Plakhotnik, 'The Radical FEMEN and the New Women's Activism', *Krytyka Magazine* 11:12 (2015), 157–8.
25. Gayatri Chakravorty Spivak, 'Can the Subaltern Speak?', in Donna Landry and Gerald M. MacLean (eds.), *The Spivak Reader* (Routledge, 1996).
26. Teresa Zackodnik, *Press, Platform, Pulpit: Black Feminist Publics in the Era of Reform* (University of Tennessee Press, 2011).

CHAPTER 8: SONGS

1. A playlist of feminist songs, including some discussed in this chapter, is available at https://open.spotify.com/playlist/5uCxpVJfbGpDmIVVdkYhOf. Readers who want to suggest new content can tweet the author on @suff66.
2. Ellen Key, *Love and Marriage*, trans. Arthur G. Chater (G. P. Putnam, 1911), 246.
3. Negar Mottahedeh, *Whisper Tapes: Kate Millett in Iran* (Stanford Briefs, 2019).
4. Elinor Accampo, *Private Life, Public Image: Motherhood and Militancy in the Self-Construction of Nelly Roussel, 1900–1922* (University of California Press, 2000), 218.
5. Anna J. Cooper, *A Voice from the South* (Oxford University Press, 1988).
6. Ethel Smyth, *The Memoirs of Ethel Smyth* (Viking, 1987), 297.
7. Julie C. Dunbar, *Women, Music, Culture: An Introduction* (Routledge, 2011), 134.
8. Smyth, *Memoirs*, 342.
9. Amanda Smith, *An Autobiography: The Story of the Lord's Dealings with Mrs. Amanda Smith, the Colored Evangelist* (Garland, 1987), 260, 265.
10. Ibid., 414–15, 324. See also Patricia Ann Schechter, *Exploring the Decolonial Imaginary: Four Transnational Lives* (Palgrave Macmillan, 2012), 11.
11. Jacqueline Warwick, '"He Hit Me, and I Was Glad": Violence, Masochism, and Anger in Girl Group Music', in Laurie Stras (eds.), *She's So Fine: Reflections on Whiteness, Femininity, Adolescence and Class in 1960s Music* (Routledge, 2010).
12. Jill Nickel and Sheri Maeda, 'Put Another Nickel In', *Quest* (Fall 1976).
13. Eileen M. Hayes, *Songs in Black and Lavender: Race, Sexual Politics, and Women's Music* (University of Illinois Press, 2010), 70.
14. Donna Pieters, *BWM16 – Heart of the Race Oral History Project*, Black Cultural Archives, Brixton. I'm grateful to D-M Withers for this transcription.
15. *Womansound* 2 (1984), cited in Women's liberation music archives, https://womensliberationmusicarchive.co.uk/s/. On women's liberation music, see D-M Withers, *Feminism, Digital Culture and the Politics of Transmission: Theory, Practice and Cultural Heritage* (Rowman & Littlefield International, 2015), 95–112.
16. Jane Armstrong, 'Radio', in Alison Bartlett and Margaret Henderson (eds.), *Things That Liberate: An Australian Feminist Wunderkammer* (Cambridge Scholars, 2013), 153.

17. Robin Morgan, *Going Too Far: The Personal Chronicle of a Feminist* (Vintage Books, 1978).
18. Janice G. Raymond, *The Transsexual Empire* (Women's Press, 1980), 104; Will Self and Stephen Whittle, *Perfidious Man* (London: Viking, 2000); D-M Withers, 'Laboratories of Gender: Women's Liberation and the Transfeminist Present', *Radical Philosophy* 2:4 (2019).
19. Sandy Stone, 'The *Empire* Strikes Back: a Posttranssexual Manifesto', in Julia Epstein and Kristina Straub (eds.), *Bodyguards: The Cultural Politics of Gender Ambiguity* (Routledge, 1991).
20. Chris Mulvey, in Barbara Harford and Sarah Hopkins (eds.), *Greenham Common: Women at the Wire* (Women's Press, 1984), 92.
21. Anna Reading, 'Singing for My Life', in Anna Reading and Tamar Katriel (eds.), *Cultural Memories of Nonviolent Struggles: Powerful Times* (Palgrave Macmillan, 2015).
22. Katrina, in Harford and Hopkins, *Greenham Common*, 167.
23. Jayne, in ibid., 15.
24. Margaret L. Laware, 'Circling the Missiles and Staining Them Red: Feminist Rhetorical Invention and Strategies of Resistance at the Women's Peace Camp at Greenham Common,' *NWSA Journal* 16:3 (2004), 33. See also Margaretta Jolly, *Sisterhood and After: An Oral History of the UK Women's Liberation Movement, 1968–Present* (Oxford University Press, 2019).
25. Sarah Green, in Harford and Hopkins, *Greenham Common*, 54.
26. 22-year-old Helen Thomas was killed during Greenham protests in 1989, after being struck by a police horse-box; her activism is commemorated in Welsh by the song 'Cân i Helen'.
27. Natalya Lusty, 'Riot Grrrl Manifestos and Radical Vernacular Feminism', *Australian Feminist Studies* 32:93 (3 July 2017), 219–39.
28. Warwick, '"He Hit Me, and I Was Glad"', 102. Courtney Love's version of 'He Hit Me' is widely available by online search.
29. Kevin C. Dunn, 'Pussy Rioting', *International Feminist Journal of Politics* 16:2 (2014), 317–34.
30. Katharine McGregor, 'Indonesian Women, the Women's International Democratic Federation and the Struggle for "Women's Rights", 1946–1965', *Indonesia and the Malay World* 40:117 (2012), 193–208.
31. Danilyn Rutherford, 'Unpacking a National Heroine: Two Kartinis and Their People', *Indonesia*, no. 55 (1993), 23–40.
32. Louise Edwards, 'International Women's Day in China: Feminism Meets Militarised Nationalism and Competing Political Party Programs', *Asian Studies Review* 40:1 (2016), 1–17.

33. Rita Mae Brown, 'The Good Fairy', *Quest* 1 (1974), 60.
34. Nancy A. Hewitt (ed.), *No Permanent Waves: Recasting Histories of U.S. Feminism* (Rutgers University Press, 2010).
35. Johanna Siméant and Christophe Traini, *Bodies in Protest: Hunger Strikes and Angry Music* (Amsterdam University Press, 2016), 107–8.

CONCLUSION: GLOBAL FEMINISMS.

1. Hiratsuka Raichō, cited in Dina Lowy, *The Japanese 'New Woman': Images of Gender and Modernity* (Rutgers University Press, 2007), 10.
2. Barbara Molony, 'Women's Rights, Feminism, and Suffragism in Japan, 1870–1925', *Pacific Historical Review* 69:4 (2000), 639–61.
3. *Ce Qui Est* ('That Which Is'), cited in Bonnie S. Anderson, 'The Lid Comes Off: International Radical Feminism and the Revolutions of 1848', *NWSA Journal* 10:2 (1998), 1–12.
4. Kathy Davis, *The Making of Our Bodies, Ourselves: How Feminism Travels across Borders* (Duke University Press, 2008), 201.
5. Aletta Jacobs, *Politics and Friendship: Letters from the International Woman Suffrage Alliance, 1902–1942*, ed. Mineke Bosch and Annemarie Kloosterman (Ohio State University Press, 1990); Francisca de Haan, '"Tapestries of Contacts": Transnationalizing Women's History', *Journal of Women's History* 26:2 (2014), 200–208; Francisca de Haan, 'Continuing Cold War Paradigms in Western Historiography of Transnational Women's Organisations: The Case of the Women's International Democratic Federation (WIDF)', *Women's History Review* 19:4 (2010); Elisabeth Armstrong, 'Before Bandung: The Anti-Imperialist Women's Movement in Asia and the Women's International Democratic Federation', *Signs* 41:2 (2016), 305–31; Maria DiCenzo *et al.*, 'Mediating the National and the International: Women, Journalism and Hungary in the Aftermath of the First World War', in Ingrid Sharp and Matthew Stibbe (eds.), *Women Activists Between Peace and War: Europe 1918-1923* (Bloomsbury, 2017); Marie Sandell, *The Rise of Women's Transnational Activism: Identity and Sisterhood between the World Wars* (I. B. Tauris, 2015); Leila J. Rupp, *Worlds of Women: The Making of an International Women's Movement* (Princeton University Press, 1997); Katherine M. Marino, 'Transnational Pan-American Feminism: The Friendship of Bertha Lutz and Mary Wilhelmine Williams, 1926–1944', *Journal of Women's History* 26:2 (2014), 63–87.

6. Sandell, *Rise of Women's Transnational Activism*, 97.
7. Raewyn Connell, 'Transsexual Women and Feminist Thought: Toward New Understanding and New Politics', *Signs* 37:4 (2012).
8. Shulamith Firestone, *The Dialectic of Sex: The Case for Feminist Revolution* (The Women's Press, 1979), 97; Karin Schrader-Klebert, *Die Kulturelle Revolution der Frau* (1969), cited in Quinn Slobodian, 'Guerrilla Mothers and Distant Doubles: West German Feminists Look at China and Vietnam, 1968–1982', *Studies in Contemporary History/Zeithistorische Forschungen* 12 (2015).
9. Papusa Molina, 'Recognizing, Accepting and Celebrating Our Differences', in Gloria Anzaldúa (ed.), *Making Face, Making Soul: Creative and Critical Perspectives by Feminists of Color* (Aunt Lute Foundation Books, 1990).
10. Benita Roth, *Separate Roads to Feminism: Black, Chicana, and White Feminist Movements in America's Second Wave* (Cambridge University Press, 2004).
11. Judith A. Allen, *The Feminism of Charlotte Perkins Gilman: Sexualities, Histories, Progressivism* (University of Chicago Press, 2009), 331–49.
12. Betty Friedan, *'It Changed My Life': Writings on the Women's Movement* (Harvard University Press, 1998), 229.

Further Reading

INTRODUCTION

Francisca de Haan *et al.* (eds.), *Women's Activism: Global Perspectives from the 1890s to the Present* (Routledge, 2013).

Ellen Carol Dubois *et al.*, 'Circling the Globe: International Feminism Reconsidered, 1910 to 1975', *Women's Studies International Forum*, 2009.

Kathryn Gleadle and Zoë Thomas, 'Global Feminisms, *c.* 1870–1930: Vocabularies and Concepts – A Comparative Approach', *Women's History Review* 27:7 (2018), 1209–24.

Nancy A. Hewitt (ed.), *No Permanent Waves: Recasting Histories of U.S. Feminism* (Rutgers University Press, 2010).

Karen Offen (ed.), *Globalizing Feminisms, 1789–1945* (Routledge, 2010).

Sylvia Paletschek and Bianka Pietrow-Ennker, *Women's Emancipation Movements in the Nineteenth Century: A European Perspective* (Stanford University Press, 2004).

Florence Rochefort, *Histoire Mondiale des Féminismes* (Que Sais-Je?, 2018).

Bonnie G. Smith, *Women's History in Global Perspective* (University of Illinois Press, 2004).

Becky Thompson, 'Multiracial Feminism: Recasting the Chronology of Second Wave Feminism', *Feminist Studies* 28:2 (2002), 337–60.

CHAPTER 1: DREAMS

Padma Anagol, *The Emergence of Feminism in India, 1850–1920* (Ashgate, 2005).

Winifred Breins, *The Trouble Between Us: An Uneasy History of White and Black Women in the Feminist Movement* (Oxford University Press, 2006).

Antoinette Burton, *Burdens of History: British Feminists, Indian Women, and Imperial Culture, 1865–1915* (University of North Carolina Press, 1994).

Laura Engelstein, *The Keys to Happiness: Sex and the Search for Modernity in Fin-de-Siècle Russia* (Cornell University Press, 1992).

Bharati Ray, *Early Feminists of Colonial India: Sarala Devi Chaudhurani and Rokeya Sakhawat Hossain* (Oxford University Press, 2012).

Kimberly Springer, *Living for the Revolution: Black Feminist Organizations, 1968–1980* (Duke University Press, 2005).

Natalie Thomlinson, *Race, Ethnicity and the Women's Movement in England, 1968–1993* (Palgrave Macmillan, 2016)

CHAPTER 2: IDEAS

Tani E. Barlow, *The Question of Women in Chinese Feminism* (Duke University Press, 2004).

Silvia Bermúdez and Roberta Johnson (eds.), *A New History of Iberian Feminisms* (University of Toronto Press, 2018).

Arianne Chernock, *Men and the Making of Modern British Feminism* (Stanford University Press, 2010).

Ellen Fleischmann, *The Nation and Its 'New' Women: The Palestinian Women's Movement, 1920–1948* (University of California Press, 2003).

James Keating, 'Piecing Together Suffrage Internationalism: Place, Space, and Connected Histories of Australasian Women's Activism', *History Compass* 16:8 (2018), 1–15.

Karen Offen, *Debating the Woman Question in the French Third Republic, 1870–1920* (Cambridge University Press, 2018).

Leila J. Rupp, *Worlds of Women: The Making of an International Women's Movement* (Princeton University Press, 1997).

CHAPTER 3: SPACES

Bonnie S. Anderson, *Joyous Greetings: The First International Women's Movement, 1830–1860* (Oxford University Press, 2001).

Maud Bracke, *Women and the Reinvention of the Political: Feminism in Italy, 1968–1983* (Routledge, 2014).

Cheryl Johnson-Odim and Margaret Strobel (eds.), *Expanding the Boundaries of Women's History: Essays on Women in the Third World* (Indiana University Press, 1992).

Shana Penn and Jill Massino (eds.), *Gender Politics and Everyday Life in State Socialist Eastern and Central Europe* (Palgrave Macmillan, 2009).

Barbara Hamill Sato, *The New Japanese Woman: Modernity, Media, and Women in Interwar Japan* (Duke University Press, 2003).

Mona L. Siegel, *Peace on Our Terms: The Global Battle for Women's Rights After the First World War* (Columbia University Press, 2020).

Sharon L. Sievers, *Flowers in Salt: The Beginnings of Feminist Consciousness in Modern Japan* (Stanford University Press, 1983).

Megan Threlkeld, *Pan American Women: U.S. Internationalists and Revolutionary Mexico* (University of Pennsylvania Press, 2014).

CHAPTER 4: OBJECTS

Lila Abu-Lughod, *Remaking Women: Feminism and Modernity in the Middle East* (Princeton University Press, 1998).

Alison Bartlett and Margaret Henderson (eds.), *Things That Liberate: An Australian Feminist Wunderkammer* (Cambridge Scholars, 2013).

Mary Cullen and Maria Luddy (eds.), *Female Activists: Irish Women and Change, 1900–1960* (Woodfield Press, 2001).

Miranda Garrett and Zoë Thomas (eds.), *Suffrage and the Arts: Visual Culture, Politics and Enterprise* (Bloomsbury Visual Arts, 2019).

Barbara Green, *Feminist Periodicals and Daily Life: Women and Modernity in British Culture* (Palgrave Macmillan, 2017).

Marilyn Lake, *Getting Equal: The History of Australian Feminism* (Allen & Unwin, 1999).

Lisa Tickner, *The Spectacle of Women: Imagery of the Suffrage Campaign, 1907–14* (University of Chicago Press, 1988).

CHAPTER 5: LOOKS

Lila Abu-Lughod, *Do Muslim Women Need Saving?* (Harvard University Press, 2013).

Margot Badran, *Feminists, Islam and Nation: Gender and the Making of Modern Egypt* (Princeton University Press, 1995).

Laura Bier, *Revolutionary Womanhood: Feminisms, Modernity, and the State in Nasser's Egypt* (Stanford University Press, 2011).

Ian Fletcher *et al.* (eds.), *Women's Suffrage in the British Empire: Citizenship, Nation, and Race* (Routledge, 2012).

Tanisha C. Ford, *Liberated Threads: Black Women, Style, and the Global Politics of Soul* (University of North Carolina Press, 2015).

Patricia Grimshaw, *Women's Suffrage in New Zealand* (Auckland University Press, 2013).

Shanaz Khan, *Zina, Transnational Feminism, and the Moral Regulation of Pakistani Women* (UBC Press, 2011).

Joan Wallach Scott, *The Politics of the Veil* (Princeton University Press, 2007).

CHAPTER 6: FEELINGS

Ann Taylor Allen, *Feminism and Motherhood in Western Europe, 1890–1970: The Maternal Dilemma* (Palgrave Macmillan, 2007).

Ute Frevert, *Women in German History: From Bourgeois Emancipation to Sexual Liberation* (Berg, 1988).

Kimberley Manning, 'Making a Great Leap Forward? The Politics of Women's Liberation in Maoist China', *Gender & History* 18:3 (2006), 574–93.

Katherine M. Marino, *Feminism for the Americas: The Making of an International Human Rights Movement* (University of North Carolina Press, 2019).

Francesca Miller, *Latin American Women and the Search for Social Justice* (University Press of New England, 1991).

Mina Roces and Louise Edwards (eds.) *Women's Movements in Asia: Feminisms and Transnational Activism* (Routledge, 2010).

Lynne Segal, *Radical Happiness: Moments of Collective Joy* (Verso, 2017).

Zheng Wang, *Finding Women in the State: A Socialist Feminist Revolution in the People's Republic of China, 1949–1964* (University of California Press, 2017).

CHAPTER 7: ACTIONS

Alison Bartlett, 'Feminist Protest and Maternity at Pine Gap Women's Peace Camp, Australia 1983', *Women's Studies International Forum* 34:1 (2011), 31–8.

Keisha N. Blain, *Set the World on Fire: Black Nationalist Women and the Global Struggle for Freedom* (University of Pennsylvania Press, 2018).

Myra Marx Ferree, *Varieties of Feminism: German Gender Politics in Global Perspective* (Stanford University Press, 2012).

Kumari Jayawardena, *Feminism and Nationalism in the Third World* (Kali for Women, 1986).

Sumita Mukherjee, *Indian Suffragettes: Female Identities and Transnational Networks* (Oxford University Press, 2018).

Judy Tzu-Chun Wu, *Radicals on the Road: Internationalism, Orientalism, and Feminism during the Vietnam Era* (Cornell University Press, 2013).

CHAPTER 8: SONGS

Angela Y. Davis, *Blues Legacies and Black Feminism: Gertrude Ma Rainey, Bessie Smith, and Billie Holiday* (Knopf Doubleday, 2011).

Eileen M. Hayes, *Songs in Black and Lavender: Race, Sexual Politics, and Women's Music* (University of Illinois Press, 2010).

Margaretta Jolly, *Sisterhood and After: An Oral History of the UK Women's Liberation Movement, 1968–Present* (Oxford University Press, 2019).

Negar Mottahedeh, *Whisper Tapes: Kate Millett in Iran* (Stanford Briefs, 2019).

Rachel Rinaldo, *Mobilizing Piety: Islam and Feminism in Indonesia* (Oxford University Press, 2013).

Rochelle Goldberg Ruthchild, 'From West to East: International Women's Day, the First Decade', *Aspasia* 6:1 (2012), 1–24.

CONCLUSION: GLOBAL FEMINISMS

Sara Ahmed, *Living a Feminist Life* (Duke University Press, 2017).

Cinzia Arruzza, Tithi Bhattacharya and Nancy Fraser, *Feminism for the 99%: A Manifesto* (Verso Books, 2019).

Heather Eaton and Lois Ann Lorentzen (eds.), *Ecofeminism and Globalization: Exploring Culture, Context, and Religion* (Rowman & Littlefield, 2003).

Akwugo Emejulu and Francesca Sobande (eds.), *To Exist Is to Resist: Black Feminism in Europe* (Pluto Press, 2019).

Terese Jonsson, *Innocent Subjects: Feminism and Whiteness* (Pluto Press, 2020).

Bonnie J. Morris and D-M Withers, *The Feminist Revolution: The Struggle for Women's Liberation* (Virago, 2018).

Index

A

B

M

N

X

Y

Z

Economics: The User's Guide
Ha-Joon Chang

Human Evolution
Robin Dunbar

Revolutionary Russia: 1891–1991
Orlando Figes

The Domesticated Brain
Bruce Hood

Greek and Roman Political Ideas
Melissa Lane

Classical Literature
Richard Jenkyns

Who Governs Britain?
Anthony King

How to See the World
Nicholas Mirzoeff

The Meaning of Science
Tim Lewens

Social Class in the 21st Century
Mike Savage

The European Union: A Citizen's Guide
Chris Bickerton

The Caliphate
Hugh Kennedy

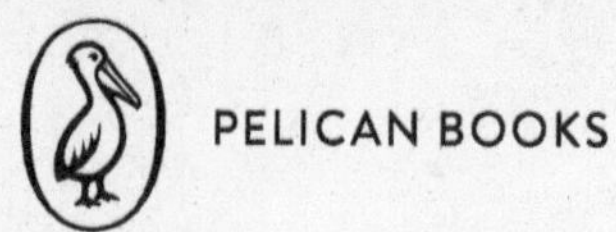

Islam:
The Essentials
Tariq Ramadan

Basic Income:
And How We Can Make It Happen
Guy Standing

Think Like an Anthropologist
Matthew Engelke

Hermeneutics:
Facts and Interpretation in the Age of Information
John D. Caputo

Being Ecological
Timothy Morton

Object-Oriented Ontology:
A New Theory of Everything
Graham Harman

Marx and Marxism
Gregory Claeys

The Human Planet:
How We Created the Anthropocene
Simon L. Lewis and Mark A. Maslin

Think Again:
How to Reason and Argue
Walter Sinnott-Armstrong

Parenting the First Twelve Years:
What the Evidence Tells Us
Victoria L. Cooper, Heather Montgomery, Kieron Sheehy

Social Mobility:
And Its Enemies
Lee Elliot Major and Stephen Machin

National Populism:
The Revolt Against Liberal Democracy
Roger Eatwell and Matthew Goodwin

A Political History of the World
Jonathan Holslag

A Short History of Brexit
From Brentry to Backstop
Kevin O'Rourke

Our Universe:
An Astronomer's Guide
Jo Dunkley

The Art of Statistics:
Learning from Data
David Spiegelhalter

Chinese Thought:
From Confucius to Cook Ding
Roel Sterckx

This is Shakespeare
Emma Smith

What We Really Do All Day
Jonathan Gershuny and Oriel Sullivan

The Government of No One
Ruth Kinna

Plunder of the Commons
Guy Standing

Artificial Intelligence
Melanie Mitchell

Can We Be Happier?
Richard Layard

The Road to Conscious Machines
Michael Wooldridge

Feeding Britain
Tim Lang

Feminisms
Lucy Delap